D1142186

TWENTIETH CENTURY VIEWS

The aim of this series is to present the best
in contemporary critical opinion on major
authors, providing a twentieth century perspective on their changing status in an era
of profound revaluations.

Maynard Mack, *Series Editor*
Yale University

D R Y D E N

A COLLECTION OF CRITICAL ESSAYS

Edited by

Bernard N. Schilling

A SPECTRUM BOOK

Prentice-Hall, Inc., *Englewood Cliffs, N. J.*

Second printing ...... June, 1965

LIBRARY OF CONGRESS CATALOG CARD NO.: 63-15413

Printed in the United States of America

C

Table of Contents

Table of Contents

Notes on the Editor and Authors

Introduction

by Bernard N. Schilling

The title of this series applies with timely force to John Dryden. Of the greater English poets he has stood most in need of the balanced judgment, the informed reappraisal that our place in time has made possible. Modern literary study, unlike that of the nineteenth century, proceeds from the text before it rather than from something that we insist on believing about poetry to begin with. Our responses are more direct to a poem's demands and we seem nearer than Matthew Arnold himself to that disinterestedness which he made a condition of the right critical temper. We are therefore freer to discover Dryden's merits and to respond without prejudice to the kind of poet he was.

We speak of the twentieth century view as right and of nineteenth century opinion as wrong—needing total correction. Yet the work of Scott, Lowell, and Saintsbury, for example, was concerned to do justice to Dryden, while our century for a time kept a low estimate of his character and achievement. In 1901 *The Sewanee Review* carried an article, "Dryden after Two Centuries," that surveyed his career with respect, but still feared that as a poet Dryden suffered from the kind of poetry he was called upon to write. The St. Cecilia odes alone show him in the great English poetic tradition. In 1923 Mr. Allardyce Nicoll's compact volume on *Dryden and His Poetry* puts forward as the chief question to be answered, "Was Dryden a poet?" If the answer differs from that of Arnold, the question shows that, as Mr. Eliot had said two years before, the twentieth century is still the nineteenth to most readers of poetry. So recently as 1939 Mr. C. S. Lewis surpassed the temperate reservations of Arnold in castigating Dryden as gross and vulgar, incapable of creating poems sound in structure, although producing occasional passages acceptable as poetry.

Yet the reader of our selections will find that the extreme nineteenth century judgment of Dryden as laid down by W. D. Christie and Matthew Arnold has been largely reversed. Christie's *Memoir* prefixed to the Globe Edition of Dryden's poems in 1870 followed in part the errors of Macaulay and did immense harm to Dryden's reputation as a man. The numerous and explicit contemporary attacks against Dryden, based on political or religious bias, were seldom answered by the poet or his friends, and Christie seems to take these denunciations at their face value. Mr. James Osborn in his indispensable *John Dryden: Some Biographical Facts and Problems* cautions the unwary reader of Christie, lest he conclude "that Dryden had the character of a chameleon and the appetites of a viper." Osborn notes that the severe *Memoir* had appeared in standard school editions, insuring a large and receptive audience. Arnold's judgment of Dryden, expressed in a famous essay, "The Study of Poetry" (1880), and elsewhere, was likewise influential, teaching nine readers out of ten to consider him a prosaic poet. Sharing in the general nineteenth century disesteem for the eighteenth, Arnold sees Dryden and Pope as classics of English prose, having the qualities of an age of prose and reason. Since poetry must have its origin in the soul and heart of man, a writer like Dryden can hardly be considered a poet at all, the higher, truer flights of poetry being impossibly beyond the range of his nature. To counter this extreme position, the twentieth century has tended to return to the eighteenth and the sensible criticism of Samuel Johnson. The reader will see how frequently in this volume modern opinion relies upon or takes seriously the largeness of Johnson's view.

We have so far used the term "twentieth century" as if the entire period from the death of Queen Victoria were involved. Yet despite the usefulness of the Noyes edition of 1909 and A. W. Verrall's *Lectures on Dryden* (1914), for example, our period does not begin until after the first World War. In the *Johnsonian News Letter* of June, 1956, Mr. James L. Clifford states what is now accepted: ". . . for the twentieth century the new appreciation of Dryden may be said to stem from the enthusiastic advocacy in 1920 and 1921 of two critics, Mark Van Doren and T. S. Eliot." After the appearance of Van Doren's book *The Poetry of John Dryden,* Eliot's review, and his later praise of Dryden as poet, dramatist, and critic, the interest in Dryden profited from the tercentenary of his birth (1931) which gave new impetus to studies already under way. Dryden was also the beneficiary, if not partly the cause, of renewed approval of the English Augustans generally, and did not suffer when Classicism was championed over Romanticism by T. E. Hulme and others. Let us take then, as twentieth century views of Dryden, the efforts beginning with Van Doren and Eliot to estimate more precisely the qualities of Dryden as man and poet. The selections that follow perform three essential tasks: they refute charges of extreme inconsistency, of vacillation from one camp to another, of mercenary or cowardly search for personal advantage; they show that Dryden's mind was vigorous and clear within its limits, commanding the literary tradition up to his time; they declare finally that Dryden was a genuine poet of considerable range and versatility, with a high degree of architectonic skill in his best poems.

Turning now to Van Doren, we find a work that in spite of clear limitations is a serious attempt to do justice to Dryden as a poetic artist, one who is most at home in "the poetry of statement." The chapters devoted to Dryden's occasional, lyric, and narrative verse, together with a review of the satires and religious poems published between 1681 and 1687, compose the heart of the volume. The writer supports his judgments with copious illustrations, so that he offers in addition to his own commentary, a considerable anthology of Dryden as well, adding greatly to the interest and usefulness of his work. When supplemented by the championship of Mr. Eliot, the position of Van Doren's book was secure. The review praises Van Doren and his subject, asserting that "Dryden is distinguished principally by his poetic ability." Mr. Eliot begins and ends by rejecting the limited tastes and fashions of the nineteenth century, and of "what is left of the nineteenth in the name of the twentieth century." Taste seems about to grow more fluid, to be ready for a new mold, ready now to pass "into a new freedom."

At this point we may give some honor to our antagonist Matthew Arnold, who usefully remarked that we should not allow personal or historical judgments to obscure the true end of criticism; we must see the object as it really is. If we do not permit gratitude to obscure judgment, we see that Van Doren's importance is more historical than real, that, as he would be the first to admit, he had introduced rather than exhausted his subject, leaving many essential problems for later solution. Such a volume written now would employ a wider range of critical resources, arriving at more advanced conclusions. But if, with the help of Eliot, Van Doren released us from the nineteenth century, we must then ask what criticism has in fact done with its "new freedom." Much less for Dryden, the answer is, than for the other members of that great triumvirate of English Augustans, Swift and Pope. The nineteenth century lay heavy on the reputation of Swift, but modern students have rid themselves of the excesses of Thackeray, for example, learning to see the work of Swift unobscured by personal or biographical considerations. The perhaps deliberately maintained enigmas of Swift's mind and character may continue to elude us, but they have called forth an impressive body of new commentary, much of it now indispensable. Voyage IV of *Gulliver's Travels* alone has engaged a large proportion of our most learned and discerning critical talent. Though we still await a twentieth century perspective on the life of Pope, the great satires and ethical poems have inspired a true "God's plenty" of interpretive criticism.

Dryden has not enjoyed such good fortune, and criticism has yet to establish his true meaning and value. We should be more fully aware of his stature as one of the great professionals of literature, a man ideally suited by temper and equipment for the task before him, one who could attempt the dominant literary forms at will and emerge in triumph over his rivals and contemporaries. Although he did in fact learn more from life and experience than from books, we need to follow his apparently unsystematic reading in greater detail, to understand more fully what he made of it. We should study anew the line of his artistic development, marking a steady progress from early conventional verse toward the mature poetical strategies of *Mac Flecknoe, Absalom and Achitophel,* and beyond.

Dryden was a man of silent dignity and reserve, of strength and independence, of sense and intelligence. He had the qualities needed for his time and so was able, as Mr. Brower shows, to absorb its intellectual resources, to respond to its principles and give them a striking poetic synthesis. While not contemptible in his birth or the ties of marriage, he was yet a *novus homo,* new to a highly stratified society aristocratic in its assumptions. He had his way to make, he had to entertain his world while achieving the highest level then attainable of professional versatility and competence. He was a public servant, at once custodian and interpreter of traditional values—the conscience of his time.

Dryden could move toward fulfillment on so many lines because he was confident, entirely at ease within assumptions and demands that might have stunted the growth of a less flexible temper. Despite the apparent handicap of prevailing rule and theory, emphasized in Mr. Morgan's essay, Dryden constantly worked at new forms and devices, his poetic practice adaptable and various. Though capable of immense variety, he fastened inevitably upon the heroic couplet, absorbed the advances made in its use before him, and achieved a masterly control of its resources. Just as Dryden felt entirely free amid the required political order of his day, so did his imagination work unhindered within the most restricted of stanzaic forms. He would never have settled for a political order or a poetic form that hampered him. Luckily for himself, his age, and the history of English poetry, he was free though committed, at ease in conformity—able therefore, to do as he pleased.

When we have fully studied again the process of his development as a poet, we shall understand more clearly how he came to achieve his easy mastery of the couplet, why he was ready, like a champion athlete in Saintsbury's phrase, when the crisis following the Popish Plot gave Dryden the supreme opportunity of his career. While criticism has recently been able to assess more satisfactorily the great political satires, the religious poems and other achievements of his later career await the informed, perceptive, and sophisticated interpretation demanded by their subtlety and range.

If we seem to lament our present distance from an ideal knowledge of Dryden from beginning to end, we have available nonetheless a number of studies which show the way to a more balanced estimate of his temper as a man, and to subtler, fuller readings of his poetic achievement.

In 1934, *The Intellectual Milieu of John Dryden* by Louis I. Bredvold presented a study of Dryden's characteristic thought and its seventeenth century background, seen mainly through the religious poems, in which the poet's sincerity and consistency clearly emerge. Mr. Bredvold makes his case so well that the reader must wonder why anyone should have thought anything else about Dryden, why for so long a time such denigration, not to say derision and contempt, was expressed for his personal character. A glance at the violent attacks upon Dryden in his own period will show at least the origin of his sufferings. In *The Medal of John Bayes*, Mr. James Osborn remarks how "scurrilous and obscene" even the best of these onslaughts could be. Anything in Dryden's life, early or mature, that might discredit or humiliate him, was seized upon and distorted. For a more just appraisal the reader should turn to a recent biography by Charles Ward. In *The Life of John Dryden*, Mr. Ward analyzes the "extent and virulence" of the attacks on Dryden after *Absalom and Achitophel* in 1681. After his acceptance of Roman Catholicism in 1685, the poet had again to endure suspicion of venality, although "no available evidence will sustain a charge either of insincerity or of personal self-seeking." As for Dryden's political views, far from having been a changeable turncoat, in 1688 "he could look back upon more than a quarter of a century of consistent support of hereditary monarchy," expecting no reward for himself "except his own consciousness of loyalty to a principle." Mr. Ward does well to end his biography by recalling the tribute of a fellow-poet and dramatist. Congreve, "who would have known," assures us that Dryden was in the last degree humane and compassionate, of a temper modest and forgiving.

With the man himself more clearly in outline, we may see greater justice done henceforth to the poet. To facilitate this, the reader will be grateful for the excellent background provided in the essays by Mr. Brower and Mr. Morgan. We are glad to have Dryden's importance as the essential forerunner of Pope so clearly shown, together with his magisterial solution of the problems created in part by his material and in part by the prevailing literary theory. The poet's versatility emerges again as we glance at an early poem in Mr. Wasserman's informed and ingenious reading, at his best play, at the great poems of the 1680's, and finally at the products of his old age. While the odes have never been so studiously neglected as the religious poems, for example, we are obliged to Mr. Tillyard and Mr. Hollander for readings that should help to alleviate Mr. Morgan's reservations about them.

Mr. Miner, in turn, shows how far we may advance our reading of the great satires if we consider them as poetic wholes "controlled" by metaphorical language. After dealing harshly with Van Doren and Eliot, he skillfully illustrates from the opening lines of *Absalom and Achitophel* Dryden's striking use of metaphor. Yet despite our pleasure in this witty passage for itself, we must appreciate "Dryden's ability to create wholes in which structure, ideas, values, tone, and metaphors are but aspects of each other." Applied to *Absalom and Achitophel*, this discernment enables us to follow the metaphors of the opening lines throughout the entire allegory of the poem which is controlled by the single general metaphor of biblical history. Mr. Miner's valuable insight has many possibilities and we must hope that it will be more extensively used for advanced readings in an area of Dryden's poetic universe still too generally neglected: the religious poems. Dryden's controlling metaphors often express and bring unity to the body of his thought, and if this had been Mr. Miner's chief line of inquiry, he might have enlarged his appreciation of *Absalom and Achitophel.* Amid its complexities the poem makes a fervent plea for the divinity of order, an order that is sustained by God throughout His created universe and which in turn must be kept by man throughout all the institutions that govern his own life in the world. On one side, the continuity and stability of order are carried by an architectural figure, comparing the universe and the earthly monarchical state to a building. A second comparison of the state to a human body employs the metaphor of disease and its cure, to present the danger that threatens a given society if changes or "cures" are too sudden or radical. Just as a long-established, if weakened, building must not be torn from its foundations, so must an ailing body politic not have to endure the shock of a treatment which may be worse than the disease it is meant to cure. At a turning point in *Absalom and Achitophel* Dryden shows the degree to which his metaphors do in fact control the body of his thought, as he combines them in a passage often quoted but which is none the less intellectually inseparable from the poem as a whole:

> If ancient fabrics nod, and threat to fall,
> To patch the flaws, and buttress up the wall,
> Thus far 't is duty: but here fix the mark;
> For all beyond it is to touch our ark.
> To change foundations, cast the frame anew,
> Is work for rebels, who base ends pursue,
> At once divine and human laws control,
> And mend the parts by ruin of the whole.
> The tamp'ring world is subject to this curse,
> To physic their disease into a worse.

Let us agree then that our greatest advance in the twentieth century toward justice to Dryden comes from seeing him as a poet, not of "striking passages or of noble fragments," but of large design. If we ask ourselves, Why read Dryden today? the answer is simply that we have found him a true poet, by whom, as Johnson aptly puts it, we are "taught *sapere et fari,* to think naturally and express forcibly." Johnson goes on to say, in a famous sentence: "What was said of Rome, adorned by Augustus, may be applied by an easy metaphor to English poetry embellished by Dryden, *lateritiam invenit, marmoream reliquit,* he found it brick, and he left it marble." If we bear in mind that marble is not necessarily *better* than brick, this is a shrewd description of the public and oratorical music in which Dryden excels.

Mr. Wright's charming tribute to the "last poet of a golden/Order" may then be allowed the final word.

John Dryden

by T. S. Eliot

If the prospect of delight be wanting (which alone justifies the perusal of poetry) we may let the reputation of Dryden sleep in the manuals of literature. To those who are genuinely insensible of his genius (and these are probably the majority of living readers of poetry) we can only oppose illustrations of the following proposition: that their insensibility does not merely signify indifference to satire and wit, but lack of perception of qualities not confined to satire and wit and present in the work of other poets whom these persons feel that they understand. To those whose taste in poetry is formed entirely upon the English poetry of the nineteenth century—to the majority—it is difficult to explain or excuse Dryden: the twentieth century is still the nineteenth, although it may in time acquire its own character. The nineteenth century had, like every other, limited tastes and peculiar fashions; and, like every other, it was unaware of its own limitations. Its tastes and fashions had no place for Dryden; yet Dryden is one of the tests of a catholic appreciation of poetry.

He is a successor of Jonson, and therefore the descendant of Marlowe; he is the ancestor of nearly all that is best in the poetry of the eighteenth century. Once we have mastered Dryden—and by mastery is meant a full and essential enjoyment, not the enjoyment of a private whimsical fashion—we can extract whatever enjoyment and edification there is in his contemporaries—Oldham, Denham, or the less remunerative Waller; and still more his successors—not only Pope, but Phillips, Churchill, Gray, Johnson, Cowper, Goldsmith. His inspiration is prolonged in Crabbe and Byron; it even extends, as Mr. Van Doren cleverly points out, to Poe. Even the poets responsible for the revolt were well acquainted with him: Wordsworth knew his work, and Keats invoked his aid. We cannot fully enjoy or rightly estimate a hundred years of English poetry unless

"John Dryden." From *Selected Essays of T. S. Eliot* (New York: Harcourt, Brace & World), pp. 264-274. Copyright 1932, 1936, 1950 by Harcourt, Brace & World; © 1960 by T. S. Eliot. Reprinted by permission of Harcourt, Brace & World and Faber and Faber, Ltd.

we fully enjoy Dryden; and to enjoy Dryden means to pass beyond the limitations of the nineteenth century into a new freedom.

> All, all of a piece throughout!
> Thy Chase had a Beast in View;
> Thy Wars brought nothing about;
> Thy Lovers were all untrue.
> 'Tis well an Old Age is out,
> And time to begin a New.

> .   .   .   .   .

> The world's great age begins anew,
> The golden years return,
> The earth doth like a snake renew
> Her winter weeds outworn:
> Heaven smiles, and faiths and empires gleam
> Like wrecks of a dissolving dream.

The first of these passages is by Dryden, the second by Shelley; the second is found in the *Oxford Book of English Verse,* the first is not; yet we might defy anyone to show that the second is superior on intrinsically poetic merit. It is easy to see why the second should appeal more readily to the nineteenth, and what is left of the nineteenth under the name of the twentieth, century. It is not so easy to see propriety in an image which divests a snake of "winter weeds"; and this is a sort of blemish which would have been noticed more quickly by a contemporary of Dryden than by a contemporary of Shelley.

These reflections are occasioned by an admirable book on Dryden which has appeared at this very turn of time, when taste is becoming perhaps more fluid and ready for a new mold.[1] It is a book which every practitioner of English verse should study. The consideration is so thorough, the matter so compact, the appreciation so just, temperate, and enthusiastic, and supplied with such copious and well-chosen extracts from the poetry, the suggestion of astutely placed facts leads our thought so far, that there only remain to mention, as defects which do not detract from its value, two omissions: the prose is not dealt with, and the plays are somewhat slighted. What is especially impressive is the exhibition of the very wide range of Dryden's work, shown by the quotations of every species. Everyone knows *Mac Flecknoe,* and parts of *Absalom and Achitophel;* in consequence, Dryden has sunk by the persons he has elevated to distinction—Shadwell and Settle, Shaftesbury and Buckingham. Dryden was much more than a satirist; to dispose of him as a satirist is to place an obstacle in the way of our understanding. At all events, we must satisfy ourselves of our definition of the term satire; we

[1] *John Dryden* by Mark Van Doren (New York: Harcourt, Brace & World, Inc.).

must not allow our familiarity with the word to blind us to differences and refinements; we must not assume that satire is a fixed type, and fixed to the prosaic, suited only to prose; we must acknowledge that satire is not the same thing in the hands of two different writers of genius. The connotations of "satire" and of "wit," in short, may be only prejudices of nineteenth century taste. Perhaps, we think, after reading Mr. Van Doren's book, a juster view of Dryden may be given by beginning with some other portion of his work than his celebrated satires; but even here there is much more present, and much more that is poetry, than is usually supposed.

The piece of Dryden's which is the most fun, which is the most sustained display of surprise after surprise of wit from line to line, is *Mac Flecknoe*. Dryden's method here is something very near to parody; he applies vocabulary, images, and ceremony which arouse epic associations of grandeur, to make an enemy helplessly ridiculous. But the effect, though disastrous for the enemy, is very different from that of the humor which merely belittles, such as the satire of Mark Twain. Dryden continually enhances: he makes his object great, in a way contrary to expectation; and the total effect is due to the transformation of the ridiculous into poetry. As an example may be taken a fine passage plagiarized from Cowley, from lines which Dryden must have marked well, for he quotes them directly in one of his prefaces. Here is Cowley:

> Where their vast courts the mother-waters keep,
> And undisturbed by moons in silence sleep. . . .
> Beneath the dens where unfledged tempests lie,
> And infant winds their tender voices try.

In *Mac Flecknoe* this becomes:

> Where their vast courts the mother-strumpets keep,
> And undisturbed by watch, in silence sleep.
> Near these, a nursery erects its head,
> Where queens are formed, and future heroes bred;
> Where unfledged actors learn to laugh and cry,
> Where infant punks their tender voices try,
> And little Maximins the gods defy.

The passage from Cowley is by no means despicable verse. But it is a commonplace description of commonly poetic objects; it has not the element of surprise so essential to poetry, and this Dryden provides. A clever versifier might have written Cowley's lines; only a poet could have made what Dryden made of them. It is impossible to dismiss his verses as "prosaic"; turn them into prose and they are transmuted, the fragrance is gone. The reproach of the prosaic, leveled at Dryden, rests upon a confusion between the emotions considered to be poetic—which is a matter allowing considerable latitude of fashion—and the *result* of personal emotion in poetry; and also there is the emotion *depicted* by the poet in some kinds of poetry, of which the *Testaments* of Villon is an example. Again, there is the intellect, the originality and independence and clarity of what we vaguely call the poet's "point of view." Our valuation of poetry, in short, depends upon several considerations, upon the permanent and upon the mutable and transitory. When we try to isolate the essentially poetic, we bring our pursuit in the end to something insignificant; our standards vary with every poet whom we consider. All we can hope to do, in the attempt to introduce some order into our preferences, is to clarify our reasons for finding pleasure in the poetry that we like.

With regard to Dryden, therefore, we can say this much. Our taste in English poetry has been largely founded upon a partial perception of the value of Shakespeare and Milton, a perception which dwells upon sublimity of theme and action. Shakespeare had a great deal more; he had nearly everything to satisfy our various desires for poetry. The point is that the depreciation or neglect of Dryden is not due to the fact that his work is not poetry, but to a prejudice that the material, the feelings, out of which he built is not poetic. Thus Matthew Arnold observes, in mentioning Dryden and Pope together, that "their poetry is conceived and composed in their wits, genuine poetry is conceived in the soul." Arnold was, perhaps, not altogether the detached critic when he wrote this line; he may have been stirred to a defense of his own poetry, conceived and composed in the soul of a mid-century Oxford graduate. Pater remarks that Dryden:

> Loved to emphasize the distinction between poetry and prose, the protest against their confusion coming with somewhat diminished effect from one whose poetry was so prosaic.

But Dryden was right, and the sentence of Pater is cheap journalism. Hazlitt, who had perhaps the most uninteresting mind of all our distinguished critics, says:

> Dryden and Pope are the great masters of the artificial style of poetry in our language, as the poets of whom I have already treated—Chaucer, Spenser, Shakespeare, and Milton—were of the natural.

In one sentence Hazlitt has committed at least four crimes against taste. It is bad enough to lump Chaucer, Spenser, Shakespeare, and Milton together under the denomination of "natural"; it is bad to commit Shakespeare to one style only; it is bad to join Dryden and Pope together; but the last absurdity is the contrast of Milton, our greatest master of the *artificial* style, with Dryden, whose *style* (vocabulary, syntax, and order

of thought) is in a high degree natural. And what all these objections
come to, we repeat, is repugnance for the material out of which Dryden's
poetry is built.

It would be truer to say, indeed, even in the form of the unpersuasive
paradox, that Dryden is distinguished principally by his *poetic* ability.
We prize him, as we do Mallarmé, for what he made of his material. Our
estimate is only in part the appreciation of ingenuity: in the end the
result *is* poetry. Much of Dryden's unique merit consists in his ability to
make the small into the great, the prosaic into the poetic, the trivial into
the magnificent. In this he differs not only from Milton, who required a
canvas of the largest size, but from Pope, who required one of the small-
est. If you compare any satiric "character" of Pope with one of Dryden,
you will see that the method and intention are widely divergent. When
Pope alters, he diminishes; he is a master of miniature. The singular skill
of his portrait of Addison, for example, in the *Epistle to Arbuthnot*, depends upon the justice and reserve, the apparent determination not to
exaggerate. The genius of Pope is not for caricature. But the effect of the
portraits of Dryden is to transform the object into something greater, as
were transformed the verses of Cowley quoted above.

> A fiery soul, which working out its way,
> Fretted the pigmy body to decay:
> And o'er informed the tenement of clay.

These lines are not merely a magnificent tribute. They create the object
which they contemplate. Dryden is, in fact, much nearer to the master of
comic creation than to Pope. As in Jonson, the effect is far from
laughter; the comic is the material, the result is poetry. The Civic
Guards of Rhodes:

> The country rings around with loud alarms,
> And raw in fields the rude militia swarms;
> Mouths without hands; maintained at vast expense,
> In peace a charge, in war a weak defence;
> Stout once a month they march, a blust'ring band,
> And ever, but in times of need, at hand;
> This was the morn, when issuing on the guard,
> Drawn up in rank and file they stood prepared
> Of seeming arms to make a short essay,
> Then hasten to be drunk, the business of the day.

Sometimes the wit appears as a delicate flavor to the magnificence, as in
Alexander's Feast:

> Sooth'd with the sound the king grew vain;
> Fought all his battles o'er again;
> And thrice he routed all his foes, and thrice he slew the slain.

The great advantage of Dryden over Milton is that while the former is always in control of his ascent, and can rise or fall at will (and how masterfully, like his own Timotheus, he directs the transitions!), the latter has elected a perch from which he cannot afford to fall, and from which he is in danger of slipping.

> food alike those pure
> Intelligential substances require
> As doth your Rational; and both contain
> Within them every lower faculty
> Of sense, whereby they hear, see, smell, touch, taste,
> Tasting concoct, digest, assimilate,
> And corporeal to incorporeal turn.

Dryden might have made poetry out of that; his translation from Lucretius is poetry. But we have an ingenious example on which to test our contrast of Dryden and Milton: it is Dryden's "Opera," called *The State of Innocence and Fall of Man*, of which Nathaniel Lee neatly says in his preface:

> Milton did the wealthy mine disclose,
> And rudely cast what you could well dispose:
> He roughly drew, on an old-fashioned ground,
> A chaos, for no perfect world were found,
> Till through the heap, your mighty genius shined.

In the author's preface Dryden acknowledges his debt generously enough:

> The original being undoubtedly, one of the greatest, most noble, and most sublime poems, which either this age or nation has produced.

The poem begins auspiciously:

LUCIFER.   Is this the seat our conqueror has given?
> And this the climate we must change for Heaven?
> These regions and this realm my wars have got;
> This mournful empire is the loser's lot:
> In liquid burnings, or on dry to dwell,
> Is all the sad variety of hell.

It is an early work; it is on the whole a feeble work; it is not deserving of sustained comparison with *Paradise Lost*. But "all the sad variety of hell"! Dryden is already stirring; he has assimilated what he could from Milton; and he has shown himself capable of producing as splendid verse.

The capacity for assimilation, and the consequent extent of range, are conspicuous qualities of Dryden. He advanced and exhibited his variety by constant translation; and his translations of Horace, of Ovid, of Lucretius, are admirable. His gravest defects are supposed to be displayed in his dramas, but if these were more read they might be more praised. From the point of view of either the Elizabethan or the French drama they are obviously inferior; but the charge of inferiority loses part of its force if we admit that Dryden was not quite trying to compete with either, but was pursuing a direction of his own. He created no character; and although his arrangements of plot manifest exceptional ingenuity, it is the pure magnificence of diction, of poetic diction, that keep his plays alive:

> How I loved
> Witness ye days and nights, and all ye hours,
> That danced away with down upon your feet,
> As all your business were to count my passion.
> One day passed by, and nothing saw but love;
> Another came, and still 'twas only love:
> The suns were wearied out with looking on,
> And I untired with loving.
> I saw you every day and all the day;
> And every day was still but as the first:
> So eager was I still to see you more. . . .

> While within your arms I lay,
> The world fell mould'ring from my hands each hour.

Such language is pure Dryden: it sounds, in Mr. Van Doren's phrase, "like a gong." *All for Love,* from which the lines are taken, is Dryden's best play, and this is perhaps the highest reach. In general, he is best in his plays when dealing with situations which do not demand great emotional concentration; when his situation is more trivial, and he can practice his art of making the small great. The back-talk between the Emperor and his Empress Nourmahal, in *Aureng-Zebe,* is admirable purple comedy:

EMPEROR.   Such virtue is the plague of human life:
> A virtuous woman, but a cursèd wife.
> In vain of pompous chastity y' are proud:
> Virtue's adultery of the tongue, when loud.
> I, with less pain, a prostitute could bear,
> Than the shrill sound of virtue, virtue hear.
> In unchaste wives—
> There's yet a kind of recompensing ease:

> Vice keeps 'em humble, gives 'em care to please:
> But against clamorous virtue, what defence?
> It stops our mouths, and gives your noise pretence. . . .

> What can be sweeter than our native home?
> Thither for ease, and soft repose, we come;
> Home is the sacred refuge of our life:
> Secure from all approaches but a wife.
> If thence we fly, the cause admits no doubt:
> None but an inmate foe could force us out.
> Clamours, our privacies uneasy make:
> Birds leave their nests disturbed, and beasts their
>   haunts forsake.

But drama is a mixed form; pure magnificence will not carry it through. The poet who attempts to achieve a play by the single force of the word provokes comparison, however strictly he confine himself to his capacity, with poets of other gifts. Corneille and Racine do not attain their triumphs by magnificence of this sort; they have concentration also, and, in the midst of their phrases, an undisturbed attention to the human soul as they knew it.

Nor is Dryden unchallenged in his supreme ability to make the ridiculous, or the trivial, great.

> Avez-vous observé que maints cercueils de vieilles
> Sont presque aussi petits que celui d'un enfant?

Those lines are the work of a man whose verse is as magnificent as Dryden's, and who could see profounder possibilities in wit, and in violently joined images, than ever were in Dryden's mind. For Dryden, with all his intellect, had a commonplace mind. His powers were, we believe, wider, but no greater, than Milton's; he was confined by boundaries as impassable, though less strait. He bears a curious antithetical resemblance to Swinburne. Swinburne was also a master of words, but Swinburne's words are all suggestions and no denotation; if they suggest nothing, it is because they suggest too much. Dryden's words, on the other hand, are precise, they state immensely, but their suggestiveness is often nothing.

> That short dark passage to a future state;
> That melancholy riddle of a breath,
> That something, or that nothing, after death.

is a riddle, but not melancholy enough, in Dryden's splendid verse. The question, which has certainly been waiting, may justly be asked: whether, without this which Dryden lacks, verse can be poetry? What is man to decide what poetry is? Dryden's use of language is not, like that of Swinburne, weakening and demoralizing. Let us take as a final test his elegy upon Oldham, which deserves not to be mutilated:

> Farewell, too little and too lately known,
> Whom I began to think and call my own;
> For sure our souls were near allied, and thine
> Cast in the same poetic mould with mine.
> One common note on either lyre did strike,
> And knaves and fools we both abhorred alike.
> To the same goal did both our studies drive;
> The last set out the soonest did arrive.
> Thus Nisus fell upon the slippery place,
> Whilst his young friend performed and won the race.
> O early ripe! to thy abundant store
> What could advancing age have added more?
> It might (what nature never gives the young)
> Have taught the numbers of thy native tongue.
> But satire needs not those, and wit will shine
> Through the harsh cadence of a rugged line.
> A noble error, and but seldom made,
> When poets are by too much force betrayed.
> Thy generous fruits, though gathered ere their prime,
> Still showed a quickness; and maturing time
> But mellows what we write to the dull sweets of rhyme.
> Once more, hail, and farewell; farewell, thou young,
> But ah! too short, Marcellus of our tongue!
> Thy brows with ivy and with laurels bound;
> But fate and gloomy night encompass thee around.

From the perfection of such an elegy we cannot detract; the lack of suggestiveness is compensated by the satisfying completeness of the statement. Dryden lacked what his master Jonson possessed, a large and unique view of life; he lacked insight, he lacked profundity. But where Dryden fails to satisfy, the nineteenth century does not satisfy us either; and where that century has condemned him, it is itself condemned. In the next revolution of taste it is possible that poets may turn to the study of Dryden. He remains one of those who have set standards for English verse which it is desperate to ignore.

The Intellectual Milieu
of John Dryden

by Louis I. Bredvold

Dryden has received generous recognition for his stylistic achievement, for the way in which he has put the stamp of his genius upon the language of England, in both prose and poetry. Dr. Johnson's famous dictum that "by him we were taught *sapere et fari,* to think naturally and express forcibly," appears to be also the standard critical opinion of our own day. Thus Mr. Bonamy Dobrée, in an essay occasioned by the tercentenary of Dryden's birth, states that the "chief work" of his "long, patiently arduous life consisted in creating a language fit for civilized Englishmen to use." [1] And Mr. T. S. Eliot has expressed the opinion that "it is hardly too much to say that Dryden found the English speechless, and he gave them speech; and they accordingly acknowledged their master; the language which we can refine, enrich, distort or corrupt as we may, but which we cannot do without. No one, in the whole history of English literature, has dominated that literature so long, or so completely. And even in the nineteenth century the language was still the language of Dryden, as it is today." [2] If this criticism errs, it is on the side of generosity, and it is possible that some of the credit here given to Dryden may in the future be distributed more equitably among his contemporaries and predecessors.

But the content of Dryden's work, his cast of mind, and his intellectual equipment have received little attention, except in disparagement. Mr. Allan Lubbock, for instance, has recently asserted that Dryden's

whole body of work can be explained as the child of a deep enthusiasm, which made him attach but little importance to religion or politics, or even to many aspects of literature itself. What excluded everything else

"The Intellectual Milieu of John Dryden." Chapter I, "Introduction," and Chapter VI, "Conclusion," of *The Intellectual Milieu of John Dryden* (Ann Arbor: The University of Michigan Press, 1934) by Louis I. Bredvold, pp. 3-15, 151-154. Copyright 1934 by the University of Michigan Press. Reprinted by permission of the University of Michigan Press.

[1] *Variety of Ways* (Oxford, 1932), p. 9.
[2] *John Dryden* (New York, 1932), p. 24.

was the love of expression for its own sake. He devoted himself therefore
to increasing the efficiency of his instruments.[3]

That is to say, Dryden was an expert craftsman with an uninteresting
mind. But this is the judgment of the twentieth century; readers in the
past have been able to say more for Dryden. Roscommon found weighty
things in *Religio Laici:*

> Let free, impartial men from Dryden learn
> Mysterious secrets of a high concern,
> And weighty truths, solid convincing sense,
> Explained by unaffected eloquence.[4]

Or, if Roscommon's praise is ruled out as the partiality of a friend, there
is the passage in Walter Savage Landor's verse letter to Wordsworth:

> Our course by Milton's light was sped,
> And Shakespeare shining over head:
> Chatting on deck was Dryden too,
> The Bacon of the rhyming crew;
> None ever crost our mystic sea
> More richly stored with thought than he;
> Tho' never tender nor sublime,
> He wrestles with and conquers Time.[5]

We need not infer from these lines that Dryden should, in Landor's
judgment, be placed among the great philosophical poets, with Lucretius
and Dante, with whom he assuredly does not belong. But the confession
of so discerning a reader as Landor may remind us that there are stores
of thought in Dryden's work which should not be ignored in an explanation and appraisal of his literary achievement. There is, indeed, something anomalous in a criticism which concerns itself with natural thinking and forcible expression without deigning to note *what* is thought
and expressed. Such criticism is either sophistical itself, or applicable
only to sophists. And the unpleasant assumption underlies much of the
criticism, much even of the praise, of Dryden, that he was a sophist and
to be dealt with accordingly; that, with the possible exception of some
of his literary criticism, his mind was neither sincere nor significant nor
interesting.

   This depreciation of Dryden's mind is in large measure due to certain
preconceptions—long current—regarding his moral and intellectual

---

[3] *The Character of John Dryden,* Hogarth Essays (London, 1925), p. 6.
[4] Dryden, *Works,* X, 34.
[5] Landor, *Works* (London, 1853), II, 667.

character, which must be dealt with briefly before we enter upon the proper subject of this study. There are at least three such common preconceptions which the student encounters as obstacles in his approach to Dryden: that Dryden was a hireling, whose political and religious affiliations were determined by bribes and pensions; that in his most serious work he never rose intellectually above the level of ephemeral journalism; and that the inconsistencies and contradictions with which his work abounds are conclusive evidence of a lack of intellectual character and significance.

I

Dryden's pensions as Poet Laureate and Historiographer Royal were constantly harped upon in his own time by hostile pamphleteers, and they have since then inspired suspicion in many of his biographers and critics—with the exceptions of Malone, Scott, and Saintsbury. Very little was known about them, but such fragmentary information as came to light from time to time was always given the most sinister interpretation. The full facts are now in print,[6] and many of these insinuations can be proved gratuitous. The time has come when it is possible to reconsider the question of Dryden's character, both intellectual and moral, with a more open and receptive mind.[7]

The poet should be heard in his own defense; he has important testimony to give regarding the moral and intellectual seriousness of his nature. Perhaps he replied too seldom to the contemporary pamphleteers who vilified him. "Anything, though never so little," he wrote in his old age, "which a man speaks of himself, in my opinion is still too much." [8] He had too much dignity to be egotistically voluble, but he often spoke incidentally about his work and himself with admirable candor, without either false modesty or false pride. These passages in his writings merit some attention from any critic who engages to explain the poet's personality.

It would appear from some of them that Dryden regarded himself as a man of greater moral dignity than tradition since his time has allowed him. Two passages may suffice to illustrate this point. In *A Discourse concerning the Original and Progress of Satire* (1693), addressed to the Earl of Dorset, he questions the legitimacy of the lampoon, "a dangerous

---

[6] In the *Calendar of Treasury Books* for the reigns of Charles II and James II.

[7] The present author has attempted two studies in this direction: "Political Aspects of Dryden's *Amboyna* and *The Spanish Fryar*," *Essays and Studies in English and Comparative Literature*, in University of Michigan Publications, Language and Literature, VIII (1932), 119-132; and "Notes on John Dryden's Pension," *Modern Philology*, XXX (1933), 267-274.

[8] *Essays*, ed. W. P. Ker (Oxford, 1900), II, 80.

sort of weapon, and for the most part unlawful." But possibly, he continues, we may be permitted to use it in revenge,

> . . . when we have been affronted in the same nature, or have been any ways notoriously abused, and can make ourselves no other reparation. And yet we know, that, in Christian charity, all offences are to be forgiven, as we expect the like pardon for those which we daily commit against Almighty God. And this consideration has often made me tremble when I was saying our Saviour's prayer; for the plain condition of the forgiveness which we beg is the pardoning of others the offences which they have done to us; for which reason I have many times avoided the commission of that fault, even when I have been notoriously provoked. Let not this, my Lord, pass for vanity in me; for it is truth. More libels have been written against me, than almost any man now living; and I had reason on my side, to have defended my own innocence. I speak not of my poetry, which I have wholly given up to the critics: let them use it as they please: posterity, perhaps, may be more favourable to me; for interest and passion will lie buried in another age, and partiality and prejudice be forgotten. I speak of my morals, which have been sufficiently aspersed: *that* only sort of reputation ought to be dear to every honest man, and is to me. But let the world witness for me, that I have been often wanting to myself in that particular; I have seldom answered any scurrilous lampoon, when it was in my power to have exposed my enemies: and, being naturally vindicative, have suffered in silence, and possessed my soul in quiet.[9]

Dryden quite evidently was not afraid in his own time to lay public claim to some of the nobler virtues.

In our second passage Dryden defends his sincerity in the matter of party loyalty. Accused as he was of having been hired to write *The Duke of Guise,* he replied in his *Vindication* (1683):

> . . . If I am a mercenary scribbler, the Lords Commissioners of the Treasury best know: I am sure, they have found me no importunate solicitor; for I know myself, I deserved little, and, therefore, have never desired much. I return that slander, with just disdain, on my accusers: it is for men who have ill consciences to suspect others; I am resolved to stand or fall with the cause of my God, my king, and country; never to trouble myself for any railing aspersions, which I have not deserved; and to leave it as a portion to my children,—that they had a father who durst do his duty, and was neither covetous nor mercenary.[10]

Such a reply Dryden's Whig enemies presumably regarded as sheer effrontery and hypocrisy; but the facts regarding his pension bear him out. From 1677 to 1684 he received annually only one half of his stipulated pension; and the payments were neither hastened nor increased on

[9] *Ibid.,* pp. 79-80.
[10] *Works,* VII, 173-174.

account of his political services. There is no evidence that the government offered him any inducement to write on politics. We may reasonably assume that he wrote as he did because he believed that his own security as an Englishman along with that of the nation depended on the defeat of the Whigs. In this spirit, certainly, he addressed the Earl of Rochester in the dedication to *The Duke of Guise* (1683):

> . . . If ever this excellent government, so well established by the wisdom of our forefathers, and so much shaken by the folly of this age, shall recover its ancient splendour, posterity cannot be so ungrateful as to forget those who, in the worst of times, have stood undaunted by their king and country, and, for the safeguard of both, have exposed themselves to the malice of false patriots, and the madness of a headstrong rabble. But since this glorious work is yet unfinished, and though we have reason to hope well of the success, yet the event depends on the unsearchable providence of Almighty God, it is no time to raise trophies, while the victory is in dispute; but every man, by your example, to contribute what is in his power to maintain so just a cause, on which depends the future settlement and prosperity of three nations.[11]

Rochester, as first lord of the Treasury, was in a position to know to what degree Dryden's Tory zeal was mercenary; if Rochester thought the poet was to be purchased for a price, that price was merely the regular payment of one half of the annual pension of the Laureate.[12] Mercenary men know better how to reap their reward. Everything points rather to Dryden's deep devotion and dignified loyalty to the Tory cause, which he identified with the best interests of his king and his country.

II

It would seem difficult enough for any man, in such an unsettled age as the seventeenth century in England, to have remained indifferent to the political and religious embroilments of his age. But Dryden was first of all a poet, and he considered it fatal for a poet to cut himself off from the intellectual life of his age and nation. His statement of the qualifica-

[11] *Ibid.*, p. 16.

[12] Dryden's famous undated letter to Rochester, appealing for "half a year of my salary" or "some small employment . . . either in the Customs, or in the Appeals of the Excise, or some other way," apparently brought him no results. The John Dryden who was appointed, on December 17, 1683, as Collector of Customs in the port of London, was not the poet: see Charles E. Ward, "Was John Dryden Collector of Customs?" *Modern Language Notes*, XLVII (1932), 246-249, and *Calendar of Treasury Books, 1689-1692*, p. 1886. It should be observed also that Dryden's letter to Rochester appears to have been an isolated appeal, made only in circumstances of dire extremity.

tions necessary for the practice of poetry should be a fair indication of the nature of his own intellectual regimen.

Dryden's career as a man of letters turned out vastly different from what he wished it. His creative energy was diverted from his great ambition, to write an epic, and dissipated in a multitude of miscellaneous tasks. If we must find a flaw in his character, this is perhaps the great and serious one, that, in spite of his love for literature and his desire for fame in it, he was not heroic enough to achieve what he himself, correctly or incorrectly, thought should be his greatest work. But there can be no question of his deep desire to write an epic, or of his considered preparation for that task. It was a task which he understood to involve extensive learning and ripe wisdom as well as genius. In the realm of literary theory Dryden was still, in some respects, in the afterglow of the Renaissance; he considered the great epic the supreme achievement of the mind of man. The epic poet, as any reader of Sidney and Spenser would know, must be a legislator, a moralist, a philosopher; as Sidney said, he is the monarch of all sciences. In this old humanistic tradition of the Renaissance, which required the man of genius to acquire learning and judgment, Dryden had been educated, and he was never able to unlearn this lesson.

"I am of opinion," he said in the *Defence of an Essay of Dramatic Poesy* (1668), "that they cannot be good poets, who are not accustomed to argue well. False reasonings and colours of speech are the certain marks of one who does not understand the stage; for moral truth is the mistress of the poet as much as of the philosopher; Poesy must resemble natural truth, but it must *be* ethical." [13] In 1674 he excluded Settle from the communion of orthodox and true poets, because he lacked learning, because he was a sottish "mere poet":

> Fanciful poetry and music, used with moderation, are good; but men who are wholly given over to either of them, are commonly as full of whimsies as diseased and splenetic men can be. Their heads are continually hot, and they have the same elevation of fancy sober, which men of sense have when they drink. So wine used moderately does not take away the judgment, but used continually, debauches men's understandings, and turns them into sots, making their heads continually hot by accident, as the others are by nature; so, mere poets and mere musicians are as sottish as mere drunkards are, who live in a continual mist, without seeing or judging any thing clearly.
>
> A man should be learned in several sciences, and should have a reasonable, philosophical, and in some measure a mathematical head, to be a complete and excellent poet; and besides this, should have experience in all sorts of humours and manners of men; should be thoroughly skilled in conversation, and should have a great knowledge of mankind in general.

[13] *Essays*, ed. W. P. Ker, I, 121.

Mr. Settle having never studied any sort of learning but poetry, and that but slenderly, as you may find by his writings, and having besides no other advantages, must make very lame work on't; he himself declares, he neither reads, nor cares for conversation; so that he would persuade us he is a kind of fanatic in poetry, and has a light within him, and writes by an inspiration; which (like that of the heathen prophets) a man must have no sense of his own when he receives; and no doubt he would be thought inspired, and would be reverenced extremely in the country where Santons are worshipped.[14]

These were not mere transient principles, professed only for the castigation of Settle. "It requires Philosophy," he wrote in 1677, "as well as Poetry, to sound the depth of all the passions." [15] And in 1679, referring to the necessity for a dramatist or an epic poet to know the "manners" of men, this knowledge, he said, is "to be gathered from the several virtues, vices, or passions, and many other commonplaces, which a poet must be supposed to have learned from natural Philosophy, Ethics, and History; of all which, whosoever is ignorant, does not deserve the name of poet." [16] In 1693 he described the qualifications of the poet who "may build a nobler, a more beautiful and more perfect poem, than any yet extant since the Ancients":

. . . a man, who, being conversant in the philosophy of Plato, as it is now accommodated to Christian use, (for, as Virgil gives us to understand by his example, that is the only proper, of all others, for an epic poem,) who, to his natural endowments, of a large invention, a ripe judgment, and a strong memory, has joined the knowledge of the liberal arts and sciences, and particularly moral philosophy, the mathematics, geography, and history, and with all these qualifications is born a poet; knows, and can practise the variety of numbers, and is master of the language in which he writes.[17]

In an epic poet, he says a few pages on, "one who is worthy of that name, besides an universal genius, is required universal learning." [18] Such were the comprehensive qualifications of an epic poet, as Dryden understood them in an age before specialization.

Not that Dryden was a great scholar comparable to Gray or Milton, or that he set himself the hard task of keeping up with all the mathematical discoveries of the seventeenth century; what is contended here is that Dryden had a generous conception of the learning necessary to a poet and that his intellectual interests, thus closely integrated to his calling, were both wide and genuine. "Every page," said Johnson, who surmised

[14] *Works*, XV, 406-407.
[16] *Ibid.*, p. 214.
[18] *Ibid.*, p. 43.

[15] *Essays*, ed. W. P. Ker, I, 183.
[17] *Ibid.*, II, 36.

that Dryden acquired his extensive knowledge rather from conversation than from reading, "every page discovers a mind very widely acquainted both with art and nature, and in full possession of great stores of intellectual wealth." [19] We must not be deluded by the charming small talk of the study which Dryden so often gives us—the careful balancing of the advantages and disadvantages of rhyme, the problem of the comic subplot, the synaloephas of Chapman's *Homer,* the "turns" of Mr. Waller and Sir John Denham to which Sir George Mackenzie had called his attention, the examination of tropes and figures and catachreses—we must not be deluded into supposing that his vital intellectual, or even artistic, interests were narrowly confined to matters of style and language. Dryden said often enough that style is more than technique, that "it must proceed from a genius, and a particular way of thinking"; his discussions of the styles of Lucretius, Horace, Juvenal, and Persius, touching as they do on the lives, social and political circumstances, personal characteristics, and philosophical tenets of these authors, are illustrative of both his theory and practice; and they might well be taken as models for appreciations of the style of Dryden himself. For Dryden believed that the man of letters must study many subjects besides style. He not only knew his *belles lettres,* but ranged extensively among the most unliterary books; he has a wealth of quotation, allusion, and anecdote, much of it from obscure sources as yet untraced by any editor of his work. To describe such a man as a mere polisher of phrases, and devoid of wide-ranging and serious intellectual interests is a grave error in criticism; it is to give the reader exactly the wrong clue.

III

Dr. Johnson, who was by temperament and reading one of the best qualified critics Dryden has ever had, has remarked that "his compositions are the effects of a vigorous genius operating upon large materials." [20] It is the purpose of this study to inquire into the intellectual traits of that genius, and into the nature of the materials upon which it operated. It is our purpose to discover to what extent and in what ways Dryden was intellectually representative of his age; to ascertain what his essential temperament was, and to find what currents of thought in his time were especially congenial to him; in short, whether he belonged to any significant intellectual milieu.

Changeableness is beyond dispute one of the dominant characteristics of his mind. But we must be careful not to conclude hastily that this

[19] *Lives of Poets,* ed. Birkbeck Hill (1905), I, 417.
[20] *Ibid.,* p. 457.

observation is in itself a moral appraisal; it may be profitable to adopt a more neutral procedure than the time-worn one of dwelling on Dryden's inconsistencies in criticism, religion, and politics, and explaining them as prudential accommodations to changing fashions. We shall better understand the nature of his mind if, to begin with, we consider some less important episode, such as cannot by any chance raise suspicions of a sordid motive. A passage in the dedication to *Aureng-Zebe* (1676) may serve. Some of the ladies had criticized as unnatural the conduct of Indamora and Melesinda in the last act. The problem was not one of vast importance, but Dryden gallantly consented to examine their representations:

> That which was not pleasing to some of the fair ladies in the last act of it, as I dare not vindicate, so neither can I wholly condemn, till I find more reason for their censures. . . . I have made my Melesinda in opposition to Nourmahal, a woman passionately loving of her husband, patient of injuries and contempt, and constant in her kindness, to the last; and in that, perhaps, I may have erred, because it is not a virtue much in use. Those Indian wives are loving fools, and may do well to keep themselves in their own country, or, at least, to keep company with the Arrias and Portias of old Rome: Some of our ladies know better things. But, it may be, I am partial to my own writings; yet I have laboured as much as any man, to divest myself of the self-opinion of an author; and am too well satisfied of my own weakness, to be pleased with anything I have written. But, on the other side, my reason tells me, that, in probability, what I have seriously and long considered may be as likely to be just and natural, as what an ordinary judge (if there be any such among those ladies) will think fit, in a transient presentation, to be placed in the room of that which they condemn. The most judicious writer is sometimes mistaken, after all his care; but the hasty critic, who judges on a view, is full as liable to be deceived. Let him first consider all the arguments, which the author had, to write this, or to design the other, before he arraigns him of a fault; and then, perhaps, on second thoughts, he will find his reason oblige him to revoke his censure. Yet, after all, I will not be too positive. *Homo sum, humani a me nihil alienum puto.* As I am a man, I must be changeable: and sometimes the gravest of us all are so, even upon ridiculous accidents. Our minds are perpetually wrought on by the temperament of our bodies; which makes me suspect, they are nearer allied, than either our philosophers or school-divines will allow them to be. I have observed, says Montaigne, that when the body is out of order, its companion is seldom at his ease. An ill dream, or a cloudy day, has power to change this wretched creature, who is so proud of a reasonable soul, and make him think what he thought not yesterday. And Homer was of this opinion, as Cicero is pleased to translate him for us—
>
> > Tales sunt hominum mentes, quali pater ipse
> > Jupiter auctifera lustravit lampade terras.

Or, as the same author, in his "Tusculan Questions," speaks, with more modesty than usual, of himself: *Nos in diem vivimus; quodcunque animos nostros probabilitate percussit, id dicimus.* It is not therefore impossible, but that I may alter the conclusion of my play, to restore myself into the good graces of my fair critics; and your lordship,[21] who is so well with them, may do me the office of a friend and patron, to intercede with them on my promise of amendment.[22]

Were ever fair ladies so perplexed by banter? And could anything be more characteristic of Dryden?

But, in small affairs as in great, Dryden's hesitancy is something more positive than indecision; it is less a weakness of will than a richness and suppleness of intellect. Dryden dearly loved a debate; he ornamented his plays with stretches of resonant argument, and his genius sustained both sides with such impartiality that we are often puzzled which is intended to receive the palm of victory. There are those who regard as the final test of an idea its coherent relation within a unified system. Dryden preferred to see it tested in a vigorous combat with its opposite, each side putting forth its utmost force. He wrote, accordingly, not treatises, but essays and dialogues. Three of his most important works are in the latter form, in spite of the fact that in each case Dryden had a partisan interest. In *An Essay of Dramatic Poesy* Neander is his spokesman; but the ideas of Neander are presented with no more force and art than those of the other three interlocutors. Political ideas are expressed in *Absalom and Achitophel* very largely by discussion and argument, and no one can say that the Whiggism there presented, whatever its morality may be, is intellectually contemptible. The plan of *The Hind and the Panther* permitted of a vigorous recapitulation of the arguments used on both Catholic and Anglican sides in the enormous pamphlet war of the time. And one might add that *Religio Laici,* even though not a debate, is a balancing of conflicting ideas, and that, Protestant though it be, it gives a clear and forceful expression of the main Catholic criticism of the Protestant doctrines regarding religious authority. As Dr. Johnson has observed, Dryden's mind was "always curious, always active." His apparent indecision is evidence, not of weakness, but of strength, of energy, of a versatile understanding. It is his distinction and his virtue.

This is only to speak after Dryden. He has himself told us that his temper was the opposite of the dogmatic and the magisterial, the traits of Hobbes and Lucretius, from whom he carefully distinguished himself in the Preface to *Sylvae* (1685):

If I am not mistaken, the distinguishing character of Lucretius (I mean of his soul and genius) is a certain kind of noble pride, and positive asser-

---

[21] The Earl of Mulgrave.
[22] *Works,* V, 197-200.

tion of his opinions. He is everywhere confident of his own reason, and assuming an absolute command, not only over his vulgar reader, but even his patron Memmius. . . . These are the considerations, which I had of that author, before I attempted to translate some parts of him. And accordingly I laid by my natural diffidence and scepticism for a while, to take up that dogmatical way of his, which, as I said, is so much his character, as to make him that individual poet." [23]

It would be easy to multiply passages to show that Dryden understood the skeptical and diffident nature of his own mind. But more than that, Dryden recognized that his temperament found support and expression in a philosophy; he has repeatedly claimed kinship with skeptical tendencies in ancient and modern thought. Regarding the *Essay of Dramatic Poesy* he declared that

. . . my whole discourse was sceptical, according to that way of reasoning which was used by Socrates, Plato, and all the Academics of old, which Tully and the best of the Ancients followed, and which is imitated by the modest inquisitions of the Royal Society. That it is so, not only the name will show, which is *an Essay*, but the frame and composition of the work. You see it is a dialogue sustained by persons of several opinions, all of them left doubtful, to be determined by the readers in general.[24]

Such was his defense of the *Essay* in 1668. In his Preface to *An Evening's Love* (1671) he asked, "Why should there be any *Ipse dixit* in our poetry, any more than there is in our philosophy?" Finally, in the Preface to *Religio Laici* (1682) he tells us explicitly that he was "naturally inclined to skepticism in philosophy."

Such was the intellectual cast of Dryden. His contact with philosophical skepticism enabled him to rationalize his natural diffidence of temper. Though he has no claim to originality as a thinker, he did possess a loose group of ideas and philosophical doctrines which he understood and to which he felt himself affined. They constitute an essential part of his personality, both as a man and as a writer; to them Dryden was attracted by his "genius," his "particular way of thinking," and through them his intellectual character was formed. Their pervasive influence is evident wherever Dryden made any important intellectual decisions, whether in politics, religion, or philosophy—most evident, perhaps, in his conversion to Catholicism. They drew him quite naturally into certain currents of thought of the century. He lived in an age of philosophical skepticism; every reader of any pretensions to cultivation knew Montaigne and Charron intimately, and almost every scholar had read Sextus Empiricus. Neither Dryden nor his age can be fully understood

[23] *Essays*, ed. W. P. Ker, I, 259-260.
[24] *Ibid.*, p. 124.

apart from this Pyrrhonism, diffused in every department of thought, lending itself to the most diverse purposes, appearing sometimes in strange guises and in the most unexpected places.

This study has not attempted to trace the "growth of a poet's mind." Occasionally it has been possible to establish points of chronology in Dryden's reading, in his intellectual interests, and in the settlement of his convictions; but most of our data remain too vague chronologically to establish any definite stages in the development of his thought. On the whole, it seems most likely that his ideas underwent no very violent change, but merely a clarification, as he added gradually to his stock of ideas in philosophy, religion, and politics, and as one after another the problems of his time pressed for a solution. Thus we do not know whether he made the acquaintance of philosophical skepticism before or after he became a Royalist in politics; it is entirely possible that he had been both skeptical and conservative for some time before he became aware of any connection in principle between the two tendencies. The growth of his thought to maturity appears to have been slow and uncertain, but on the whole, from his point of view at least, sound. Though he tarried to examine everything and try everything, yet from a sufficient distance and with perspective, his somewhat erratic and zigzag course does move with consistency toward a goal; he was a robust individuality, with strong instincts. If, from one point of view, the history of his mind is a clarification of his ideas and a reduction of them to some sort of order, from another it appears to be the triumph of his instincts and his temperament over the multitude of intellectual distractions, such as Hobbism, materialism, Deism, and other temptations of the time, each of which for a season exercised its fascination upon his intelligence. Dryden was not a philosopher in the strict sense of the word; the organizing force in his nature, which gives unity to his work, is as much his temperament as his reason.

He was not a discoverer of new ideas; his whole intellectual biography consists of his ardent and curious examination and testing of those ideas which were current in his age. He is consequently easily misunderstood if detached from his intellectual milieu. And both his temperament and his intellectual character must be defined in terms of what he rejected as well as of what he appropriated. For, although it may be admitted that he was fortunate to live in an age that provided him with precisely those ideas which he could make peculiarly his own, nevertheless the offerings of his age were no simpler than those of any other; and his success in achieving something like centrality and consistency in his intellectual life testifies to both the seriousness and the strength of his mind. His intellectual reactions are as thoroughly characteristic of him as his style, and manifest the same qualities of the man.

The final value of a study of Dryden's adventures among ideas lies, no doubt, in what it contributes to an understanding of the poet's personality. His versatility has long been recognized, usually with the qualifying suspicion or assumption that it precludes his having had any high purpose. But Dryden tried very seriously to find himself, and he eventually succeeded, even though at a mature age. Only a mind thus vigorously exercised could have produced prose and poetry of such solid and enduring value as he has left. The weft of his style crossed a strong warp of thought, skillfully laid to form the base of the completed pattern.

When Dryden said that he laid by his "natural diffidence and scepticism for a while" to take up the dogmatical way of Lucretius for the purpose of translating him, he indicated his own essential quality both of mind and temperament. His philosophical skepticism has been discussed at large in this study. His native diffidence of manner has been attested to by Congreve, who knew him in his old age:

> He was of very easy, I may say, of very pleasing access; but something slow, and as it were diffident in his advances to others. He had something in his nature that abhorred intrusion into any society whatsoever. Indeed it is to be regretted that he was rather blamable in the other extreme; for, by that means, he was personally less known, and consequently his character might become liable both to misapprehensions and misrepresentations.
>
> To the best of my knowledge and observation, he was, of all the men that ever I knew, one of the most modest, and the most easily to be discountenanced in his approaches, either to his superiors or equals.[25]

It is apparent how deeply the skeptical way of thinking was rooted in his whole nature, what an admirably fitted philosophical medium it was for the expression of his inborn temperament. A man whose intellectual possessions are so obviously his birthright should not be hastily set down as insincere.

As Dryden's sincerity may be discovered in his appropriation of exactly those ideas of his age which fitted him, so his consistency is to be understood from the historical development of those ideas. Some of the extensive ramifications of Pyrrhonism in the thought of the seventeenth century have been traced in the preceding pages of this study. It is obvious that the man who in that century found himself inclined to philosophical skepticism was likely to find his views to some extent determined thereby in such distantly related subjects as religion and politics. For if Pyrrhonism has made many "libertines" and "free-thinkers," it has had a far more distinguished following among serious-minded men of con-

---

[25] Dedication to Dryden's *Dramatic Works* (1717).

servative tendencies in Church and State. Among the many great names representative of this comprehensive and important tradition of the century Dryden's is not the least. A survey of the history of the whole tradition reveals, therefore, as no mere analysis or commentary can, the fundamental and intimate relationship between Dryden's philosophical skepticism and his conservatism and traditionalism in religion and politics. The consistency of his thought is perhaps better not regarded as entirely a matter of logic; it is the consistency of a man who came to understand one of the profound impulses of his age, through which also he could define and express his own temperament and convictions.

If such considerations as these are sound, Dryden is even on the intellectual side a significant and an imposing figure. He represents an important aspect of the seventeenth century. His poems on religion should be studied along with Montaigne, Charron, Pascal, Bishop Huet; his poems on politics would profit the historian of political thought as much as the writings of Hobbes—certainly more than the treatises of Filmer. But any work of first-rate historical importance has also some intrinsic value as an enrichment of the experience of later generations. Conservatives and liberals we shall always, fortunately, have with us. Those who belong to the same camp recognize and salute one another, however widely they may differ on particular doctrines in economics, politics, or theology; they are somehow like-minded and understand one another. Dryden has always had, and probably for a long time to come will have, some small following of those who delight not only in relishing his phrases, but also in thinking his thoughts. For such readers his work is one of the classic expressions of the conservative temperament.

The Medal of John Bayes

by James M. Osborn

Most of the attacks on Dryden are painfully dull reading. The majority of them contain nothing but the same stock charges against him, such as his early verses on Cromwell, the ignominy of Rose Alley, or more personal insults repeated from the *Rehearsal*. A contrast to these lampoons is *The Medal of John Bayes* (1682), which, though equally scurrilous and obscene, is deservedly the best known and most quoted poetical assault on Dryden.

This superiority in matter and manner is explained by the fact that Shadwell has been accepted as the author. Malone discovered the first evidence, the copy that belonged to Narcissus Luttrell,[1] which bears the autograph note, "6ᵈ. By Thomas Shadwell. Agt Mʳ Dryden. very severe 15 May." But later this ascription was challenged by a distinguished authority on Restoration literature, George Thorn-Drury.[2] He questioned Shadwell's authorship on four grounds: first, that the publisher of the libel, Richard Janeway, "had not been concerned in the issue of any single scrap of Shadwell's identified work": secondly, that

As Shadwell had been his most conspicuous victim among the literary men, his name was most readily associated with anything and everything in the nature of a retort, and that it is for this and for no other reason that he has been saddled with *The Medal of John Bayes* [and other anti-Dryden libels].

To substantiate this argument, Thorn-Drury gave the dates of several other lampoons which came after *The Medal of John Bayes*.[3] On this

---

"The Medal of John Bayes." From *John Dryden: Some Biographical Facts and Problems* (New York: Columbia University Press, 1940) by James M. Osborn, pp. 155-167. Copyright 1940 by Columbia University Press and © 1963 by the University of Florida Press. Reprinted by permission of the author and the University of Florida Press. Slightly revised by the author for this edition.

[1] Now in the Dyce Library at South Kensington.

[2] RES, I (1925), 190-92.

[3] *Satire to His Muse by the Author of Absalom and Achitophel*, advertised in *The True Protestant Mercury*, July 22-26, 1682; *The Tory Poets*, dated by Luttrell "Sept. 4" [1682]; *The Address of John Dryden Laureat, to His Highness the Prince of Orange*, 1689. Luttrell's copy is dated January 30, 1689/90.

basis he contended that "it is to the last degree improbable that within [this] short period . . . any one man should have produced them all and should have returned three several times to the attack upon Dryden." In the third place, Thorn-Drury called in witness the dedication of Shadwell's translation of *The Tenth Satyr of Juvenal* (1687). In this he found neither "scurrilous violence or obscenity," nor any acknowledgment of Shadwell's authorship of *The Medal of John Bayes* (though it is not clear why he should have expected acknowledgment of either):

> There are, I suppose it must be admitted, no limits to hypocrisy and untruthfulness, but it is very difficult to believe that a man who had shortly before disgraced himself by the disgusting obscenity of his attack upon Dryden, should, while actually addressing him in public, put forward this unctuous claim to make excuse for himself, because he is neither base nor dishonest.

Finally, there is the core of the argument, Thorn-Drury's attempt to depreciate Luttrell's authority. He did this by labeling it "a single unsupported statement," in contrast to which "there is not to be found, as far as I am aware, a trace of a suggestion of his authorship of it throughout the full and free exchange of abuse which the religious and political differences of the time provoked; the above inscription is, in fact, the ground, and the only ground, for heaping upon Shadwell the disgrace of this scurrilous production." It must be admitted that Thorn-Drury made a plausible case against Luttrell's ascription, but nonetheless I believe that Shadwell was indeed the author.

Answering the points in order, I shall first examine the argument based on Janeway. That he published nothing else for Shadwell is suggestive rather than conclusive: Janeway's press was very active in the Whig interest and was useful for many writers who wished for maximum anonymity. The poem before us is so obscene and vitriolic that the author may well have preferred to send it to a party printer rather than merely to take the chance of concealment behind title-page anonymity. Moreover, Thorn-Drury neglected to take into account Shadwell's publishing habits during this decade: after he ceased writing for Herringman, in 1678, and until he settled with Knapton, in 1689, Shadwell did not, so far as I can discover, use the same publisher twice consecutively.

Next, the matter of the many poetical libels fathered on Shadwell. It is true that nameless brats are usually laid at the doors of notorious rakes, but in the present instance this circumstance does not invalidate the authority of Luttrell's ascription. The fact that other libels were attributed to Shadwell *after* the appearance of *The Medal of John Bayes* in no way detracts from the likelihood that Shadwell wrote the first and most powerful of them: indeed, this explanation strengthens the case for

Shadwell's authorship, for it is entirely consistent with the qualifications propounded by Thorn-Drury. *The Medal of John Bayes* is ascribed to Shadwell on positive evidence, and there are no corresponding grounds for the attribution of succeeding libels to him.

The interpretation of the epistle to Sedley before *The Tenth Satyr of Juvenal* seems to me to have been oversimplified by Thorn-Drury. Written five years after *The Medal of John Bayes* and the publication of *Mac Flecknoe* (regardless of its composition date, we must remember that a poem circulated in manuscript has a restricted audience compared to the same poem in print), this dedication was framed consciously as a "vindication," the very word Shadwell used. Although he could not foresee how many centuries he would live as monarch of Dullness, Shadwell realized that he had been caricatured unmercifully and was deeply hurt by what he regarded as the injustice of Dryden's exaggerations. Five years earlier his method had been to meet abuse with abuse; but now that the quarrel had died down to embers, his method changed into an attempt to prove that Tom Shadwell was not such a bad fellow after all.

> I hope Sir [he wrote to Sedley] you will not think me guilty of Arrogance in my own Vindication, especially since there have been such strong endeavours to depress me, and by those who had least reason to do it.
>
> But sure he goes a little too far in calling me the dullest, and has no more reason for that, than for giving me the *Irish* name of *Mack,* when he knows I never saw *Ireland* till I was three and twenty years old, and was there but four Months. . . . But he is not content with [pronouncing me dull], but has another fling at me for playing upon the *Lute.* I must confess that that and all other Gentlemen-like Exercises, which I was capable of Learning, my Father was at the charge of, and let the Libeller make his best of it.
>
> I was provoked to this first [venture in translation] by the supposed *Author* of *Mack-Fleckno,* who saies in another Pamphlet; that to his knowledge, I understand neither Greek nor Latin, though in *Bury* School in *Suffolk,* and *Cajus* Colledge in *Cambridge,* the places of my Youthful Education, I had not that reputation, and let me tell him he knows the contrary.[4]

Having taken this tack, Shadwell naturally avoided saying anything at all about his earlier attempts to repay blow for blow. His whole purpose now was to show that Dryden's shafts were never deserved. Thus it was the very essence of Shadwell's remarks to omit references to his attack on Dryden, though he nowhere denies or even implies that he failed to retaliate to the best of his ability. In the absence of an implied denial

---

[4] *Works,* ed. Summers, V, 292. These quotations show how well acquainted the two poets were with incidents in each other's life.

this "vindication" is a slender thread upon which to hang the contention that Shadwell did not write *The Medal of John Bayes*.[5]

And now for the core of the argument, the authority that should be accorded to Luttrell's title-page inscription. Luttrell's habit of jotting on title pages clearly reveals that he was unusually well informed. I have approached the matter by collecting data from over two thousand of Luttrell's books and have found no instance where Luttrell's ascriptions are mistaken in the case of such a well-known figure as Shadwell. Luttrell's note is positive evidence of established quality, which cannot be controverted except by evidence equally positive. So far none has been produced. Neither Thorn-Drury nor any other scholar has put forward as author any other candidate who is worth consideration. If during "the full and free exchange of abuse which the religious and political differences of the time provoked," the poem had been ascribed to another writer, Thorn-Drury would certainly have urged this candidate in Shadwell's place. The negative evidence *against* Shadwell is not a whit stronger than the negative evidence *for* him. Moreover, we should not lose sight of the fact that another writer with an equal knowledge of Dryden's affairs and an equal capacity for virulence in verse could not easily be found in 1682.[6]

In addition to the previous arguments, an important new piece of evidence has recently been brought forward by Dryden's bibliographer, Mr. Hugh Macdonald.[7] In the library of Trinity College, Cambridge, is a copy of *The Medal of John Bayes,* on the title page of which an unknown contemporary recorded his reaction to the abusive poem. It reads, "Shadwell is run mad." With this statement corroborating that of Luttrell, I believe we must accept Shadwell as the author until there are new grounds for thinking otherwise.

Once Shadwell is acknowledged as the author, it is necessary to re-examine with care the passages in *The Medal of John Bayes* that tell us anything about Dryden. Sprinkled in the poem or in the preliminary *Epistle to the Tories,* there are about a score of such passages, of which half a dozen or so are repetitions of old charges that had been bandied about by Dryden's opponents for more than ten years. Before going on to the dozen passages which contain new biographical information about Dry-

---

[5] Even if Shadwell *had* categorically denied the authorship, Thorn-Drury's argument could be turned inside out: why should we be expected to accept Shadwell's denial of *The Medal of John Bayes* any more than Shadwell accepted Dryden's denial of *Mac Flecknoe*?

[6] D. M. McKeithan, in his study of "The Authorship of *The Medal of John Bayes,*" (*Texas Studies in English,* pp. 92-97, 1932), has examined passages of this poem in comparison with Shadwell's acknowledged verse.

[7] *Essays and Studies by Members of the English Association,* XXI (1935), 59. In his *Dryden Bibliography* (1939), which appeared after this study was written, Mr. Macdonald points out (p. 233) the contemporary evidence of *A Journal from Parnassus* connecting Shadwell with *The Medal of John Bayes.*

den, it is pertinent to glance at Shadwell's restatement of these stock charges.[8]

The first of them, mentioned in the *Epistle to the Tories* and expanded in the poem, is that Dryden, ever prompt to discover dullness in others, was himself "lumpish and flegmatick" in conversation. Shadwell was especially sensitive to this contradiction, for he had won a name as a clever conversationalist, and so was doubly insulted that a whole poem should celebrate him as the monarch of Dullness. His vanity punctured and his wit impugned, Shadwell sought revenge with personal abuse. His task was comparatively easy, because fourteen years earlier Dryden had confessed in print that he was backward in company:

> I know I am not so fitted by nature to write comedy: I want that gaiety of humour which is required to it. My conversation is slow and dull; my humour saturnine and reserved; in short, I am none of those who endeavour to break jests in company, or make reparties.[9]

To what degree Dryden described himself fairly it is now impossible to determine, but his admission was used for several decades by his opponents as a stick with which to beat him.

The next circumstance of which Shadwell reminded Dryden was his relations with the actress Ann Reeves.[10] From the many contemporary references to this affair, we may safely conclude that she was the poet's mistress, although to the credit of both it must be acknowledged that amidst the loose living of the age Dryden was apparently constant in his affections: for unlike his notorious contemporaries, Dryden's name is never linked by gossip with that of any other woman of the theater or the town.[11] Even Shadwell pays tribute to his "constancy in Love," although the venereal consequences cannot be substantiated.

Mention of the Reeves affair is followed by this paragraph:

> You who would know him better, go to the Coffee-house (where he may be said almost to inhabit) and you shall find him holding forth to half a score young fellows, (who clap him on the back, spit in his mouth, and loo him on upon the *Whiggs,* as they call 'em) puft up, and swelling with their

---

[8] Shadwell's critical opinions, such as that Dryden "has an easiness in Rime, and a knack at Versifying," or that his dedications are full of "nauseous flattery," have been passed over as not coming within the scope of this present inquiry.

[9] *Defence of an Essay of Dramatic Poesy*, in Ker, *Essays of Dryden*, I, 116. This trait is again mentioned many years later in a letter to the Earl of Chesterfield, dated February 17, 1696/7: "I have humoured my natural bashfulness by not addressing you sooner." *The Letters of Chesterfield* (1829), pp. 376-79.

[10] See Thorn-Drury's discussion of the subject, *Covent Garden Drollery*, 1928, p. 135.

[11] There is a little-known story that Dryden and Henry Cromwell competed for a mistress and that Cromwell won. For a refutation of it see "Dryden, Pope and Curll's Corinna," in *Notes and Queries*, First Series, XII, 277-79.

praise: and the great Subject of his Discourse shall be of himself, and his *Poetry;* What Diet he uses for *Epick* what for *Comick;* what course he is in for *Libel,* and what for *Tragedy.*

That Dryden did "inhabit" Will's has become a commonplace in all accounts of him. We also know that he got on easily with younger men: Southerne, Congreve, Walsh, Lockier are a few that immediately come to mind. Dryden was past fifty at this time, so the contrast between him and the rising generation of wits was easily noticed. Yet there are passages in the 1668 *Letter to Edward Howard* by the unidentified "R. F." and also in the *Rehearsal* which provide earlier analogues for this reference to the flattering attentions of "half a score young fellows."

The joke about "What Diet he uses for *Epick* and what for *Comick*" is repeated in full anecdotal form lower down the page:

> 'Tis not two years since he consulted with an Eminent and Learned Physician of this Town; telling him, he was obliged to write a Play, and finding himself very dull, desired he would prescribe him a Diet, and course of Physick fit for his Malady: the Dr. merrily asked him Whether 'twas *Comedy* or *Tragedy* he designed? he answered, *Tragedy;* the Dr. replyed, The Steel Diet was most proper for *Tragedy;* whereupon the Poet desired to have it prescribed, and did undergo it for six weeks.

It would be tempting to believe this anecdote, for such pseudo-science and credulity were possible in an age when modern empirical medicine was just beginning. However, a likely source for the tale makes speculation futile. I refer to the well-known passage in the *Rehearsal* where Bayes describes his preparations for literary composition:

> If I am to write familiar things, as Sonnets to *Armida,* and the like, I make use of Stew'd Prunes only; but when I have a grand design in hand, I ever take Phisic, and let blood: for, when you would have pure swiftness of thought, and fiery flights of fancy, you must have a care of the pensive part. In fine, you must purge the Belly.[12]

Even so late as 1730, in Lamotte's *Essay on Poetry and Painting,* the anecdote was repeated that Dryden customarily was "blooded and purged" before sitting down to serious work. Both Shadwell and Lamotte follow their source too closely to warrant belief that their testimony is independent of the *Rehearsal.*

---

[12] *Rehearsal,* ed. Summers, p. 18. From a letter to Tonson (*Letters,* ed. Ward, No. 26) we learn that, whatever his affection for stewed prunes, Dryden was apparently very fond of damsons: "Pray, Sir, let [my wife] know that I am well; and for feare the few damsins shou'd be all gone, desire her to buy me a sieve-full, to preserve whole, and not in mash."

Another stock charge repeated from the *Rehearsal* was that Dryden depended on other men's work for his wit and his plots:

> All written Wit thou seizest on as prize;
> But that will not thy ravenous mind suffice;
> Though men from thee their inward thoughts conceal,
> *Yet thou the words out of their mouths wilt steal.*

There could be no better measure of the paucity of valid complaints against Dryden than the fuss made over his careful reworking of the *materia poetica.* Yet in the twenty years between the *Rehearsal* and Langbaine's 1691 *Account of the English Dramatick Poets* this was one of the chief accusations against him.[13]

So much, then, for the conventional items of abuse; and now to consider the original information to be found in this pamphlet. The second paragraph of the *Epistle to the Tories* contains two anecdotes that have an air of verisimilitude about them. The first is as follows:

> You may know he is no concealer of himself, by a story which he tells of himself, *viz.* That (when he came first to Town) being a young raw fellow of seven and Twenty, as he call'd himself when he told the story, he frequenting but one Coffee-house, the Woman (it seems finding him out) put Coffee upon him for Chocolate, and made him pay three pence a dish for two years together: till at length, by what providence I know not, he discovered the Cheat.

Surrounded as it is by violent abuse, this story is so feeble that no reason can be suggested for the prominence given to it except that it is true. Certainly the phrases "a story which he tells of himself," "as he called himself when he told the story," "it seems," "by what providence I know not," have the ring of authenticity about them. They may be mere devices of conscious art, but when taken in conjunction with the mild pointlessness of the anecdote itself, the combined factors make me believe that Shadwell was really repeating an incident once recounted to him by Dryden.

This story is followed by what Shadwell considered a jesting explanation of Dryden's incredible stupidity:

> . . . there is somewhat to be said for it; for (as he said of himself at the same time) the opening in his head (which in Children usually closes about the age of three) did not close in him till he was seven and twenty; which may be the reason he has had such a devilish soft place there ever since.

[13] For a somewhat fuller treatment of these charges of plagiarism, see Osborn, *Dryden Facts and Problems* (1940), pp. 221-23.

The reasons already given for accepting the anecdote of the coffee hoax incline me to believe that Shadwell based his quip about the "devilish soft place" on what he considered to be a fact. The tardy closing of the fontanelle is a not uncommon occurrence, but only in very abnormal cases has the fontanelle been known to remain soft until manhood. If Dryden suffered from this trouble it was probably caused by rickets, usually the result of diet deficient in vitamin D and lack of sunlight.[14] Although the connection is not implicit, it is suggestive that Dryden was one of the slowest to mature of all the great poets.

Leaving the preliminary prose epistle and turning to the poem itself, we are arrested by a phrase in line 13, "this Cherry-cheeked Dunce of fifty-three." At this time Dryden was actually only fifty-one, an error devoid of importance. The adjective "cherry-cheeked" is, however, one to be remembered, as it is in many ways the happiest description of Dryden that has come down to us. The touch of color cannot be discerned in the dark portraits of Kneller and is lacking in most other references to "Poet Squab." [15]

Allied with a point already discussed—Dryden's lack of mirth in company—is the charge that his repartee consisted chiefly of bawdy talk:

> An old gelt Mastiff has more mirth than thou,
> When thou a kind of paltry Mirth would'st show.
> Good humour thou so awkwardly put'st on,
> It sits like Modish Clothes upon a Clown;
> While that of Gentlemen is brisk and high,
> When Wine and Wit about the room does flie.
> Thou never mak'st, but art a standing Jest;
> Thy Mirth by foolish Bawdry is exprest. . . .

To substantiate the allegation Shadwell quotes an obscene remark supposedly made by Dryden "At *Windsor* in the company of several persons of Quality, Sir G[eorge] E[therege] being present." [16] Considering the standards of the time, especially those of Sedley, Etherege, and others, I see no reason to doubt this story. The general charge of bawdy talk, it will be recalled, had previously been made in the *Rehearsal*. Dryden was always thoroughly responsive to his audience, and in this instance as

---

[14] I am indebted for this medical opinion to Clarence W. Lieb, M.D.

[15] Malone (*Life of Dryden*, p. 430n) mentions Radcliffe's *News from Hell* (1682):

> "Laureate who was both learn'd and *florid*.
> Was damn'd long since for *silence horrid*."

And in *The City Mouse and the Country Mouse* (Malone, p. 431n) is a reference to Bayes's "rosy-coloured" appearance.

[16] Dryden apparently visited Windsor on several occasions. See the discussion of his absences from London, Osborn, *op. cit.*, pp. 199-200.

elsewhere we can be sure that he gave the company what it wanted to hear.

Shadwell next developed still another theme from the *Rehearsal*, that Dryden "boasts of Vice which he did ne'er commit." The contemporary readers of the poem probably did not notice that this allegation directly contradicts the claims previously made about his conduct with Anne Reeves. But consistency is not to be sought for in abuse.

Of course the Rose Alley beating was the delight of Dryden's foes, and throughout the following years it served as a cudgel with which to chastise the old poet in print. Shadwell alluded to it several times, but only once in a way that is of interest to posterity:

> After the drubs, thou didst of late compound,
> And sold for th'weight in Gold each bruise and wound. . . .

The only other reference to monetary compensation for this disgraceful episode is dated thirty years after the event and is found in Defoe's *Review*, the issue of May 17, 1712: Here the story goes that Buckingham "can'd him very smartly; *there Sir,* said the Duke, *is for your ill Manners;* and *here, Sir,* says he, *is for your Wit,* and threw him a Purse with Thirty Guineas at the same Time." [17] But there is no reason to connect Buckingham with the event, and even Rochester's part in the beating is open to question. The most likely explanation of such reparation would be that the Duchess of Portsmouth, probably the chief protagonist in the ambuscade, may have discovered that, not Dryden, but Mulgrave was responsible for the satire and afterward may have attempted to salve the bruises of the poet in the manner reported by Shadwell. Conjecture on the subject is futile, yet Shadwell's statement must not be disregarded.

Leaving these small points, let us turn to the main biographical passage—more than thirty lines which chronicle in detail the unfortunate incidents of Dryden's early years. This much-quoted passage begins with the lines:

> At *Cambridge* first your scurrilous Vein began,
> When sawcily you traduc'd a *Nobleman,*
> Who for that Crime rebuk'd you on the head,
> And you had been Expell'd had you not fled.

As with other incidents in Dryden's early life, details are lacking of this overflow of youthful impertinence, but Shadwell probably knew what he was talking about. Dryden had left Cambridge early in 1655, and Shadwell arrived there in December. The records do not tell when

---

[17] This was first pointed out by E. G. Fletcher in *MLN*, L, 366.

Dryden departed, and his movements in this year are entirely conjectural. Even if the incident occurred some time before Shadwell came into residence, he had ample opportunity to pick up the tale from contemporaries who knew both him and Dryden. Dryden was punished at least once during his college years, in July, 1652,[18] and this event may have provided the foundation for Shadwell's story.

The next lines describe Dryden's move to London:

> The next step of Advancement you began,
> Was being Clerk to *Nolls* Lord *Chamberlain,*
> A Sequestrator and Committee-man.

For years this triplet was the chief authority for the tradition that Dryden held a small position on Thurloe's staff. The public records have yielded confirmation, although little more than the bare fact can be ascertained from them.[19]

After the Restoration Dryden was forced to seek new employment, and his progress is continued in the already-quoted lines:

> He turn'd a Journey-man t'a * Bookseller;
> Writ Prefaces to Books for Meat and Drink,
> And as he paid, he would both write and think.
>
> * Mr. Herringman, *who kept him in his House for that purpose.*
> [Original note.]

Shadwell's claims that Dryden worked for Herringman and lived in his house are still unconfirmed and probably never can be proved positively. Yet here again the known facts are consistent with Shadwell's statements.[20]

In similar fashion Shadwell alluded to Dryden's relations with Sir Robert Howard:

> Then by th'assistance of a § Noble *Knight,*
> Th'hadst plenty, ease, and liberty to write.
> First like a *Gentleman* he made thee live;
> And on his Bounty thou didst amply thrive.
> But soon thy Native swelling Venom rose,
> And thou didst him, who gave thee Bread, expose.

[18] "His crime was, his disobedience to the Vice-master, and his contumacy in taking his punishment inflicted by him." Conclusion-book, Trinity College, Cambridge, quoted by Malone, *Life of Dryden,* p. 16.

[19] For a discussion of the evidence that Dryden was an employee of the Commonwealth government see Osborn, *op. cit.,* pp. 168-70. Charles Ward seems excessively cautious on this matter, *Life of Dryden* (1961), p. 17.

[20] For a detailed examination of this subject see Osborn, *op. cit.,* pp. 170-77.

> 'Gainst him a scandalous Preface didst thou write,
> Which thou didst soon expunge, rather than fight.
>
> § *Sir R. H. who kept him generously at his own House.*
> [Original note.]

As I have already pointed out, other evidence confirms Shadwell's statement about Dryden's residence under Howard's roof and tells us that
Dryden slept in a "serge bed." Dryden's own statements leave no doubt
of his indebtedness to Howard during the early 1660's.[21] The literary
quarrel with Howard is still obscure in some particulars but it is clear
that the "scandalous Preface," that is, the *Defence of an Essay of Dramatic Poesy,* was indeed "expunged." If the quarrel was terminated by
the threat of a duel, as Shadwell implies, no corroboration can be found
in contemporary writings.

The last incidents that Shadwell relates from Dryden's early career
concern his patroness Anne, Duchess of Monmouth:

> (When turn'd away by him in some small time)
> You in the Peoples ears began to chime,
> And please the Town with your successful Rime.
> When the best Patroness of Wit and Stage,
> The Joy, the Pride, the wonder of the Age,
> Sweet *Annabel* the good, great, witty, fair;
> (Of all this Northern Court, the brightest Star)
> Did on thee, *Bayes,* her sacred beams dispence,
> Who could do ill under such influence?
> She the whole *Court* brought over to thy side,
> And favour flow'd upon thee like a Tide.
> To her thou soon prov'dst an * *ungrateful Knave;*
> So good was she, not only she forgave,
> But did oblige anew, the faithless Slave.

> * *When he had thrice broken his Word, Oath, and Bargain with
> Sir* William Davenant, *he wrote a Letter to this great Lady to
> pass her word for him to Sir* William, *who would not take his
> own; which she did. In his Letter he wisht God might never
> prosper him, his Wife or Children, if he did not keep his Oath and
> Bargain; which yet in two months he broke, as several of the
> Dukes Play-house can testifie.* [Original note].

Since Dryden frequently acknowledged his gratitude and indebtedness
to "charming Annabel," Shadwell's lines tell nothing that is very new.

---

[21] See especially the Letter to Howard before *Annus Mirabilis:* "You have not only
been careful of my fortune, which was the effect of your nobleness, but you have been
solicitous of my reputation, which is that of your kindness."

They do, however, illustrate well Shadwell's mastery in the art of distortion: on the ground that Dryden was helped by his patroness, we are told that the poet's success was primarily due to her influence.

But the footnote is a different matter: this oath taking is an entirely unknown incident and has never been examined by any of Dryden's or Davenant's biographers. We know little of Dryden's relations with Davenant, except the two passages, one in the Preface to the *Tempest* (1670) and the other in the essay *Of Heroique Plays* (1672), in which Dryden paid tender tribute to his late collaborator and predecessor in the office of laureate. The episode is related with such an air of verisimilitude and show of detail, especially the effective phrase "as several of the Dukes Play-house can testifie," that it cannot be lightly disregarded. Can we believe there is any truth in it? The answer to this question is important, for it is the crux of our re-examination of the poem.

Once Shadwell is accepted to be the author of this poem, the logical consequences must be faced. The careers of the two poets paralleled each other so closely that each had an opportunity for intimate knowledge of incidents in the other's life: both were at Cambridge, both were in the government service, both had connections with Herringman the publisher, both circulated in the same company of wits and literary noblemen, and both were important figures in the theater. Thus when *Mac Flecknoe* and *The Medal of John Bayes* were written, the authors had ample knowledge of their subject matter.

The detailed examination of Shadwell's poem which we have just made substantiates this fact. In every instance where outside evidence can be produced, Shadwell's anecdotes are consistent with the established details. He distorted and exaggerated, but like every good satirist he based his abuse on a kernel of truth. Because the outside evidence always supports and never contradicts what Shadwell says, even those incidents where corroborative evidence is lacking must be accepted until they can be disproven. The course for future biographers is therefore clear. The anecdotes concerning Dryden's drinking coffee for chocolate, his lodging with Herringman, his expedition to Windsor with Etherege, his tangle with Davenant, and the others, may take their place in Dryden's biography until they are contradicted by new discoveries.

And while logic is being vigorously applied, one other point should not be forgotten: Shadwell conspicuously omits any reference to the circumstances of Dryden's marriage with Lady Elizabeth Howard. Other passages in the abuses are personal enough and obscene enough to show that he was not holding back any slanderous charge from a sense of delicacy. This negative evidence strongly suggests the conclusion that the story of certain unpleasant circumstances attendant on the marriage was not true. Shadwell had found enough authentically scandalous anecdotes about Dryden without resorting to rumor or fabrication to lengthen his list.

An Allusion to Europe:
Dryden and Poetic Tradition

by Reuben A. Brower

> He professed to have learned his poetry from Dryden, whom, when-
> ever an opportunity was presented, he praised through his whole life
> with unvaried liberality; and perhaps his character may receive
> some illustration if he be compared with his master.
>
> (Samuel Johnson, *Life of Pope*)

Any talk of Pope's achievement as a poet or of his relation to poetic
tradition must begin with the tradition of Dryden. Like Dryden he was
catholic in his tastes, and he enjoyed an easy commerce with the poetry
of the past and present. From his early reading and imitations and translations, it is clear that Pope had direct and lively contact with Homer
and the greater Roman and English poets and with many lesser English
and French poets of his own generation and of the century before him.
Feeling no nineteenth century compulsion to be merely original, he took
pleasure in imitating the poets he read and admired, one and all. Speaking years later of his youthful epic *Alcander,* he remarked to Spence,

> I endeavoured [said he, smiling], in this poem, to collect all the beauties
> of the great epic writers into one piece: there was Milton's style in one
> part, and Cowley's in another: here the style of Spenser imitated, and
> there of Statius; here Homer and Virgil, and there Ovid and Claudian.

Although it is highly probable that without Dryden's example Pope
would have discovered a voice of his own and a way of mastering this
embarrassment of poetical riches, the fact remains that he "learned his
poetry" from Dryden and that as Johnson also says,

> By perusing the works of Dryden, he discovered the most perfect fabric
> of English verse, and habituated himself to that only which he found the
> best. . . .

"An Allusion to Europe: Dryden and Poetic Tradition." From *Alexander Pope:
The Poetry of Allusion* (Oxford: The Clarendon Press, 1959) by Reuben A. Brower,
pp. 1-14. Copyright © 1959 by the Oxford University Press. Reprinted by permission
of the Clarendon Press, Oxford.

From Dryden he learned how to imitate without loss of originality, how to make use of the resources of other poets and other poetic modes and yet remain himself and the same. The poetic education he received was more than technical training in versification and practice in the ancient literary art of skillful borrowing. While searching "the pages of Dryden for happy combinations of heroic diction" or more musical cadences, he was also finding his relation to the poetry of the European past and to the mind of Europe. By following Dryden and surpassing him, Pope became after Chaucer, Shakespeare, and Milton the most European of English poets. Reduced to its simplest terms, his problem was how to connect the old world of Homer and Virgil and Horace, or of Spenser and Milton, with the actual society of eighteenth century London in which he and his readers were living. His success as a poet depended directly on Dryden's achievement in solving a similar problem for the very different society and literary public of the Restoration.

As literary histories of the Neoclassical period remind us far too often, it is easier to bury Dryden than to praise him. So much depends on the tradition we choose to place him in and on the standards by which we measure poetic success. If we follow Dr. Johnson and set Dryden in the succession of Waller and Denham, we arrive at a pious tribute to the "reformer of our numbers." If we follow F. R. Leavis and trace "the line of wit," we bring out Dryden's undeniable limitations as compared with Donne or Marvell. (Leavis' strategy was justified in relation to his aims and results: he has made us aware that "serious wit" did not end with the Metaphysicals.) But if we are to make a positive estimate of Dryden's achievement, we should include in his ancestry English poets of the earlier and later Renaissance and their ancient predecessors, and we need to maintain a keen sense of what Dryden accomplished for his contemporaries. So viewed, Dryden marks the reaffirmation of "Europe" in English poetry and culture after an experiment in insularity and at a time of artificial essays in continental "Classicism."

Again, it would be easy to arrive at a rather tepid estimate of Dryden's career—true enough, but hardly of much concern to readers with a live interest in either history or poetry. Dryden's reaffirmation matters— aesthetically and historically—because it is a poet's affirmation, realized in the shaping of new modes of expression and in the writing of poetry which is imaginatively various and unified. His direct critical propaganda for French and Latin literary standards counts for relatively little in the continuing life of the Renaissance tradition. A more adaptable Arnold, like Pope,

> He won his way by yielding to the tyde.

By "indirection," by creating his unique satirical mode, Dryden reaffirmed important European values, while engaging the most lively concerns of his readers. It is to this poetic feat that I want to draw attention.

Dryden's accomplishment is more remarkable in view of the situation in which he wrote. Charles had been "restored," and with him an audience that was alien to the most vigorous of the surviving older poets. Milton withdrew; Cowley retired without producing much of the "wit" he prescribed. Marvell dived as a Metaphysical and came up as a satirist; but as a poet he belonged to another world. Although Dryden talked sentimentally of "retiring," he was unequivocally the "first" man of this

> Laughing, quaffing, and unthinking time.

His success lay in his ability to draw on a wide range of English and European literary traditions while "speaking home" to this audience of Court and City. A glance at his development as a dramatist will suggest how he attained a style which had this twofold effectiveness.

In the period between *Astraea Redux* and *Absalom and Achitophel*, while Dryden was mightily pleasing his auditors in the theater, he struck out two more or less distinct styles which were blended in the successes of his maturity: one, the "heroic"; and the other, the style of public address which he somewhat scornfully regarded as Horatian. Whatever we call them, both styles bear traces of their mixed European and English origin. In the process of making his outrageous experiments in drama, the Heroic Plays, Dryden invented a style that gave an impression of ancient epic grandeur; at times, in narratives of quite incredible exploits, the impression became almost convincing, thanks to the skill with which Dryden combined Virgilian allusions with rather obvious echoes of Virgilian rhythm.

In the last and best of these plays, *Aureng-Zebe,* we first hear distinctly what Mark Van Doren calls Dryden's "grouping" of couplets, an enlargement of rhythm which comes when he had been reading Shakespeare, and, more significantly, soon after his reworking of *Paradise Lost.* Milton's example, along with Sylvester's and Cowley's, helped fix the Old Testament-ecclesiastical strain in Dryden's mature heroic style, as it finally emerged in *Absalom and Achitophel.* In tone the style is unmistakably a "translation out of the original tongues."

While Dryden was cultivating a manner that had almost no appropriateness to his auditors—except by a law of literary contraries—he was learning to speak to them with directness and ease in his prologues and epilogues. Here he acquired his mastery of more varied tones; and here "the great reform" of language and rhythm was most happily realized. The language is "such words as men did use" (in an age less polished than our own); and the molding of speech idiom to the patterns of the couplet is admirable. After the tepid velleities of Waller—the "crooner" of the couplet—Dryden's prologues mark a partial recovery of the toughness and "juice" of Jonsonian English. But though they are highly original, they are linked via Jonson with an earlier tradition. The prologue, as used by Jonson to give instruction in literary taste, is a theatrical form of the Roman epistle. Dryden's later blend of the prologue-satirical style with the heroic is anticipated in the insolent debates of the plays and in the prologues themselves. Given a very slight excuse, Dryden will sound off with an ancient literary parallel, or a debased parody of one. Part of the game of amusing his listeners consisted in deliberately talking over their heads.

The "huddled notions" of Dryden's satiric mode lay in readiness when the Monmouth "conspiracy" offered the occasion his genius had been waiting for. He could now compose heroic narrative and dialogue while talking to his familiar audience. What is remarkable is that in scoring a journalistic and political success he produced poetry of a high order. Here is a representative passage, the commemoration of Titus Oates, the Presbyterian "weaver's issue" who testified that the Jesuits were plotting to murder Charles II:

> Yet, Corah, thou shalt from oblivion pass:
> Erect thyself, thou monumental brass,
> High as the serpent of thy metal made,
> While nations stand secure beneath thy shade.
> What tho' his birth were base, yet comets rise
> From earthy vapours, ere they shine in skies.
> Prodigious actions may as well be done
> By weaver's issue, as by prince's son.
> This arch-attestor for the public good
> By that one deed ennobles all his blood.
> Who ever ask'd the witnesses' high race,
> Whose oath with martyrdom did Stephen grace?
> Ours was a Levite, and as times went then,
> His tribe were God Almighty's gentlemen.
> Sunk were his eyes, his voice was harsh and loud,
> Sure signs he neither choleric was nor proud:
> His long chin prov'd his wit; his saintlike grace
> A church vermilion, and a Moses' face.
> His memory, miraculously great,
> Could plots, exceeding man's belief, repeat;
> Which therefore cannot be accounted lies,
> For human wit could never such devise.
> Some future truths are mingled in his book;
> But where the witness fail'd, the prophet spoke:
> Some things like visionary flights appear;
> The spirit caught him up, the Lord knows where;
> And gave him his rabbinical degree,
> Unknown to foreign university.

(632-59)

To see the imaginative unity of these lines is to see the blending of Dryden's earlier styles and to feel the active pressure of older literary traditions. As in most satirical verse, the lines are held together in part by the broad illogic of irony: Dryden makes a series of triumphant assertions, every one of them the opposite of the truth from the Court point of view. But it is Dryden's "intonation" that sets his mark on the lines and gives them life and singleness of effect. His note is clearly heard in "arch-attestor," with its upper level of churchly associations, and in "prodigious," which nicely combines Latin solemnity with the literal Latin meaning of "monstrous." Dryden has anticipated the high level of this commemoration by suggesting that it belongs to a Homeric catalogue; he then addresses Oates in a line so nobly reminiscent of Virgil that it is hardly recognizable as parody:

> Yet, Corah, thou shalt from oblivion pass. . . .

The occasionally Latin flavor of the diction is also vaguely suggestive of Virgilian epic, while at many points the language is more or less biblical, ranging from near-quotation to expressions with religious or churchly associations. Working within a fairly narrow range of allusion Dryden maintains a declamatory tone that is both biblical-ecclesiastical and Roman-heroic. But the "venom" of the address depends on the contrast of another tone which is unmistakably the voice of the prologues, insolently vulgar and knowingly unliterary:

> Ours was a Levite, and as times went then,
> His tribe were God Almighty's gentlemen.

The blend of manners is most subtle in the lines of greatest imaginative variety:

> Yet, Corah, thou shalt from oblivion pass:
> Erect thyself, thou monumental brass,
> High as the serpent of thy metal made,
> While nations stand secure beneath thy shade.

The focus of the ironies is also the focus of opposing styles and of the widest range of literary and religious associations, the ironies arising mainly from the double references of "monumental" and "brass." Taking "monumental" on its high Latinate side, in a Virgilian address, we feel that this beneficent hero is "monumental" in greatness. Or we may read the whole line as a preposterous parody of Horace's

> Exegi monumentum aere perennius. . . .

But biblical and ecclesiastical connotations of "brass" and "monuments" suggest that our hero is worthy of a "monumental brass" in an English church, the rude command implying that this monument, contrary to decent custom and the laws of gravity, will rise of its own power. Finally, "brass" in its vulgar sense reminds us that such effrontery is otherwise "monumental."

In these lines Dryden's satirical mode appears at its characteristic best. There are the black-and-white oppositions of irony with rhetorical and metrical emphasis striking in unison. There is the smack of life and vulgarity in a word from "Jonsonian" London, the word which imparts the ironic intention and gives force to Dryden's thrust. But the irony is most concentrated in a word of Classical origin which is rich in literary and historical connotations and which suggests the Roman oratorical tone.

These features appear in close combination in many of the best lines in Dryden's satirical verse:

> A fiery soul, which, working out its way,
> Fretted the pigmy body to decay,
> And o'er-inform'd the tenement of clay.

(The reminiscences of Aristotle and Plato, Bishop Fuller, and Carew have often been pointed out.) Or consider:

> Besides, his goodly fabric fills the eye
> And seems design'd for thoughtless majesty;
> Thoughtless as monarch oaks that shade the plain,
> And, spread in solemn state, supinely reign.
> Heywood and Shirley were but types of thee,
> Thou last great prophet of tautology.

or

> But gentle Simkin just reception finds
> Amidst this monument of vanish'd minds:

or

> Thou leap'st o'er all eternal truths in thy
> Pindaric way!

Finally, a delicious blend of neo-Platonic fancy and shrewd analysis in these lines on the Church of England:

> If, as our dreaming Platonists report,
> There could be spirits of a middle sort,
> Too black for heav'n, and yet too white for hell,
> Who just dropp'd halfway down, nor lower fell;
> So pois'd, so gently she descends from high,
> It seems a soft dismission from the sky.

From these examples and from our analysis, it is clear that "allusive irony" is a more adequate term than "mock-heroic" for Dryden's satirical mode, whether in *Absalom and Achitophel* and *Mac Flecknoe* or in passages of incidental satire in his argumentative verse. His mode is allusive in a wide variety of ways: in close imitation or parody of other writers, in less exact references to language, styles, and conventions of other literatures—Classical, biblical, and French—in drawing on the large materials of philosophy and theology, in playing on popular parallels between contemporary religious and political situations and those of ancient history, sacred and secular. Through this mode Dryden makes his "affirmation of Europe."

A solemn claim and a preposterous one, if we think of the mode as devices for heightening style. The difference between allusive irony and the heroic trimmings added to the *Annus Mirabilis* lies in the imaginative union of tones and levels of meaning that I have been describing: "thou monumental brass"! The vulgar thrust is inseparable from the reference to high literary styles and to heroic behavior and ecclesiastical splendor.

That the union of styles was more than an academic trick is further shown by the success of the poem with contemporary readers. As compared with Restoration plays or lampoons and gazettes, *Absalom and Achitophel* spoke to more of the interests of the reading public in 1681, and, as Beljame observed, to *more* of the public. Although the Classical heroic was especially flattering to the aristocrats' view of themselves, Latin culture was the common possession of educated men, whatever their political and religious allegiances might be. Dryden, Milton, and Marvell have at least this in common. The Old Testament flavor, satirically amusing to the Court, was richly meaningful and insidiously attractive to Nonconformists. And the colloquial idiom brought the high talk down to the level where Court and City lived. By responding so naturally to the double claims of both his audience and his development as a poet, Dryden "made himself heard" and created a fresh form of art in English poetry.

By this fact alone, he affirmed an important European value to his audience: that poetic craft matters. Dryden's admiration for what Boileau had done for French satire is a sign of his belief that he had performed a similar service for English satire. Boileau would have recognized as art of a high order the poise and finish of Dryden's mode:

> At his right hand our young Ascanius sate,
> Rome's other hope, and pillar of the State.
> His brows thick fogs, instead of glories, grace,
> And lambent dulness play'd around his face.

The poise is evident in the balance between crude burlesque in "thick fogs" and the subtle gravity of "lambent dulness"; the finish is felt in the melodious and resilient verse. But the smoothness is not merely fashionable: it functions poetically in the strategy of civilized irony. The reader is momentarily beguiled into taking the lines as an exquisite compliment. Dryden had a right to claim that like Boileau he was bringing into modern satire a Virgilian refinement of "raillery." In the fine Latin wit of "lambent dulness" or "spread in solemn state, *supinely* reign," Dryden is "alluding" to a culture and the fineness of response which it fostered.

It is no great compliment to describe Dryden's achievement as a triumph of Neoclassicism, if we mean by Neoclassicism mechanical use of conventions borrowed from Boileau or Rapin. Dryden's achievement is not one of "meeting requirements"; the conventions "at work," as in the lines just quoted, are expressive of larger aesthetic and cultural values. In writing verse which combined the normality and vigor of good talk with a musical pattern that was the apt accompaniment of ironic wit and in using language which was equally alive in its reference to immediate interests and to literary tradition, Dryden expressed a community in attitude and standards of art with European poets and critics. Some of these attitudes and standards—the detachment, the refinement of ironic censure, the insistence on design and precise mastery of language —were particularly salutary for readers too well pleased with *Hudibras* and for writers who mistook ease for art. But Dryden did not sacrifice the vigor of Butler to "correctness." The Augustan reform as initiated by Dryden, unlike that of Addison, kept close contact with a masculine audience. Dryden's allusive mode shows a positive strength in Neoclassicism which the odious term and its theories completely conceal.

Let us consider more particularly how this mode worked, how and why epic allusions offered Dryden a way of expressing important values. In ironic contexts, the more or less close imitations of epic introduced a standard of manners and actions by which the exploits of politicians and poetasters might be measured. Fomenters of Popish plots and rash rebellions and slipshod writers were exposed to ancient and biblical ideals of prince and prophet, and their operations were socially and intellectually "placed." In contexts less purely ironic, as in parts of the Shaftesbury and Monmouth "characters," the allusions to Classical and biblical heroic had another effect. The magnificence imparted by the

Miltonic flavor was not merely literary. For Shaftesbury had great abilities as a judge and diplomat; Monmouth had noble looks and manners, and Dryden himself confessed a "respect" for "his heroic virtues." By granting their loftiness some degree of pride the satirist, too, attained a largeness of temper: "Preposterous plottings, but rather splendid persons!" Nevertheless, as Dr. Johnson observed, there are limits in heroic allegory: "Charles could not run continually parallel with David." But though the David–Aeneas incarnation cannot be taken seriously, the tone adopted in addressing Charles and attributed to him and his courtiers did have a certain validity. The parallel between state manners and Roman aristocratic manners was justified, even in Restoration England. In public discourse, the English aristocracy, like the Roman, had a hereditary right to high oratory. And heroic poetry had been by a long tradition an aristocratic possession.

The grand yet lively eloquence that characterizes and satirizes Shaftesbury and Buckingham is thus quite different from the inflated and dully insistent rant of the Heroic Plays, for Dryden had found the one kind of situation in which a Restoration poet might adopt the heroic style. As spokesman for aristocracy, Established Church, and monarchy, he could rightly assume the Roman dignity of Renaissance epic. As the critic of the King's enemies, he could parody his own heroic style and so express still another true relationship between contemporary events and the heroic ideal. The discovery of relationships which were true for Dryden both as poet and citizen made it possible for him to use his accumulated literary skills with a new freedom. His satirical poetry exhibits a fluidity and force and a concentrated range of reference which his earlier verse had rarely shown.

Why may we reasonably describe this success as "European"? Not simply because Dryden's satiric mode was widely and often precisely allusive to European writers and styles and to English writers who were most consciously European in their styles and critical standards. Nor simply because he satisfied a Continental standard of literary craft, although this is significant. But rather because he brought the larger light of European literature and a European past into verse of local public debate. He invited his readers, including Nonconformists, to take a less parochial attitude toward the persons and events of contemporary history. We have only to compare *Absalom and Achitophel* or *The Medall* with Marvell's satires to appreciate the imaginative value of linking these smaller and greater worlds. The Marvell of the *Ode* on Cromwell had brought to political history a similar largeness of scene and a poise of values much finer than Dryden's. But breadth of vision and sureness of rhythm are missing in *Last Instructions to a Painter,* although the poem has some of the obvious earmarks of epic satire. The spectacle is rather painful: the earlier Marvell could not address this world without sacrificing many of his virtues as a poet. Dryden could; with losses, too, if his poetry is measured by the standard of the Cromwellian *Ode;* but he managed to translate to his audience something of the larger historic vision, the noble manner, and the justness of style of the Renaissance tradition in which the younger Marvell wrote. He was a vigorous civilizer among the sons of Belial.

Dryden did something else for his generation that Marvell and Milton, much less Cowley, could not do: he reaffirmed the public role of the poet, the Greco-Roman conception of the poet as the voice of a society. It is true that Dryden succeeded only too well in fixing the public tone as the Augustan norm; but the voice we hear is not solely that of the party or class or church. Thanks to Dryden the tone of Augustan poetry is less parochial than it might have been: it is resonant with echoes of other literary worlds, of larger manners and events. Minor Augustan poetry is dead for modern readers not because it was too "general," but because it was too local.

In praising Dryden for reaffirming the European tradition in his satirical mode, it is well to recall the conditions of our praise. The eighteenth century is littered with epics, odes, and philosophical poems that are traditional in the academic sense; the "forms" and the "diction" are too often reminiscent of the best writers of Greece and Rome. Dr. Johnson's remark on Gray's *Odes* is the appropriate comment on such products: "They are forced plants raised in a hotbed; and they are poor plants; they are but cucumbers after all." Dryden's achievement matters because the verse through which he draws on the European tradition satisfies us as other poetry does by offering concentrated and surprising richness of relationship: we feel that language is being "worked" for all its worth. (The allusive mode is for Dryden what the symbolic metaphor was for the Metaphysicals.) But Dryden's use of tradition satisfies also a condition of another sort. In the act of writing poetry that was far from provincial in implication, Dryden engaged the most active political and intellectual interests of his immediate audience. The particular issues are of little concern for us at present; but we can recognize their importance in the late seventeenth century, and see that the genral issues involved are of a sort that is central in any conceivable society. There are local successes in literature that are instructive to later generations: Dryden's is one of them.

But Pope and the poets who were contemporary with him were not prepared to take instruction from Dryden the controversialist, since they quite consciously removed themselves from the field of public debate. Although political pamphleteering of a violent sort continued throughout the age of Anne, the typical watchwords of the new world of *belles lettres* were "politeness" and "retirement." That Pope could inhabit this Addisonian world of well-bred amenities and moderate enthusiasms and yet rise above it to a serious criticism of life, he owes in part to Dryden's forceful example.

Dryden's most valuable gift to Pope was the creation of his generously allusive mode with all of its wider cultural implications. (I am not overlooking "the couplet": the style is inseparable from its rhythmic form.) With his shrewd flair for craft, Pope realized the principle within the mode, and possessing a finer responsiveness to the poetry of the past, both Classical and English, he enriched his satire with more subtle and more various kinds of reference. His obvious imitations of epic in the *Rape of the Lock* and the *Dunciad* are of less importance than his blending of the heroic with other literary styles and nonliterary idioms into the complex modes appropriate to his two very different "mock-epics." Although some single traditional style or genre is dominant in each of Pope's major works, from the *Pastorals* and the *Rape of the Lock* to the satirical epistles and the *Dunciad,* his poetry is freshly and variously allusive to poets of many traditions and many periods. At random one can think of allusions to Spenser, Ovid, Catullus, to Shakespeare, Milton, and Crashaw, to Rochester, Denham, and Addison. From Dryden Pope also learned the art of self-parody, which he exploited with amusing thrift. He alludes with overtones of wit to his own pastoral insipidities, to the landscape-painting of *Windsor Forest,* to the Ovidian theatrical rhetoric of *Eloisa to Abelard,* and of course to the heroics of his *Iliad.*

As in Dryden, the Roman heroic is always breaking in; and though the modulation of tone is infinitely various in the *Moral Essays* and the *Satires,* the tone of Roman cultivation—more refined and more truly Horatian, less downright and less pompous than in Dryden—still prevails. With the changes in state and society that had been taking place since the Glorious Revolution, the tone had acquired a validity which it could hardly have had in the Restoration. It might well be argued that the actual society in which Pope wrote was considerably nearer to the ideal of the original Augustan Age than that of Charles II. Burlington, Bolingbroke, and Bathurst, in public and private life, were certainly less unlike their ideal literary selves than Charles and Rochester. But if the society was not more Augustan, Pope was: his work taken as a whole shows that he had mastered the intellectual and aesthetic ideals which for the Age of Anne were embodied in the Age of Augustus and Virgil and Horace. In Pope's verse, the cultivated tone and the oblique reference to Roman grandeur and decorum symbolize an ideal of culture which he is frequently expressing by other more explicit means. The symbolic force of the allusive mode which he had first learned from Dryden can be felt wonderfully in his address to Burlington in the fourth *Moral Essay:*

> You show us, Rome was glorious, not profuse.
> And pompous buildings once were things of Use.
> Yet shall (my Lord) your just, your noble rules

> Fill half the land with Imitating Fools;
> Who random drawings from your sheets shall take,
> And of one beauty many blunders make;
> Load some vain Church with old Theatric state,
> Turn Arcs of triumph to a Garden-gate;
> Reverse your Ornaments, and hang them all
> On some patch'd dog-hole ek'd with ends of wall,
> Then clap four slices of Pilaster on't,
> That, lac'd with bits of rustic, makes a Front;
> Or call the winds thro' long Arcades to roar,
> Proud to catch cold at a Venetian door;
> Conscious they act a true Palladian part,
> And, if they starve, they starve by rules of art.
>
>   (23-38)

After that, the tradition of Dryden needs no further justification; renewed and refined, it speaks for itself.

Dryden's Drudging

by Edwin Morgan

Thy Genius, bounded by the Times, like mine,
Drudges on petty Draughts, nor dare design
A more exalted Work, and more Divine.

(To Sir Godfrey Kneller, 1694)

I am still drudgeing on: always a poet, and never a good one.

(Letter to Mrs. Steward, February 2nd, 1699)

I

Whatever homage may have been paid to John Dryden in the last thirty years, there is little doubt that his poetry is neither widely read nor greatly enjoyed. It is easy enough to become convinced of his historical importance, but there comes the point at which every reader of Dryden's verse stops and asks himself, "What would happen if I were to read this as a human being? Can I find out what sort of poetry it really is, if it is poetry?" If the reader then disjects what Mayakovsky called the professorial bicycle-spectacles in order to see at a more natural and human rate, he may well find it still none the simpler to pick out the poetry as he goes along, or to be surer of its value than he was before. Poet and period seem here to be unusually inseparable. For this reason it is not merely the romanticist who is worried by the unsolved question of Dryden's stature as a poet; there is a general interest in asking how far the quality of his verse requires to be either explained or excused (as he himself excused it) by reference to environment rather than to innate capacity. The question may also claim to have some relevance at the present time, since the combination in Dryden of vigor, hardness, and clarity is something that contemporary poets are likely to take an increasing interest in, as the suggestional-exploratory-ametrical mode begins to have completed its work.

"Dryden's Drudging" by Edwin Morgan. From *The Cambridge Journal* VI, No. 7 (April 1953), 414-429. Reprinted by permission of Bowes & Bowes, Publishers, Ltd.

Why, then, these "petty Draughts"? Milton wrote his own epic; Dryden wished to, but only translated the *Aeneid;* Pope contributed a *Dunciad;* Cowper sang the Sofa; and Blake and Wordsworth, in the total absence of great subjects at the end of this deterioration, had to try creating great subjects for themselves. Dryden, we may feel, was uttering in 1694 a timely complaint. But against the complaint we must set the complacence. The century from Dryden to Johnson, though shot periodically by regrets or velleities after the manner of these lines to Kneller, expressed consistently its deeply felt sense of advances gained, culture retrieved, and anarchy dispelled. To grasp the one virtue of stability, it sold many others, and finally forgot the price it had paid. "There was therefore before the time of Dryden," Johnson wrote in his Life of the poet, "no poetical diction, no system of words at once refined from the grossness of domestick use, and free from the harshness of terms appropriate to particular arts. . . . To him we owe the improvement, perhaps the completion of our metre, the refinement of our language, and much of the correctness of our sentiments." That Dryden would have agreed with this, substituting Waller perhaps for his own name, is evident from many references in his essays. He regarded the times, from the point of view of language, as entering into a period of civilization and grace after the harshness and barbarity of Elizabethans, Jacobeans, and Metaphysical wits. Donne received his praise as a monarch of wit, but, as he says, would the satires not appear "more charming, if he had taken care of his words, and of his numbers?" We cannot but feel, too, that his praise of Shakespeare is very different from ours, and very much a part of his time, when he says: "Never did any author precipitate himself from such height of thought to so low expressions, as he often does." The truth seems to be that the age thought itself blessed and propitious in a three-fold sense, which at first glance might indeed pass for an admirable benefit but which proved a dangerous and insensitive circumscription of the poetic art.

The first aspect was metrical: Dryden, said Dr. Johnson, improved and perhaps completed our meter. As Dryden wrote both blank verse and stanzaic meters in addition to heroic couplets, we must assume that Johnson really did mean meter in general, and not simply rhyming pentameters; and the apparent absurdity of his remark (paralleled elsewhere, as in his Life of Pope) will be diminished only when we remember the paramount importance to him and to his period of standards, and of the idea of achievement. In its extreme form this sense of having arrived at a happy stability after a long period of lawlessness is expressed by Dryden in the epilogue to *The Conquest of Granada* (Part II), when he says:

> If Love and Honour now are higher rais'd,
> 'Tis not the Poet, but the Age is prais'd.

> Wit's now ariv'd to a more high degree;
> Our native Language more refin'd and free.
> Our Ladies and our men now speak more wit
> In conversation, than those Poets writ.

Dryden's age looked back on the breakup of the Elizabethan and Jacobean poetry from a much closer viewpoint than ours, and with a very marked difference of emphasis on individual writers. To them it was much easier to dwell on the gradual degeneration and virtual eclipse of blank verse in the first half of their century, which we ourselves do not deny; and we must also concede that they would not have been true to themselves had they not condemned the metrical irregularities of a Donne, which apparently belonged to a careless use of language and which might have been "improved" by taking thought, without an essential alteration of the sense. We can see that the rhyming couplets of *The Second Anniversary* would be openly vicious in effect on following writers unimbued with the force to drive them continually yet not casually forward in defiance of the recurring rhyme, and that Dryden's age, laying down a stricter and a smoother measure in its couplets, was striving to make a standard, parallel to the Classical hexameter, against which it would be possible to criticize such excesses as had passed muster in a less solicitous period. Such a standard would even supplant the blank verse which in the Jacobean dramatists had seemed to break metrical bounds and become altogether too loose for dignified utterance; and in fact we notice in the blank verse of the period, except of course in Milton and in Dryden at his best, an unmistakable and adulterating infusion of the heroic measure.

For the second aspect (closely linked with the first), we must consider what Johnson called "the refinement of our language." Here again we have to be quite certain of what was meant by "refinement" in the ideas of the time. From many remarks on Shakespeare, we infer that Dryden would have thought more of him had he admitted fewer low expressions, or, as Johnson further defines them, too common or too technical terms. When we take a different view today, and look on the heroic style itself as one of a particular emptiness and absurdity, largely because of its generalizing vocabulary and windily "high tone," we have to remember that at the time an important stop seemed to have been put to the intolerable congestion and obscurity of Metaphysical conceits on the one hand and to the prevailing Elizabethan and Jacobean fondness for vivid, concrete but "vulgar" terms of description in both prose and verse on the other hand. Refinement carries its own dangers (always how unexpected by the refiners!), and is paid for by two unwanted effects, the lifeless and the ludicrous. But it was perfectly characteristic of the period to congratulate itself on the exercising of proper control here as in the question of meter, and demanding a standard of vocabulary for poets who wished to write within the newly narrowed gamut of public taste and propriety. It was chiefly an avoidance of the obscure, and of what was thought to be the incongruous, and its claim was to have produced a general vehicle of expression, which by means of slight and regulated modulations could serve for the utterance of almost the whole variety (but see Dr. Johnson on Thomson and Young) of what was the poet's proper material.

The third advance concerned "the correctness of the sentiments" of poetry. Much more anxious than we are about the ideas and themes and statements proper to poetic expression, the Augustan period believed strongly in a limiting of these within bounds suggested by the more general temper of the times. (Typical, perhaps, are Johnson's very careful remarks about the character of Milton's Satan, and his condemnation of Pope's *Unfortunate Lady* for the "illaudable singularity of treating suicide with respect.") It was assumed that the previous century had been reprehensible in encouraging a steady widening of the allowable subject matter and consequently the expression of many things which it was not the business of the poet to meddle with: the feigner of beauty being a juggler with truth. For example, the free treatment of virtue and vice in the great dramas with their obviously open and imaginative approach to moral problems, and the uninhibited and often extra-moral sense of the divine among the Metaphysical wits, seemed to have been happily superseded by the insistence on a scheme of morality, and the exclusion or distortion of themes and expressions calculated to upset it. In this sense *All for Love* had its own boldness, which we are apt to overlook; though it rested, perhaps, safely enough in the shadow of Shakespeare. We are given another indication of the meaning of "correctness of sentiments" by the prevalence of satire. Just as there were a few subjects and ideas now encouraged which before had received little attention (for instance theological, moral, political, and literary argument in specific and up-to-date terms) as matters for a poet's consideration, so also the demands of "correctness" led to an oblique treatment of many subjects which had formerly been open. Satire is characteristic of a period which prides itself on standards, both of conduct and of language; it is hardly necessary in a society where wide variation is not frowned on. It tends to become a stick for the back of eccentricity, and at last for mere individuality, since massive denunciations of perennial viciousness are suited only to the largest spirits, and may occur in any age, but departures from norms of civilized and regulated conduct, instead of receiving the humorous toleration of an individualistic period, irritate the sensibilities of these times, and are treated satirically, to put them out of countenance and send them packing from gracious intercourse.

It will be seen at once that disadvantages, some of them not suspected by the Augustans themselves, accompany this threefold progression. The hypnotic ubiquity of the heroic couplet need not, of course, blind us to the wide variety of successes it achieved. There is a world of modulation between Dryden's prologues and the couplets of Katherine Philips, or between either of these and *Peter Grimes.* We should also remember the possible influence of the splendid (if banished) tradition of the couplet which ran through Marlowe, Chapman, and Donne. But against the successes must be set the limitations which by the end of the eighteenth century had become painfully obvious: a stiffening of the sense of rhythm, a loss both of subtlety in verse construction and of an interest in the possibility of subtle effects, and a deadening leaning towards certain grammatical and verbal formulas encouraged by the necessity of the rhyme, under which it became very difficult to make a unit larger than the couplet cohere (triplets and alexandrines being little more than a confession of the failure of the medium). Also, the refinement of diction by the excluding method of constant general censure of uncouthness is useful only inasmuch as it purges language of real coarseness in situations where coarseness is not apt; its use by the age of Dryden stands as a warning to future attempts. It is a common criticism that the admired "poetic diction," with its habit of demanding the general, the moderate, the "proper" description, in place of the startling, the more distantly metaphorical, the inevitable-only-on-second-thought description of the preceding period, was symptomatic of a certain decline of poetic sensibility, and permitted the writing of verse tautological, inane, inert, and unoriginal in the extreme. The greater poets such as Dryden and Pope had therefore subconsciously to modify that very diction which their period thought it was extracting from their works as an ideal. In the third place, we need only note that any command laid on poets (or implied, in the existence of satire) to manage their sentiments with "propriety" is dangerous. There is nothing more ridiculous than the proper improperly introduced, just as there is often nothing finer than the improper properly introduced. Shakespeare's verbal wit in serious contexts angered Johnson; but Johnson's remark that *"Cordelia,* from the time of *Tate,* has always retired with victory and felicity" would make the stones of Stratford tremble.

In a more general and comprehensive way, how helpful or inimical was the theory of poetry emerging at that time? A key-phrase, repeated with many variants, is certainly "proper Thoughts in lofty Language drest." This, taken at its face value, and as it was written and intended to be read, might well apply to the *Aeneid,* to the *Divine Comedy,* or to *Paradise Lost,* but as we can see today, when the words have separated themselves from the immediate linguistic consciousness and become objects of historical contemplation, it might equally well be descriptive of *Don Sebastian, Venice Preserved,* or Pope's Homer, and is in fact the justifying aegis under which these latter examples foregather. It is possible now to understand in such a phrase what could not then be apparent, that it rested on a basically pernicious, if specious, division of the creative faculty. We cannot say that the poetry was a poetry of theory, since the style appeared first, and has its natural roots and growth, but the development of the theory (largely by Dryden himself) confirmed its use and blessed it for a hundred years. What sort of poetic composition does it in fact describe? It applies obviously enough to those passages, which in deference to the theory we might instance from Lucretius and Dante, not the least sleepless of poets, wherein we see the poet failing between bouts of inspiration and beating up his verse by just such mechanical means as the "dressing" of thoughts in language suggests. But can it be said to apply except in flagging, labored, transitional passages or in imaginationally undernourished verse? It recalls *An Essay on Man*; *Night Thoughts*; *The Course of Time*; *Merope*; *Festus*. The poet at his happiest will not be found selecting fine thoughts and then scouring his memory for expressions which will show off these thoughts to the best advantage ("like a dog out of the water, with a duck in his mouth," in Dryden's favorite image). He has no time for that, were he not under a profounder compulsion. He thinks in and through language: thinks words; his "thoughts" are not nearer thought than these inverted commas allow, and to him a tear may be an intellectual thing. The greatness of his work is sealed by language rather than by thought because poetry is an utterance, and nowhere is falseness of speech for the sake of thought more instantly detectable, or loftiness for the sake of propriety more suspiciously examined. The most moving of poetic statements, which we might be tempted to classify under "thoughts on life and death," may be expressions of language far removed from the magnificent, and are distinguished from other kinds of human utterance only by their quality of holding meanings and values that we never wholly expound. Thoughts we may and do trawl up from these depths, yet at the moment of being divided from their element of words they perish and their virtue which we had hoped to capture becomes a dead thing unsupported by its unique context. Were it otherwise, if the Augustan theory of writing gave a true description of the best practice, poetry would be little more than an elaborate game with dictionaries and history-books and moralists' vade mecums, and that peculiar fusing, centripetal, focusing, meditating quality of creative writing, which is not thinking, or feeling, or speaking, or singing, or dancing, but something of all these, and an activity complete and distinct in itself from all others, however feebly it can be described from outside, would appear to be productive of an unreasoned beauty at best, and at the worst of dithyrambic unintelligibility. But we know that the age of Dryden was determined to avoid at all costs the obscurity it saw (and of course rightly saw) in the Metaphysical poets and also in the Elizabethan dramatists, and to this end welcomed a scheme of writing which demanded first a perfect comprehensibleness, and then a succession of thoughts worthy of the comprehending faculty. Such writing is obtained by the method they described: proper ideas are selected, words recognized to be proper to the expression of these ideas are dug out of the poet's recollection, and, intellectually correct, down goes the expression, perhaps frigid in its generality, or threadbare by unconcernedly repetitive usage, but, as it seems, proper for the matter in hand. It is scarcely surprising that the eighteenth century should find it so necessary to satirize dullness, or that it should have added new meanings to that word. It failed to see how steadily (and with what self-acclaim!) it was marching down a well-built cul-de-sac.

II

It is now to be asked how far the work of Dryden, within such an environment as has been indicated, owes its virtues and deficiencies to the literary background.

When we look at the heroic plays, we may seem to see merely the exploiting of a genre that has proved to have no lasting appeal. Yet in spite of the declamatory method, the generalizing epithet, the mind's first verb, the punch-and-judy couplets, we are offered a progression which argues the Dryden working with unworthy materials, though not acutely or perseveringly conscious of their inadequacy. This progression is seen in the unquestioning acceptance of the heroic couplet in *The Conquest of Granada,* a sense of its drawbacks by the time of *Aureng-Zebe,* and its abandonment in *All for Love;* and in these plays a corresponding advance in dramatic power. We are forced to admit, however, that this is too simple, and that we owe the solitary outstanding play of *All for Love* rather to a fortunate group of circumstances than wholly to trends mounting up through the earlier dramas. The most fortunate of these circumstances was doubtless the amplitude of the theme, particularly as already announced by Shakespeare, a theme which might be expected to produce a poetic drama if any in the heroic style was in fact possible. Dryden, however, was wise in not relying on the theme itself to carry him through the arid heroic wilderness, and decided on the dangerous plunge into blank verse which did in fact save the play.

I have called the circumstances fortunate because of the considerable success of the style, heroic not in the narrow but in a general sense, quite distinctive at the time it appeared in 1677 and distinctive among Dryden's poetic work. On the normal working level it can be seen to derive almost equally from the rhetoric of the heroic drama and from Shakespeare; that is, it appears as an unusually dignified and solid rhetoric ("scarce rants at all," as the prologue says) eminently suited to the noble characters of the theme. But Dryden has made use of his blank verse to express something more important than this, significant though it is. As if with restraint and care unwilling to dissipate the dignity along a fa-

tally easy torrent of formless verse, attractive enough after the heroic
pinfolding, he goes exactly as far as dignity will allow along the road
of metrical emancipation, permitting himself a thinly sown variety of
enjambment, and discovering without being intoxicated by the aptness
of occasional short lines in blank verse which he had introduced with
bathetic and ludicrous effect among his earlier couplets; and the result,
in many remarkable passages, is a style which no one seems to have used
before, grave, often simple in the extreme, relying on scant or everyday
metaphor, clear, escaping from the echoes that haunt the heroic play as
a species, most fitted for the undertones of passion, the reverse of the
heroic coin, a rumination on certain aspects and causes of feeling where
the diction itself has managed to separate its existence from the more
resonant but more common body of the oratory. Perhaps the best-known
example of this style is Dolabella's speech in Act 4 Scene 1 beginning
"Men are but Children of a larger growth." But the essence of simplicity
which Dryden seems to be extracting in this play is perhaps best seen
at two other points of the action. There is Antony's dying speech to
Cleopatra in Act 5 Scene 1, niggardly of epithets, of imagery, even of
metrical feet—but not niggardly of tragic feeling:

> But grieve not, while thou stay'st,
> My last disastrous Times:
> Think we have had a clear and glorious day;
> And Heav'n did kindly to delay the Storm
> Just till our close of Ev'ning. . . .

Equally persuasive in this serious, quiet, self-sustaining style is a speech
of Cleopatra's in Act 4 Scene 1, relying again on what is only one image,
worked out slowly and as if reluctantly into its full meaning, becoming
gradually of great imaginative weight:

> Like one, who wanders through long barren Wilds
> And yet foreknows no Hospitable Inn
> Is near to succour Hunger, eats his fill,
> Before his painful March:
> So would I feed a while my famish'd Eyes
> Before we part; for I have far to go,
> If Death be far, and never must return.

This, it seems to me, is far removed from the frequently admired "When
I consider Life" speech in *Aureng-Zebe*, and is perhaps as much an advance upon that as the *Aureng-Zebe* speech is itself an advance on four
other lines which occur in the same scene:

> Oh, I could stifle you, with eager haste!
> Devour your Kisses with my hungry taste!
> Rush on you! Eat you! wander o'er each part,
> Raving with pleasure, snatch you to my heart!
>
> (*Aureng-Zebe*, Act 4 Scene 1)

To explain the success of *All for Love* we may go to Shakespeare, to the theme, or to Dryden's twenty years of experimenting; but we can scarcely deny that the effectiveness of the verse, which is at many points a new kind of effectiveness, quite opposed to the gorgeous and rondure-sweeping poetry of *Antony and Cleopatra*, must be the responsibility of the adapter.

From plays to their prologues and epilogues. Of these Dryden himself made the interesting remark:

> Expect no more when once the *Prologue's* done;
> The Wit is ended e'r the *play's* begun.
>
> (Prologue to *The Rival Ladies*, 1664)

This is of course only too often true, but in Dryden's case the emphasis is to be put not on "plays" but on "prologues," and these contain some of his most vigorous writing in a style very different from the grave manner of *All for Love*. Again posing the query, how far this vigor can be accounted for by reference to the general framework within which he wrote, we find an easy adherence to the metric, apart from a more frequent use of double and false rhymes, but an individual treatment of diction and "sentiments" by means of which Dryden made these prologues and epilogues a characteristic and legitimate form of expression. "Proper" diction he keeps for the plays, or for the prologues spoken at Oxford; elsewhere he admits a wide vocabulary, harking back to the Elizabethan in general effect though strictly contemporary in details, for the sake of a lively, colloquial, humorous, and satirical railing at the audience by sections, pit, wits, cits, and critics. The "sentiments" are often improper enough, and the bantering sometimes flogs itself into invective, but wit, a very sparkling and biting wit, plays over and lightens and sustains everything, and there is not often a fall into either dullness or prurience. To be noted here is the expansion of his imagery, much more varied than it is in the plays themselves, and contributing most to the swiftness and vivacity and realism of these prologues. The imagery is, as we might expect, of shops and trades, of citizens and players, of card games and bear gardens, of masquerades and rope dancing, judges and punks, Whigs and Tories, clubs and courts, quacks, coxcombs, cannons, coffee houses, and conventicles. But not only is vigor drawn from a busy and complex urban environment. In the combining of words Dryden has here, in spite of the theory, recaptured some of the stinging freshness of the preceding age, and he very seldom uses the stereotyped phrase when a more vivid one presents itself. Thus he often seems to gain his effect by speaking familiarly, if satirically, of contemporary events, and his language owes its reality to that direct touch:

> 'Twas a sad sight, before they march'd from home,
> To see our Warriours, in Red Wastecoats, come,
> With hair tuck'd up, into our Tireing-room.
> But 'twas more sad to hear their last Adieu,
> The Women sob'd, and swore they would be true;
> And so they were, as long as e're they cou'd:
> But powerful *Guinnee* cannot be withstood,
> And they were made of Play house flesh and bloud.
>
> (Prologue to *Marriage-a-la-Mode*, 1672)

Of the more mordant and indeed thoroughly roused invective in this style, a strong example is:

> The Clergy thrive, and the litigious Bar;
> Dull Heroes fatten with the spoils of War:
> All Southern Vices, Heav'n be prais'd, are here;
> But Wit's a luxury you think too dear. . . .
> There needs no care to put a Play-house down,
> 'Tis the most desart place of all the Town.
> We and our Neighbours, to speak proudly, are
> Like Monarchs, ruin'd with expensive War.
> While, like wise *English*, unconcern'd, you sit,
> And see us play the Tragedy of Wit.
>
> (Prologue to *Aureng-Zebe*, 1675)

And an example of a lighter, fantastic humor, extremely neat, a snap rather than a bite:

> Next summer *Nostradamus* tells, they say,
> That all the *Criticks* shall be shipt away,
> And not enow be left to damn a Play.
> To every Sayl beside, good Heav'n be kind;
> But drive away that Swarm with such a Wind,
> That not one *Locust* may be left behind.
>
> (Prologue to *Limberham*, 1678)

In the prologues and epilogues, then, there is little to which the self-exculpatory lines of Dryden need be applied. The fact that their success is a success in satirical writing leads now to a consideration of his poems. But first, of those poems which are not satirical, the following may be said. Dryden's approach to the correspondences that exist between outer nature and human feeling was purely conventional: he possessed only in very undeveloped form the interests which would have made possible a love poetry, a nature poetry, a religious or mystical poetry: he drew no inspiration from the outer world except when it impinged on his civilized consciousness through the limited externals of London society, and he did not have that curious openness and simplicity of personal emotion in the face of the normal crises of the heart which could lead even the cool and ironical spirit of Marvell into lyricism.

The songs scattered through his plays have found their admirers, and it has been suggested that we read them before we condemn them. It might rather be suggested that we *hear* them before we condemn them, since they have surely little to recommend them as poems. Their effectiveness as songs is a different matter; transplanted from their context, they betray their frigid and factitious metrical sprightliness and their convention-ridden courtoiserie, in comparison with which the airiest air of Campion is an item to be handled with delicacy and respect. The best of the songs is perhaps the simplest, "Young I am, and yet unskill'd" (from *Love Triumphant*, 1693). As for the Odes (*St. Cecilia's Day, Mrs. Anne Killigrew, Alexander's Feast*), these have been often enough and highly enough praised for a caveat of dispraise to be entered against them here. They have at best, in my experience of them, a glinting and baroque impressiveness, and at the lowest estimate they could be called labored, ungainly, heteroclite, and flashy in a half-hearted and mechanical fashion. *Mrs. Killigrew* contains some of the worst diction in Dryden, to the tune of "sylvan scenes" and "lofty trees," "blooming grace" and "beauteous face." The two musical odes are remarkably coarse-textured and rhythmically unskillful for poems of that kind, which should either arise exuberantly out of an expressional need like Milton's *At a Solemn Musick* or be fabricated with careful and constant artistic brilliance like Crashaw's *Musicks Duell*. Dryden's odes do not touch our feelings, nor do they much gladden our intellectual ear. It may be said here in extenuation that the use of the "ode" in its English variants between the times of Cowley and Gray was an unfortunate enthusiasm in an age of heroic couplets, because the heroic couplet, cultivated with fanaticism, overshadowed all lyric verse forms so completely that the subtleties of their construction were forgotten, and in its "odes" that period was producing merely chopped-up and adjectivally heightened fragments of heroic verse which only very rarely assumed any life after Cowley had left the best examples, still fixed in a diluted metaphysical solution. It is a point of some interest, I think, that odes like *Alexander's Feast* do not really show us a brighter side to the constantly satirical picture, or another verse facet of Dryden's genius, but on the contrary are clear indications of the unique superiority of the heroic couplet in the late seventeenth century, and of the decline of the lyric forms which Herrick and Milton and Marvell had tempered to virtuoso pitch.

In *Religio Laici* and *The Hind and the Panther* we have Dryden "hatter'd out with drudging works of grace." The former poem, a low-toned disquisition where the language is seldom interesting enough to redeem the intractable matter, need not long detain the literary critic, whom Dryden has already forestalled in his preface. *The Hind and the Panther,* especially in its satirical parts, has a great deal more vigor, and some striking lines and couplets, but the absurdity of its animal fable is too great for it to be taken as seriously as it would have to be. The poetry of theological disputation is of course an all-but-impossible kind of poetry, and it was not helped here by being given such an uneasy and intermittently remembered embodiment in a honey-tongued hind and a grumbling panther. In the two poems Dryden is obeying the "language-as-dress-of-thought" heresy of his time, and making the best of an extremely difficult job: the desire to be lucidly didactic leading out toward prose (*Religio Laici*), the desire to sugar the pill leading to fantasy and incredibility (*The Hind and the Panther*).

Of the other nonsatirical poems, there is a somewhat perverse satisfaction to be obtained from those early verses where we see the Metaphysical influences of his "darling Cowley" giving place gradually to the normal poetic diction of the unastonishing metaphor. There is a certain attraction in the *Elegy Upon the Death of the Lord Hastings,* with its grim echoes of the superseded microcosm, its Ptolemy and Archimedes, spheres and astrolabes, rosebud blisters and universal metempsychosis, and the massive fall of the closing couplet. In *Annus Mirabilis* the poetic diction, "the feathered train," "the first blushes of the morn," "the melting breast," "the watery field" and "the scaly herd," may have the upper hand and account for the prevailing tonelessness of the poem, but some fine stanzas and images appear when the eye of the poet seems really to be on its object, as in

> The utmost Malice of their Stars is past,
> And two dire Comets, which have scourg'd the Town
> In their own Plague and Fire have breath'd their last,
> Or, dimly, in their sinking sockets frown.

I turn now to the satirical poems, in which Dryden excelled. In his *Discourse concerning the Original and Progress of Satire* (1693) he distinguished clearly between satire which, called forth by the general badness of the times, expressed invective unsweetened, and that milder sort which aimed to laugh a vice or folly out of countenance and entertain as well as condemn. Of the first type are his translations of Persius and

Juvenal, of the second his *Absalom and Achitophel, The Medall,* and *Mac Flecknoe.*

To consider the more suave chastisement: three remarks made by Dryden will help us to understand his aim in this method. "The nicest and most delicate touches of satire consist in fine raillery." "Satire is a poem of a difficult nature in itself, and is not written to vulgar readers." "They are not the violent, whom I desire to please." These statements give us pleasure, I think, because we realize that Dryden did have the peculiar gift of being able to direct his raillery, sharply pointed as it was, against individuals who are in themselves, or in their aspects as presented to us by him, perpetual subjects of raillery to be found in every civilized society. To Dryden himself this was evidently an idea of some importance. Many times he expresses concern about the proper objects of wit, and about the misdirected energies of some of his contemporaries in letting fly denunciatory boomerangs. For the same reason he insisted on the value of a continually witty and entertaining treatment, realizing that, for poetry, such is the only alternative to the purely indignant and serious outcry. The poetry is there because Dryden felt with vigor what he was expressing, because he was using his considerable power to galvanize a fairly knowledgeable audience, and because his objects are readily set up in the imagination of succeeding readers. Satire is to bring folly into disrepute: but should it also exhort to virtue? If it does, the wit vanishes, and it was perhaps the wit that made the poem. The attempt to turn a satirical "petty Draught" into something semiheroic and positive can rarely be successful, and it is this attempt that makes *Absalom and Achitophel* less satisfying as a whole than the best parts of it suggest. There is a similar weakness in *The Medall,* and in *Mac Flecknoe* the problem is avoided. The satirist is seldom constructive or realistic; he will disguise a jeremiad as a blueprint, but his visions of good tend to be as unpersuasive as a Shelley's visions of evil. In *Absalom and Achitophel,* the series of dull and fulsome hyperboles relating to David and the state of kingship have in them something contemptible and are far from spreading a sense of the order Dryden no doubt had in mind to oppose faction and sedition. He rightly admired his portrait of Zimri; but what are we to say of David's long speech, "Thus long have I by Native Mercy sway'd"? Not only is the tone different, but the wit which sustained the portrait has quite fallen away, and the language is lifeless in comparison. The light touch has been lost, and the heavier substitute fails to impress, though it might be expected to carry a greater significance. This would suggest that the definition of a "fine raillery" is insufficient for a satire of any considerable length or ambitious form (unless of course literary parody, as in *The Rape of the Lock,* is involved), and that *Mac Flecknoe* is Dryden's masterpiece in the genre. Here he is thoroughly at home with his subject from beginning to end; his enemy is the arch-enemy of all writers who attempt Dryden's own two particular virtues of clarity and forcefulness; setting and action are perfectly suited to the matter; and there is no deadening or inhibiting compulsion to exhort.

Yet satire was in some sense, in the theory and tradition which Dryden accepted, "a species of heroic poetry"; and there are other indications that he finally favored the definition of "fine raillery" much less than the original and sterner one of invective or denunciation—a different approach to the heroic from that of *Absalom and Achitophel*. In the *Discourse* he makes the comparison of Horace and Juvenal favorable to the more rigorous master. While admitting Horace to be the greater poet over the whole of his work, he finds that Juvenal exceeds him in the force and brilliance of his satires, and these satires are of the severe kind where those of Horace are mild and (as Dryden says) "insipid." Juvenal is praised, it should be remembered, not as a satirist but clearly as a poet making of satire something equal in value to other forms of "heroic" writing. "We cannot deny," Dryden says, "that Juvenal was the greater poet, I mean in satire. His thoughts are sharper; his indignation against vice is more vehement; . . . he treats tyranny, and all the vices attending it, as they deserve, with the utmost rigour." It is after these statements that Dryden speaks of the "nicest and most delicate touches" of satire as in Horace which he says show a greater triumph of art, but we are concerned here rather with his practice than with his judgment, and we can see from his own work that his praise of Juvenal's "more vigorous and masculine wit" comes from his heart more immediately than his intellectual admiration of the "fine strokes" of Horace. He seems to be recognizing a principle which may help to account for the success of his translations, by linking the severity, swiftness, and deadliness of Juvenal's style with the seriousness of his subject matter, and suggesting that while raillery suits folly, no castigation can be too violent for the general vices of a society. In this we are brought up against the question in his own work, whether the more delicate thrusts of wit or the annihilating attacks of these late poems are farther removed from the status of "petty Draughts."

The unsatisfactory compromise that had to be effected in *Absalom and Achitophel* with material on which wit could scarcely work has already been noticed. May it not be that in the translations, where the necessity for such a compromise, in the continuous rigor of the condemnation, disappears, he found a more congenial form of utterance, and that he was able in them to preserve the usages of wit on a higher level, without descents to the makeweight of "virtuous" commentary? Certainly he himself spoke elsewhere of the viciousness of the times and the aptness of heavy satire, and in these translations we feel that here alone has his wit attached itself to an object both speedy enough and massive enough to bear it. Here he employs the heroic couplet with a perfect realization of its capabilities; the rhyme is no setback but performs again and again the office of a double blow or of the epigrammatic sting in the tail of a two-line statement: the vocabulary escapes from "diction" into very free and "improper" usages often startling and vivid, helped to this freshness no doubt by the fact that Dryden was trying to make Juvenal and Persius speak as they would had they lived in Dryden's England; and in the matter of the denunciations, with which of course we credit the originals, he appears to have found subjects, often unpleasant enough but clamoring for "strong lines" in the translator, to which his pen warmed with alacrity.[1]

As an example of the imagery, which is immediate and "free" in a sense not recommended by the theories of the time, the following lines from Persius (4th Satire):

> Him, do'st thou mean, who, spight of all his store,
> Is ever Craving, and will still be Poor?
> Who cheats for Half-pence, and who doffs his Coat,
> To save a Farthing in a Ferry-Boat?
> Ever a Glutton, at another's Cost,
> But in whose Kitchin dwells perpetual Frost?

And this, to show the extension of vocabulary, the liberty of approach it signified, and the richness of effect it made possible within the heroic couplet (5th Satire):

> Art thou of *Bethlem's* Noble College free?
> Stark, staring mad; that thou wou'dst tempt the Sea?
> Cubb'd in a Cabin, on a Mattress laid,
> On a Brown *George,* with lowsie Swobbers, fed,
> Dead Wine, that stinks of the *Borrachio,* sup
> From a foul Jack, or greasie Maple Cup?

Or from Juvenal, some lines which show the considerable musical and evocative power he was able to summon from this admission of Johnson's "low expressions" (6th Satire):

> Who lewdly Dancing at a Midnight-Ball,
> For hot Eringoes, and Fat Oysters call:
> Full Brimmers to their Fuddled Noses thrust;

---

[1] Wordsworth, who understood Dryden well although he opposed him in his critical writings, saw that "whenever his language is poetically impassioned, it is mostly upon unpleasing subjects, such as the follies, vices, and crimes of classes of men, or of individuals." (Letter to Scott, November 7th, 1805.)

> Brimmers the last Provocatives of Lust,
> When Vapours to their swimming Brains advance,
> And double Tapers on the Tables dance.

And finally, the beginning of the powerful description of the bleakness
of old age which has the intensity of Swift (10th Satire):

> Mistaken Blessing, which Old Age they call,
> 'Tis a long, nasty, darksom Hospital,
> A ropy Chain of Rhumes; a Visage rough,
> Deform'd, Unfeatur'd, and a Skin of Buff. . . .

may be instanced as proof of the congenial nature of such graver and
darker thoughts to Dryden in this period of his writing.

I have indicated the successful emergence of at least three different
styles: the serious, simplified, humane "thinking-aloud" of *All for Love;*
the light, brilliant, familiar, entertaining wit of the prologues, epilogues,
and satires; and the later enriched, emancipated, vulgarized, less subtle
but more passionate style of the Juvenal and Persius translations. With
the exception of the single play *All for Love,* these successes took place
within the accepted mediums, made use of contemporary material, and
might have Dryden's disclaimer to Kneller applied to them by extension:
they owed their vitality indeed to the ever-active mind of Dryden, but
to that mind working in full cooperation with the tendencies of the
time, and achieving distinction, by its own superiority and by a certain
"belated-Elizabethan" independence of approach, only within a restricted
sphere. When we come to apply the disclaimer, however, as it stands, to
the "more exalted work" we know he desired, and to his existing essays
in the lyric and dramatic fields, it seems less true to agree with him in
this excusing of his deficiencies by reference to the age he lived in
(though it might well have been true!) than to say that he was constitutionally and inherently unsuited for any such designs. Many people, I
think, have sought to praise Dryden for the wrong reasons, endeavoring
to find some plausibly attractive resting-place for their general feeling of
"force" or "greatness" in his work. He has suffered where lesser poets
have not, by excelling in subjects and styles often disagreeable, hard,
and unsympathetic to the ear, and from the fact that he has a difficult
and elusive personality. But the qualities of his verse are worth study,
as poets themselves have usually recognized, and in addition to the interest that should attach at the present moment to his unprofound but
unyielding poetry of discourse and scorn, he offers peculiarly the poetry
of a period in history, and evidence of the varieties of effect possible
within a narrow and unpromising critical view of the poet's function, at
a point just before that critical view had had time to harden into dogma
and self-love.

Dryden: *Epistle to Charleton*

by *Earl Wasserman*

I

Commentators on Dryden have either ignored his congratulatory
epistle "To my Honour'd Friend, Dr. Charleton," presumably because it
is felt to be of negligible value; or else they have dismissed it with the
brief gloss that its significance lies in revealing the poet's interest in the
Royal Society. Certainly the discursive surface of the poem prior to the
concluding lines makes statements about the new science, about its opposition to Scholasticism, and about its recent discoveries. But to pare
from the poem these surface statements is to ignore the subtle complexity
of its thematic concerns and to disregard, for the sake of extrinsic biography and history, the intrinsic activities of its artistry.

Even a casual reading of the epistle discloses that after his survey of
science from Aristotle to Charleton, Dryden turns to Charles II and
somehow makes a transition from notes on Charleton's theory (that
Stonehenge was a Danish palace) to a panegyric on the King. By disre-
garding the internal interrelations generated in the poem, such a reading
would therefore define the poem as merely a commentary on the new
science, to which, with considerable ingenuity, Dryden appended some
praise of Charles.

Slightly more than a year before composing the epistle, Dryden, com-
plimenting Sir Robert Howard on the publication of his poems, wrote
that once

> Of Morall Knowledge Poesie was Queen,
> And still she might, had wanton wits not been;
> Who like ill Guardians liv'd themselves at large,
> And not content with that, debauch'd their charge.
> Like some brave Captain, your successfull Pen
> Restores the Exil'd to her Crown again;

"Dryden: *Epistle to Charleton*." Chapter II from *The Subtler Language* (Baltimore:
The Johns Hopkins Press, 1959) by Earl Wasserman, pp. 15-33. Copyright © 1959 by
the Johns Hopkins Press. Reprinted by permission of the Johns Hopkins Press.

> And gives us hope, that having seen the days
> When nothing flourish'd but Fanatique Bays,
> All will at length in this opinion rest,
> "A sober Prince's Government is best."

Here one can have no difficulty in seeing that Dryden has read Howard's poetical accomplishments into the pattern of recent political events: Howard has restored Poesie to her throne and re-established calm after the hectic and irresponsible days of her exile, just as General Monck has restored Charles to the throne. There is no mistaking the political circumstances behind the passage, for they are almost explicitly stated and quite directly equated with the immediate subject. But it is likely that the political references are more than merely the subordinate halves of a metaphor, since the last two couplets equivocally assert both that Howard has restored order to letters and that Charles will restore sobriety to the state, neither assertion being subordinate to the other. For the moment Dryden has two main themes, not one, and the artistry of the lines makes them coextensive, as though they were but different manifestations of the same truth. If, then, the structure of this passage results from a mode of conception about the course of human affairs, rather than merely a mode of expression, and suggests that the recent turn of political events constituted for Dryden a basic ordinance that gives shape and meaning to other matters, it is proper to ask whether the somewhat more oblique political allusions in the epistle to Charleton do not also point to its being conceived in the same political pattern.

The very title of the epistle conditions one to read with an eye to a political context. Inigo Jones had called his earlier treatise *The Most Notable Antiquity of Great Britain, Vulgarly Called Stone-Heng, on Salisbury Plain, Restored;* and Charleton's reply appeared, in 1662, under approximately the same title, but with the addition, *restored to the Danes.* To this second work Dryden contributed his epistle to the author, *on his learned and useful works; and more particularly this of Stone-Heng, by him Restored to the true Founders.* In early 1662, when Dryden must have composed his poem, it is unlikely that the word "restored" would have failed to have as one of its main predicates the recent restoration of the Stuarts; and Dryden completes the connection between Charleton's treatise and the return of the Stuarts by repeating this word in the final line of the poem: "But, *He* Restor'd, 'tis now become a *Throne.*" Consequently, in choosing to describe Charleton's theory of the Danish origin of Stonehenge with the phrase "Restored to the true Founders" Dryden was affirming both the validity of Charleton's theory and the hereditary right of the Stuarts to their throne. In a significant sense the total poem exists in order to bring about the identification of the "Restored" of the title with the "Restor'd" of the final line.

The epistle opens with an explicit attack on Aristotle and the authoritarianism in science that stemmed from him, an attack wholly in conformity with the policies of the Royal Society. But while the subject matter of the opening is the assault of the new science on the old, the language that conveys it is borrowed from the vocabulary of politics: Aristotle's domination over thought was a "Tyranny" that "sway'd"; he alone supplied the "State" with truth; and Columbus was the first that "shook his Throne." By drawing his metaphor from politics the poet is attributing to his scientific theme the patterns and relationships that belong to affairs of state, and is therefore implying the essential analogy of the two. Consequently the initial comments on Aristotle are informed by an implied parallelism between him and Cromwell, the political terminology alone betraying the fact that the account of science is shaped by the apparent use of political history as a kind of archetypal design. No doubt it was inherent in the temper of the age to make recent political events the metaphorical base of much of its thought. Bishop Sprat, for example, was also inclined to see the analogy of scientific developments and English history: some modern scientists, he protests, in overthrowing the "Tyranny" of the ancients, have themselves assumed a "Usurpation as great as that of the others: An Action, which we that live in this Age, may resemble to some things that we have seen acted on the Stage of the World: For we also have beheld the Pretenders to publick Liberty, turn the greatest *Tyrants* themselves." [1]

The reference in the opening of Dryden's epistle, then, is double. Just as the Aristotelian domination over scientific thought was "The longest Tyranny that ever sway'd" and caused "our Ancestors" to "betray" their "free-born *Reason*," so (in the interpretation evoked by the political terminology) Cromwell's rule was the longest tyranny England had suffered. Like many of the Royalists, Dryden clearly hoped that Charles, by cooperating with Parliament, would accept a limited monarchy instead of absolutism or the one-man rule of the Protector; what is here repudiated is the governmental form in which "onely one" supplies the state with truth. By their ambivalence the words "our Ancestors" refer equally to the pre-Royal Society thinkers and to the pre-Restoration parents of the English, although the second reference, while informing the first, exists only beneath it at the moment. And behind this ambivalence must lie the assumption that Scholasticism was to the history of European thought as the Interregnum was to English political history. The words "free-born," therefore, which serve as a metaphor for the Royal Society's rejection of authoritarianism and its insistence upon the validity of empirical evidence, are also political in their primary meaning, having to do with a person born to the civil rights of a free man, rights that the English insisted were inherited from their ancient laws and constitutions, and that, Dryden is here saying, were violated by

---

[1] *History of the Royal Society* (fourth ed., 1734), p. 28. Unless otherwise indicated, it is to be understood that the place of publication is London.

Cromwell. Superimposed upon each other are the right of man to know the physical world through his inborn senses and the natural civil rights of Englishmen.

This same double reference is discernible in the comments on Columbus. Just as his discoveries shook the throne of Aristotle by confirming a new picture of the world, so General Monck also found what had been thought impossible in nature, a *"Temp'rate* in a *Torrid* Zone," a place where the "fevrish aire" was "fann'd by a cooling breez." In a later poem Dryden was to write of the English political system, "Our Temp'-rate Isle will no extremes sustain." With the return of the monarch, England looked toward the introduction of a calm into the confusion and turbulence of the Interregnum and toward the creation of another Golden Age as idyllic as the culture Columbus believed he had discovered:

> The fruitful Vales set round with shady Trees;
> And guiltless *Men,* who danc'd away their time,
> *Fresh* as their *Groves,* and *Happy* as their *Clime.*

The word "fevrish," moreover, seems too highly charged to be confined to a climatic reference, especially when we recall the frequent seventeenth century assumption of a causal relation between climate and political systems. In the sense of "infectious," *"causing* a fever," it tends to call up a secondary reference to the excited and deranged temper of Commonwealth days that spread by contagion. The final ambivalence of this type appears in the statement that had Columbus not made his voyages, "The *Western* Seas had been our utmost bound." Clearly the main intent is to say that Columbus enlarged the world for man, but *"our* utmost bound" works as ambiguously as *"our* Ancestors" so as to summon up as an additional response the seventeenth century Englishman's new pride in his colonies in the New World.

It is significant to the sense of the poem that, after this preliminary section, Dryden limits himself to contributions made by English scientists and explicitly calls attention to his patriotic pride in the fact that "Th' *English* are not the least in Worth, or Fame" as scientists, that is, as *"Assertors* of free Reason's claim." In the first movement of the poem, the political reference had been veiled behind overt statements about science; now, however, because of the obvious connection between pride in the Royal Society and pride in England, the explicit assertion of the English claim to scientific honors has brought the nationalistic theme into the open so that both science and the state may become equivalent subjects. The bifurcated structure of the heroic couplet naturally lends itself to expressing this coequality, and Dryden's technique is to pivot the two themes about a single referent, each theme controlling a line of the couplet. William Gilbert's work on the magnet has both scientific and national importance: as a scientist Gilbert "shall live, till *Load-stones* cease to draw"; and because his work contributed to practical navigation he will live during that eternity in which "*British* Fleets the boundless Ocean awe." The brothers Boyle also bind together the two themes: Robert, one of the leaders of the Royal Society, is "not less in *Nature* seen, / Than his great *Brother*," the political leader, the Earl of Orrery, is "read in *States* and *Men*." The political substratum of the first movement, made possible there by its use as the base of a metaphor, has now risen to independent significance equivalent to that of the original scientific theme, the equivalence being effected by Dryden's shift of poetic mode from metaphor to explicit doubleness of reference.

As a member of the Royal Society, physician to Charles, and author of medical treatises, Charleton of course had an established right to a place in this succession of scientists. Dryden's problem, however, is to integrate the treatise on Stonehenge with the work of other scientists by means of poetic logic rather than by mere fact, in order that the entire scientific theme of the poem may be channeled into the image of the treatise and that the treatise may thereby be transmuted into a symbol. Having written that Harvey was notable for discovering "The *Circling* streams, once thought but pools, of blood," he now shapes into a similar verbal pattern his statement that Charleton, refuting Inigo Jones's theory that Stonehenge is the remains of a Roman temple, has proved it to have been a Danish palace constructed for the election of kings: the relics, "once thought a *Temple,* You have found / A *Throne*." In addition, another analogy is constructed between Charleton's proved abilities as physician, which clearly entitle him to scientific honors, and his work as archeologist. His research on Stonehenge is only an extension of his accomplishments as physician, for

> Such is the healing virtue of Your Pen,
> To perfect Cures on *Books,* as well as *Men.*
> Nor is This Work the least: You well may give
> To *Men* new Vigour, who make *Stones* to live.

These poetic maneuverings have now shaped Charleton's treatise into the radical image of the epistle, since, by reason of its position in the historical sketch of science, it assimilates all the values previously developed in the poem, both about science and about England's glory. In this sense it is truly the subject of the poem—although not its only objective. For while it is the image that collects the entire preceding pattern concerning the new science it can also serve now as the means of unfolding the corresponding political theme which is to be celebrated and whose analogy with the scientific has already begun to emerge significantly. Rather, the ultimate objective of the epistle is to celebrate the Stuart reign in so far as it is confirmed by the providential correspondence of political developments and the progress of the new science. Charleton's archeological study gains its full glory in conforming to Stuart fortunes; and the greatness of the Stuart reign is verified by the analogous treatise. Science, then, is not the central theme of the poem; it is only a function of the theme, and to detach it is to falsify the poem. The consequence of the shifting techniques of the poem has been to implicate each of the two themes in the other and to make possible the ultimate inversion of the initial strategy. The opening political reference that had formed the basis for an extended metaphor for science had been made coequal with the scientific theme by the double roles of Gilbert and Boyle. And now, just as the poem began with the political theme serving as the vehicle for the account of science, so it will end with the scientific treatise serving as the vehicle for the political thesis.

II

In his specifically political references to Charles, Dryden writes that kings are our "Earthly Gods" (48) and that Charles' head is "Sacred" (53). On the other hand, he has emphasized the Englishman's "free-born *Reason*" and the fact that the English are "*Assertors* of free Reason's claim," allusions applicable equally to the new antischolastic English science and to English politics. Moreover, it might superficially seem a further contradiction to Charles' divinity to say that at Stonehenge he might "be *chose* again to rule the Land" (52), for the king's divinity suggests that he owes his prerogative to God's designation, and choice suggests he owes it to popular election.

Now, the source of the monarch's authority was, as might be expected, a hotly debated problem of the moment, for on the answer depended the distribution of powers and rights. The usual manner of facing the question was to turn to Scripture, especially to the histories of Saul and David; and from these accounts the chop-logic of the period was able to extract three main contradictory explanations, since Saul and David were anointed by Samuel before the people called upon them to be kings. A strong defender of a commonwealth like Harrington could explain away divine anointment by insisting that not only the designation of the monarch but also every other human act is governed by God and that therefore there is no special relevance in God's prior designation of the king. Since the "miraculous designation of Magistrates in a Commonwealth, was never understood to exclude the free suffrage of the people in their election," it is of no consequence to say "that Saul was anoynted by Samuel, before he was elected by the people"; and it is popular election alone that gives the king his power.[2] The "vote of the people is the

---

[2] James Harringon, *The Art of Law-Giving* (1659), p. 28.

voice of God." [3] At the opposite extreme the defenders of absolute monarchy could claim that popular choice is merely God's instrumental cause for fulfilling His designation as efficient cause; and therefore the king is "invested and annointed with a divine power by God himself to exercise his judgements" and through the election by the people merely to be "sole administrator" of them.[4] In this view "the Coronation of the King is only a Declaration to the people that God hath given them a King: Outward Unctions, and Solemnities used at coronations, are but only Ceremonies, which confer no power to the King, for it was his from the Lord." [5] Between these two extremes many good Royalists found it possible to argue a middle position that established divided sources of the king's prerogative. "Saul and David were both anointed by Samuel, and yet had not the crowne till the people consented"; and therefore the king is both "Gods anointed, and mans appointed," owing his power to both God and his subjects, who make their choice undetermined by the divine act and without whose consent the king cannot assume the throne. Consequently the king is "Gods anointed, and so *in re personae,* in the right of his person, exempt from all men; but he is the peoples appointed, and so *in re Coronae,* in the right of the crown, can do nothing without them." [6] There is no necessarily special political importance, then, merely in Dryden's references to Charles' divinity on the one hand and to his election and the free-born rights of the English on the other, since these would be consistent with any one of three contradictory political concepts.

And yet Dryden does carefully tip the scales to one side. Because James I had married Anne of Denmark, it may be said that the Stuart succession was distinguished by its relation to the Danes, with whom the Stuarts had always been more than friendly. Possibly for this reason, but certainly for political reasons, Charles was eager, even before his return, to establish accord with Denmark.[7] In February 1661 England signed a

---

[3] [Edward Gee] *An Exercitation concerning Usurped Powers* (1650). The official Stuart position, however, makes no allowance for popular choice in any form. In his coronation sermon the Bishop of Worcester would tolerate only divine right and hereditary succession as the grounds of monarchy and devoted much of his many hours on that occasion to inveighing against any degree of popular choice (George Morley, *A Sermon Preached at the Magnificent Coronation of . . . Charles II* [1661]).

[4] *Christus Dei, the Lords Annoynted, or a theological discourse, wherein is proved, that the regal or monarchical power of our sovereigne lord King Charles is not of humane, but of divine right, and that God is the sole efficient cause thereof, and not the people* (Oxford, 1643), p. 12. See also *Sacro-Sancta Regum Majestas: or, the Sacred and Royal Prerogative of Christian Kings* (Oxford, 1644); Edward Bagshaw, *The Rights of the Crown of England* (1660).

[5] *Scutum Regale* (1660), pp. 104, 231.

[6] *The Aphorismes of the Kingdome* (1642).

[7] See Henry L. Schoolcraft, "England and Denmark, 1660-1667," *English Historical Review*, 25 (1910), 457.

defensive alliance with Denmark, the first treaty Charles concluded with any foreign state.[8] At approximately the time Dryden must have been writing his poem young Prince Christian of Denmark was visiting the English Court. The word "Danes," therefore, must have been rich with favorable meaning during the years 1661-62 in court circles, and when Dryden wrote, "Through You, the DANES (their short Dominion lost) / A longer Conquest than the *Saxons* boast" (45-46), it probably would have been difficult for a contemporary to divorce the words from political overtones.

But more significant, Charleton's thesis that Stonehenge had been a Danish palace allowed Dryden to bend his references to Charles' divinity and popular election into an expression of the concept of a limited monarchy that many were hopeful the Stuarts would accept. Between the absolute monarchists and the complete parliamentarians there were many during the Interregnum, and especially around 1660, who looked for a perfect balance of the two powers.[9] Putting aside the inherited right to the throne and the theory of right by conquest, they held that the king is designated by God to serve as king but owes the actuality of his power to his election by the people and is limited by this fact. The defenders of this position generally traced the English parliamentary structure back to the supposedly liberty-loving Germanic peoples and the Germanic *witenagemot,* or parliament, that the Saxons were thought to have introduced into England.[10] Consequently the Danes, as a Germanic people, were traditionally associated with the origins of parliamentary monarchy, and in such works as Francis Hotoman's *Franco-Gallia* the persistence of elective monarchy in Denmark is used as evidence of Hotoman's central thesis that among all the Germanic peoples there was originally a "Free State . . . before the Loss of their Liberties," since originally the crown was "conferr'd by the Choice and Suffrages of the People." [11] In the mid-seventeenth century the theorists repeatedly noted that Denmark was one of the few continuing examples of an elective monarchy, and even the guide books of the period consistently took pains to explain that the Danish king is elected and does not inherit his

[8] *Ibid.* For the continued intimacy of Denmark and the Stuarts, see Clarendon's *History of the Rebellion.* For example, in 1645, when Charles I had reason to fear for the safety of his family, he urged the Prince to escape to Denmark for protection.

[9] See, e.g., *A Plea for limited Monarchy, as it was established in this Nation before the late War* (1660), p. 5: ". . . our former Government, eminently, included all the perfections of a Free-State, and was the Kernel, as it were, of a Commonwealth, in the shell of Monarchy." How insistent these demands were for a limited monarchy can be judged by the urgency with which some pamphleteers protested against them: *Scutum Regale* (1660); T. C., *Vox et Votum Populi Anglicani* (1660).

[10] See Samuel Kliger, *The Goths in England* (Cambridge, Mass., 1952).

[11] Francis Hotoman, *Franco-Gallia . . . Written originally . . . in the year 1574* [trans. Robert Molesworth] (1711), p. 38. See also Jean Bodin, *The Six Bookes of a Commonweale* [trans. Richard Knolles] (1606), pp. 723 ff.

throne, even though the eldest heir is customarily chosen.[12] In the English pre-Restoration disputes over the proper form of monarchy Denmark was recurrently offered as one of the chief examples of the true balance of political power. Sir Robert Filmer, for example, arguing for absolutism, protested in 1648 against Henry Parker, who, he says,

> . . . tells us now most countries have found an art, and peaceable order for public assemblies: and to the intent that princes may not be now beyond all limits and laws, the whole community in its underived majesty shall convene to do justice. . . . We do hear a great rumour in this age, of moderated and limited Kings; Poland, Sweden, and Denmark are talked of for such: and in these kingdoms, or nowhere, is such a moderated government . . . to be found.[13]

And in protesting that the popular election of Danish kings is an exaggeration, he admits grudgingly, "As for the kingdom of Denmark, I read that the senators . . . do choose their King. They have always in a manner set the King's eldest son upon the royal throne."

However, at the moment of Dryden's composition this could no longer be said of the Danish monarchy. A brief palace revolution as recently as 1660 had converted the elective kingship into a hereditary and absolute one; and it is evident from the news journals that the event was well known in England and that its impact upon the course of political theory was vividly felt,[14] so that even a few years later an allusion to Denmark

[12] E.g., Giovanni Botero, *Amphitheatridion* (Lubeck, 1600) and *Le Relationi Universali* (Venice, 1605); S. Stephanius, *De Regno Daniae et Norwegiae* (1629); J. J. Pontanus, *Rerum Danicarum Historia* (Amsterdam, 1631): Pierre d'Avity, *Nouveau Théâtre du Monde* (Paris, 1644).

[13] *The Anarchy of a Limited or Mixed Monarchy,* in *Patriarcha and Other Political Works,* ed. Peter Laslett (Oxford, 1949), p. 309. See also William Prynne, *Soveraigne Power of Parliaments and Kingdomes* (1642), appendix, pp. 80 ff.; and Algernon Sidney, *Discourses concerning Government,* chap. 3, sec. 18. Sidney adds that "The crown of Denmark was elective until it was made hereditary . . . in the year 1660."

[14] The reports of the revolution in *The Parliamentary Intelligencer* (nos. 45, 46; for 29 October and 5 November 1660) reveal how vividly the English were aware of its political importance and how intimately in terms of their own political structure they interpreted it: "This day, that good work . . . hath taken its wished effect; For his Majesty and all his royal issue Male and Female are by all the States with an unanimous consent declared Soveraign and Hereditary Princes of Denmark, so that this Kingdome which heretofore was Elective, is now become Hereditary, which is a very great alteration . . . and herein the world may read the Reward of Vertue in the blessing of God on that excellent Prince . . . his People, who all being witnesses of his admirable carriage and unparalel'd Magnanimity, have now as a Monument of eternal Gratitude, oblig'd themselves and their Posteritie, to make the Crown upon that King's head, to be his and his heirs for ever. Wherein we cannot let pass, how that people being taught by their many late Troubles, have by experience found that the best and surest way to preserve themselves and their Children safe, is to live under the Government of Hereditary Monarchs. . . ." Dryden's position at the moment is, of course, quite the reverse of this. In 1694 Lord Molesworth was to use the Danish revolution of 1660 as evidence of the virtue of elective monarchy and the danger of absolutism (*An Account of Denmark*).

would trigger a reference to the dispute between hereditary and elective monarchy.

The conjunction of Dryden's comments on the choosing of Charles and on his guardianship by the ancient Danes suggests, then, that Dryden assumes England will enjoy in the Stuarts a balance between monarchy by divine right and the elective monarchy Denmark once shared with all Germanic peoples.[15] In this sense, Charles, like David and Saul, was first "God's anointed" upon the execution of his father and then "man's appointed" on the occasion of the coronation of 1661—despite the fact that Charles himself dated his reign from 1648. It was most opportune for such a theory of mixed government that Charleton at this point supposed he had discovered Stonehenge to have been a Danish palace, thereby providing Dryden an occasion to introduce the passage on the Danes with relevance.

For its full meaning, therefore, Dryden's statement that at Stonehenge Charles might again be chosen to rule must be read in the context of the treatise in which his epistle appeared. On this score Charleton's book leaves no room for doubt about Dryden's meaning. Stonehenge, according to Charleton, was a Danish palace in which the Danes, following the Germanic practice, elected their kings. As evidence he quoted Saxo Grammaticus and Olaus Wormius to the effect that in Denmark also "are beheld certain Courts of Parliament, in which heretofore Kings were elected [he is translating Wormius' *creabantur*] with solemn State, which are surrounded with mighty Stones . . . and one . . . Stone exceeding the rest in Eminency . . . upon which (as upon a Regal Throne) they seated the newly elected Kings, by the general Suffrage of the Assembly. . . ."[16] Charleton himself seems to have been somewhat nervous about the possible political implications of his theory, especially in view of the recent Danish revolution, and sought to smile away the Danish "Election and inauguration of their Kings" by describing it as "according to a certain strange Custom, yet of eldest Date, most sacred Esteem, and but late Discontinuance, among that Martial People."[17]

Dryden, quite to the contrary, has drawn into his poem the whole tradition of the Germanic elective monarchy by making his words echo the quotation from Wormius (". . . one . . . Stone exceeding the rest in Eminency . . . upon which [as upon a Regal Throne] they seated the new elected King, by the general Suffrage of the Assembly"):

> Our *Soveraign* here above the rest might stand;
> And here be chose again to rule the Land.   (51-52)

[15] Later Dryden was to change his estimate of elective monarchy, as his references to the elective kingdom of Poland in *The Medall* testify.

[16] *Chorea Gigantum* (second ed., 1725), pp. 36-37.

[17] *Ibid.*, The Epistle Dedicatory.

Dryden has imagined Charles once again being elected to his office according to the ancient practice of all the Germanic races. But Dryden, like Charleton, has also taken cognizance of the recent significant turn of events in Denmark. Since the people had called Charles from exile, they had truly chosen their king. However, the new Denmark is now an absolute monarchy, and so when Charles stood at Stonehenge after the Battle of Worcester he was guarded by "mighty Visions [i.e., visionary figures] of the Danish Race" (56), phantom symbols of elective monarchy rising from the past as though evoked by Charles' presence to preserve him for his future election by their modern counterparts.

The consequence of Dryden's artistry has been to bring together in a single statement the frequent representation of Denmark as an elective monarchy, the frequent derivation of the English parliamentary monarchy from the Germanic peoples, the political relevance of Charleton's supposed findings, and his own wishes for a limited monarchy. Although he did not thereafter express it in terms of the union of popular choice and divine right, this was the moderate political position Dryden regularly adopted in one form or another. As he was to write later,

> Our Temp'rate Isle will no extremes sustain
> Of pop'lar Sway or Arbitrary Reign:
> But slides between them both into the best;
> Secure in freedom, in a Monarch blest.   (*The Medall,* 248-51)

This paradoxical theory of a king who owes his power to both his inherent divinity and his choice by the people—a paradox that serves as the rationale for the desired balance of powers—also provides lines 15-18 with a second area of meaning:

> Had we still paid that homage to a *Name,*
> Which onely *God* and *Nature* justly claim;
> The *Western* Seas had been our utmost bound.

In terms of the explicit allusion to science the "Name," of course, is "Aristotle," and Dryden is stating that earlier science blindly accepted Aristotle's authority (a mere name) and empty words as though they were realities (according to the motto of The Royal Society, *nullius in verba*), whereas the true concern of science is created nature and God, whose attributes nature adumbrates. But the word "homage," deeply rooted in the feudal system, is a political term and hints at a political interpretation of the lines; and the leader to whom England had recently bowed was Cromwell, who, having had no proper claim upon man's homage, is a mere name. True, the claims of God and nature, like those of anointment and appointment, could be twisted to defend almost any concept of monarchy. But in the context of the reference to the Danes and to Charleton's treatise, the sense is that the king draws his claims both from God, the king being the "Earthly" god, and from nature—the laws of nature which dictate that the king be chosen by the people, since they are "free-born," as even the English overthrow of scholastic science has shown.

Moreover, the lines "Through You, the DANES (their short Dominion lost) / A longer Conquest than the *Saxons* boast" (45-46) work in much the same manner as the opening lines of the poem, for the immediate subject, the history of theories about Stonehenge, is given a shape similar to that of English history. Just as the Danes, whose supposed title to Stonehenge had long been forgotten, have now had restored to them by Charleton's treatise the honor of having built it, and just as the Danes had once ruled briefly over England, so the Stuarts (for whom the name "Danes" becomes a kind of synonym) lost their "short Dominion" over England to Cromwell, but now, through the return of Charles, can boast of a longer conquest than the Commonwealth government. By this parallelism, then, Charleton's activities take on something of a typological relationship to recent Stuart history. The couplet therefore is like the opening movement of the poem, where the history of science was couched in the language of politics—but with a significant difference. Because of its progressive emergence, there is no pretense here of veiling the political theme. Indeed, Charleton's restoration of Stonehenge to the Danes is almost lost sight of in the obvious allusions to national history: the words "Dominion" and "Conquest" are applicable to Charleton's treatise only as hyperboles, and it is highly likely that "a short Dominion lost" must have immediately suggested the brief reign of the Stuarts and their loss of the throne during the Interregnum.

This interpretation of the epistle, then, would suggest the inadequacy of saying of it, as one critic has said, that it "is principally important as showing Dryden's early enthusiasm for natural science." Rather, at the same time that it is about Charleton and the Royal Society, it is also about the fact that all events (of which science is only a representative) providentially acclaim and are in accord with the restoration of Charles. If the first is the immediate subject, the second is the vital condition that gives it meaning and from which it cannot be separated. Therefore, it is less important to Dryden's purpose to praise Charleton than it is to show that all things testify to the glory of the crown. Were his objective solely to commend Charleton, Dryden could have profited by flatly repudiating the rival theory of Inigo Jones; but since the assumption of the poem is that all events are relative to the condition of the kingship, he can assimilate both Jones and Charleton into his poetic thesis. Not only is

Charleton's treatise true, but even Jones's book, although refuted by Charleton's, contains a kind of "truth." That is, Jones, who died in 1652 and whose treatise was first published in 1655, was accurate relative to the political conditions of the moment, since he wrote before Charles' restoration. In claiming that Stonehenge was a Roman temple, Jones had at least taken cognizance of the divinity with which Charles was invested —his having been, like David, divinely anointed long before taking his office—since kings are "our Earthly Gods." While the Stuarts were in exile one could know only their divine role; and correspondingly Jones could discover only the religious temple in Stonehenge: it then "was for a *Temple* shown" (57). In this sense, Charleton did not demolish Jones's thesis: "Such is the healing virtue of Your Pen, / To perfect Cures on *Books.*" Only after the earthly god had actually gained the throne could Charleton discover that Stonehenge had been a palace, for it was a fact that had not yet become a truth while Charles was without his crown: Charles being "Restor'd, 'tis now become a *Throne*" (58). Now, Charleton did not in fact adopt any information in Jones's volume or "cure" it in any way; and only with respect to Dryden's subtle poetic definition of the relation of the king's divinity to his monarchic power derived from election—and hence with respect to the relation he establishes between the two treatises—could it be said that "What ever *Truths* have been . . . / Redeem'd [by Jones] from *Error,* or from *Ignorance*" Charleton's work unites and still discovers more (37-40).

In yet another fashion both Jones's and Charleton's theories were strikingly appropriate to the restoration of the king, for around Dryden's lines hovers a reference to the actual coronation of a British king. Just as Stonehenge had been thought a temple and was then found a place of coronation, so when a king is crowned Westminster Abbey becomes not only a place of religious worship but also a "Royal place" (55). Consequently the conjunction of the two theses confirms the divinity of the Stuarts and its union with popular choice; and the two theories, taken together, are symbolic of a truth that had been enacted at the Abbey, another Stonehenge, in the coronation of 1661. Because of this near identity of the Abbey and Stonehenge as a consequence of their double roles, Dryden can write of the ancient ruins that "Our *Soveraign* here above the rest might stand; / And here be chose again to rule the Land."

One last allusion allows Dryden to bind securely together the theories concerning Stonehenge and Charles' personal history, and thereby to funnel all the previous values developed in the poem into the image of Stonehenge, so that it may at the same time serve as a symbol of the new science and as a metaphor for expressing the greatness of the crown. After the disastrous battle at Worcester in 1651, Charles, at the jeopardy of his life, had stopped to examine the ruins of Stonehenge, and through this event Stonehenge became directly related to the King, just as through Charleton's treatise it is related to science. Since Charles could then have been known only for his divinity, Jones's pre-Restoration thesis was valid: the temple-ruins on that occasion sheltered Charles' "Sacred Head." But at the same time, Charles' presence there was prophetic, for he was guarded in his hour of danger by the genius of this "*Royal* place" and by the visionary Danes, the symbols of the elective monarchy. The course of political events has proven that the spirit of Stonehenge, like that of Westminster Abbey, and like that of Charles himself, is twofold and inherently contains both Jones's and Charleton's findings—the temple and the palace, anointment and appointment.

The poem may now reach its climactic final couplet. The initial poetic mode has at last been completely inverted, since the new science (Charleton's treatise) has become the metaphoric base for the political theme. The remaining artistic task is simply to filter the political theme out of all the metaphoric workings in which it has evolved and to give it autonomy. The "you" of lines 45-48 refers to both Charleton and Charles, for both have restored the "Danes" and found Stonehenge a throne. Because of this ambivalence of reference, one of the two factors, Charleton, can now be removed, and Charles alone remains on the poetic scene: "Our *Soveraign* here above the rest might stand."

But ultimately all things, even Charles, become passive agencies of a supreme providence residing in the kingship itself. It is not Charleton nor even Charles who finally effects the revision of the truth about Stonehenge; rather, it is an impersonal abstraction, the monarchic restoration, that has become the active power. All other factors are but reflections of this one event and become truths only by reference to it. Consequently, it is only the status of the English crown that is the controlling force in the final couplet: with the Restoration what was formerly shown as a temple has now *become* a throne.

Dryden's fumbling and obviously insincere attempt at the Metaphysical mode in his youthful elegy on the death of Hastings makes it evident that the richly intricate world-picture on which the Metaphysical manner depended was no longer meaningful to him and had lost its power to be felt as true. A universal order of precisely corresponding planes and a conception of man as in every detail a microcosm could yield him a treasure of extravagant metaphors for a school exercise, but not a valid way of thinking. Because the older systems of order have grown attenuated in his mind, Dryden has turned in his epistle to Charleton to an analogous, and therefore publicly recognizable, but more generalized, less grand, less detailed conception of an all-pervading providence in the human realm that, operating simultaneously at all levels, makes one explicate and validate another. With this meaningful nexus

—this system of universal syntax—he can bind into a single meaningfulness the disparateness of human experience, and by embodying this order in a verbal structure he has formulated a position from which he can survey, interpret, and value the special manifestations of the plan that governs events.

On the Poetics of Terminal Tragedy:
Dryden's *All for Love*

by R. J. Kaufmann

Artists are often men who educate themselves in public and who
make their audience intimate with their own soul's struggle for moral
repose. So it was with Dryden. He was the first great English poet to
operate from an initial central emptiness. He gradually filled in this
inner void with persuasive doctrines; as his art unfolds we watch him do
this. Wise men agree his special genius was for the satiric poetry which
disciplines and instructs social belief. T. S. Eliot's fine assertion that
"Dryden found the English speechless, and he gave them speech" properly refers to his molding of a poetic idiom which makes possible civilized discussion of religious and political behavior and misbehavior in a
fashion which transcends the triad of his predecessors' failings: obscurity;
heavy didacticism; and vulgar abuse. This open, nervous, sufficient style
of Dryden's was not a birthright—it had to be earned.

If we go to Dryden's *Collected Poetry,* confident we can trace the
smooth curve of growing mastery in this deliberate professional's work,
we will be surprised. We find, instead, the unsteady verbalizings of
Annus Mirabilis (1667) back to back with *Absalom and Achitophel*
(1681), a masterpiece of impudent control and confidence. Between there
is nothing for the uninstructed except an inference of fourteen year's
silence. The truth, of course, is otherwise. Dryden spent the half generation between these two poems giving himself to the risky world of
professional theater. We can no longer afford to look upon this as an
unhappy turning away from his destiny as an artist—years of expensive
error ended by his gratifying recall to his satiric vocation. He didn't go
to the theater just to make money either, for he was no poetaster whose
liquid talents flowed into every opportune social receptacle. Dryden was
self-critical; the cumulative inadequacies of *Annus Mirabilis* as poetry
constituted a mandate to this ambitious poet to develop a finer art. He
did this in the poetic theater. It took a decade of concentrated effort

from the circumscription of the issues in his great critical essay, *A Defense of an Essay of Dramatic Poesy*, in 1668 to the splendid consolidation of his mature poetic in *All for Love* in 1678. After that Dryden was ready. Thus, the theater was not a detour for Dryden; it was a highroad to self.

But, Restoration dramatists had problems. They lived under the shadow of Shakespeare and Jonson. They wrote for a small, self-consciously circumscribed group of privileged courtiers and their monied imitators. They were obliged to interpret the newly urbanized mind to itself. They were using actresses for the first time. They felt the heavy competition of French culture. They were uncertain about the proper language for their theater, since Fletcher's facility had taken the starch out of Elizabethan blank verse, while the short-winded heroic couplet put a low ceiling on tragic characterization. Prose was for comedy. In the division of artistic labors by the Restoration dramatists, forging a critical comedy good enough to rationalize private motive and to stabilize a new sexual ethic short of rampant licentiousness and Hobbesian strife fell to Etherege, Wycherley, and Congreve, who were both gifted and interested. Congreve's culminating performance in this endeavor, *The Way of the World*, at once fulfills and exhausts the form. Dryden's important work in the theater is in the so-called heroic play or heroic tragedy.

He wrote a sequence of such plays, beginning with *The Indian Emperor* (1665), followed by *Tyrannic Love* (1669), the two-part *Conquest of Granada* (1669-70), and *Aureng-Zebe* (1675), and climaxing in *All for Love* in 1678. Dryden wrote numerous other plays thereafter till near the end of his life, but they display no sense of a continuing quest or design. His recasting of Shakespeare's *Troilus and Cressida* (1679) reveals much of the Restoration's temporal provincialism; his 1679 version of Sophocles' *Oedipus* has only its strangeness to recommend it. Some admire his *Don Sebastian* (1689-90), but the heart of his dramatic work—and it is work that profoundly affected subsequent English tragic writing—is in the heroic sequence climaxed by *All for Love*.

These plays form an organic cycle. They have a familial similarity in image and tone, they are obsessed by the same themes, and their fraternity of protagonists faces similar moral threats. This intense episode of heroic plays can be described historically as the death agony of the tragic drama in England, and as the last phase of Renaissance experimentation with high individualism. Thus these plays provide an obituary, somewhat hysterical perhaps, of tragic heroism as it had been understood. A heroism of service and *representative* initiative was replacing older conceptions of individual honor and *virtù*, but these more reckless forms of self-expression could not be given up without public ritualization— hence, heroic drama. The point is a crucial one. The grandiose and bombastic assertions of the hero in Dryden's plays are not (as they are in Marlowe's *Tamburlaine*, or even in Ford's *'Tis Pity She's a Whore*) indications of the author's eager tribute to Promethean striving and its mission of radical social renovation. Almanzor, the apparently mighty hero of *The Conquest of Granada*, fights and slays thousands with his sword. His heady self-descriptions flood the play—"The minds of Heroes their own measures are, / They stand exempted from the rules of War." (IV,ii)—and Dryden specifies in his preface that he is to be thought of as having "an excessive and over-boyling courage." Yet the lasting effect of the play is of inactivity, of too much leisure, of no true occupation, and of a constant effort at self-discipline rather than any expenditure of energy against the external world. Dryden, like Sartre in our time, is not truly political in his orientation, though he is obsessed with the consequences of political order and its negation, anarchy. There is something radically Stoical about Dryden's quest for the freedom of indifference. The description made by the great Marxist critic, George Lukacs, of Existentialist attempts at social critique as "a permanent carnival of fetishized inwardness" can be applied to Dryden's heroic plays as well. His orientation is psychological and personally redemptive. He has not the tragic writer's necessary belief in the constructive possibilities of the hero's creative defiance of a meaningful social order which he must resist and which, by resisting, he redirects.

This incapacity to believe in the continuing social utility of heroic energy is what makes Dryden's plays less than high tragedy; it is also what makes them genuinely new and thus guarantees their lesser but definite importance as drama. There are two important points to make about this: one has to do with the dramaturgical consequences of *divided vision*, the other with the distinguishing features of what we can call *terminal tragedy*.

Dryden, the first great English critic, was a close student of the past dramatic literature of England. His conviction of Shakespeare's and Jonson's greatness is as free from provinciality as it is from envy, and is of a detailed professional texture and not loose adulation. He studied their work. Tragic writing is a cultural and not merely a personal enterprise, and through its fierce disputes insights accumulate which are part of a national heritage. Tragedy seeks to embody adequately complex answers to adequately simple questions. Its quest is for root motives for action. As it matures through a tragic era, it develops an ever finer clinical technique for isolating and appraising the motivation of the protagonist. Thus it slowly kills its own mystery in this perfection of technique and this achievement of "knowledge." Shakespeare's *Coriolanus*, for example, shows us clearly what can happen when a playwright grows too expert at disclosing real as opposed to disguised personal motive. Coriolanus' delusions about his own heroic independence are so easily exposed by Shakespeare's matured powers of analysis that he is reduced from tragic stature into "a boy of tears" tied mortally to his mother's will. What is gained in explicit psychological knowledge is lost in tragic respect and terror. Dryden is the beneficiary and the victim of this earlier achievement. The great issues have been searched into, motives have been anatomized. Dryden's mind was too conventional to question these discoveries. His genius was fluidly ironic and hence too accommodating to things as they are to transcend his skepticism of men's will to the good, or of their individual power to hold out against the attractions of a pillowed throne or a soft bosom. Dryden's moral world is a hybrid of disenchanted political realism and romantic nostalgia.

This promotes his divided vision, for he has a *satiric method* and *heroic memories*. The tragic vision tends to fall into these two parts when its era is ending. Thus, Dryden saw human faults clearly, and he brought to *separate* perfection the techniques for satirizing deluded motivation which were *inseparable* components of the complex attack of *Hamlet, King Lear,* or *The Duchess of Malfi.* The crucial other half of the tragic vision, the sense of human greatness actively transforming its world, is not so much lost as distanced into the past. Dryden does not deny heroism so much as he embalms it, memorializes it in the form of terminal tragedy. His heroic stage is a museum of vital feelings honored lest they be forgotten but securely preserved from present use.

Once freed from the camouflaging accidents of exotic detail, the indispensable, central situation of Dryden's heroic plays is of a dying emperor in the midst of a dying empire. His city is beleaguered and internal dissension is rife. Outside the gates "some strange beast, its hour come round at last" knocks rudely on the portals of history. Montezuma in *The Indian Emperor,* Boabdelin in *The Conquest of Granada,* Aureng-Zebe in India, Cleopatra in Egypt, and the pagan, Maximin, vainly resisting in *Tyrannic Love* the irresistible triumph of Christianity, are all either literally "the last emperor" or clearly understood as the descendent of an order once ascendent but now moribund, like strange races who lived before the Flood. Furthermore, Dryden chooses heroes who are either superior or immune to normal social motives. They derive special strength either from an altogether foreign ethos: primitive Christian literalism; Islam; the apoliticality of the noble savage; or from worldly accomplishments, like Antony's, which are so definitive as to render indifferent any mundane claim of lesser degree than absolute love or absolute renunciation.

Dryden's recurrent images harmonize with his situations. He is addicted to terminal images of sunsets, twilight, of entropy, extinction and exhaustion, of sea monsters and antediluvian creatures left gasping on the strand, of water overflowing the land and forming lakes, of flat, undifferentiated things. This imagery reflects Dryden's own historical situation—one of gradual leveling of old distinctions in the increasing democratizing of language and behavior. In this apprehension of the supersession of the old by the new, Dryden's sympathies were profitably at war with his critical awareness. His plays dramatize this conflict, which is partly resolved by placing his central characters in remote, simplified, threatened societies with palpable enemies, so that heroic energies have clear employment but are clearly being replaced. Tribute is thus paid with no endorsement for the long future. Dryden's modern counterpart in this is William Faulkner, whose southern aristocrats are individually intact and historically irrelevant. The disorder they live in is in direct contrast to the luminous exactitude of their memories. Against the huge world mindlessly engulfing them they achieve momentary splendors of courage. Dryden's world is an engulfed world and its ethos is precisely that reserved for those engulfed. Its logic and its absolute values are those of extreme situations. The appeal of his absolute solutions—religious conversion, suicide, etc.—is recognizably modern.

Dryden's society was demoting rugged individualism even as we are. His serious drama is a critique of the unassimilable Achilles, Bryon, Essex, Macbeth type of hero whose military skills are not consequent in a peaceful society and whose mind "is for a Calm unfit." Even the once heroic God is in his plays made remote and featureless until he is depersonalized into a figure admired but not loved, a God about whom one cannot be *enthusiastic*. He thereby strips religious sentiment of its disturbing, heroic side-effects while affirming its centrality. There is something very Virgilian about Dryden's deity.

Dryden's special tone is reflected not only in his choice of heroes, situation, theme and in his repertoire of images, but also in his conception of theatrical space and scene. Many must have noticed that he treats social values without giving us any convincing scene to set them in; his depiction of the political community is shadowy and hence exercises a shadowy claim to respect. Reflecting on this, we can see that his treatment of place is informatively different from the two writers whose dramatic handling of heroic material influenced him most—Corneille and Shakespeare.

Corneille worked out his theory of indeterminate place, *lieu théâtral*, so as to permit the inclusion of a variety of actions while still, nominally, adhering to the Neoclassical demands of unity of place. Shakespeare, on the other hand, used place thematically, and hence abstracted motifs and characteristic qualities from Venice, Alexandria, a "blasted heath," or an "enchanted isle" as a means of conditioning his entire dramatic statement. He was interested in the qualities of a place as a supplementary means of dramatic signification. But Dryden practiced a theory of *neutral space*. He wanted a character to be studied in relation to a particular set of conditions independent of his framing natural or social setting. His heroes are insulated from external conditions by despair, defeat, cultural cataclysm or by a world-negating philosophy. He drains space in a quasi-scientific fashion of all significance save that which he gives it for his own experimental purposes. His theater is an arena for psychological surgery; it is as free from distractions as possible.

Thus we can see that Dryden's theatrical style is deeply in harmony with the Restoration stage with its new framing arch, its long diminishing perspectives, and hence its visual emphasis of isolated figures in the neutral space of a storied action.

To dominate such a stage required greatness. In the story of *Antony and Cleopatra,* and particularly in the figure of Antony, the epoch found its defining figure, just as the Elizabethan theater had in Hamlet, the French Classical theater in Phaedra, and the whole Western tradition in Antigone and Oedipus. Shakespeare had, of course, already treated the story with an autumnal completeness of language and insight. But his *Antony and Cleopatra* carries to their limit panoramic tendencies permitted by the open, fluid Elizabethan stage and the wonderful power of thematic linkage through image and scenic echo still understood in Shakespeare's day but lost to the more rational procedures of Dryden's time and our own. It is conventional to make set comparison of the two plays, to the predictable disadvantage of Dryden. I do not think this is very fruitful. Dryden's sense of dramatic structure is closer to Ibsen's than to Shakespeare's. He stays close to the decisive moment of dramatic change. His *All for Love* is "one long catastrophe" and hence it limits the cast of characters, abbreviates the action, concentrates effects, and formalizes character oppositions. Shakespeare's great Enobarbus, Eros, and Ventidius all three find one incarnation in Dryden's Catoesque, bluff soldier, Ventidius. Dryden's action is all after Antony's humiliating flight from battle at Actium, a "moment of truth" which decided his life and, incidentally, sharply changed Western history.

If we define the climax of a play as the point after which no essential change can occur without flaunting the structure of the action or contradicting the nature of the protagonists, it would be proper to say of *All for Love* that it is a retrospective tragedy in which the climax occurs before the action begins. There are a number of advantages to this. If everything has been decided, we are free to watch the fulfillment of "character as destiny" protected from any worries about externalities. And since something like despair has been achieved, the protagonists can be more open, they are past maintaining appearances. They are free to confront themselves, and this is exactly what Antony is made to do in *All for Love*. This gives the play the typical movement of those with a hero immobilized by sin, age, excess, metaphysical fatigue, or failure, plays like *Prometheus Bound, Oedipus at Colonus, Samson Agonistes,* and *The Masterbuilder*. These plays all stage a *psychomachia*, a war in the soul, and the lesser characters become to a degree expressions of competing parts of the conflicted mind, of the suffering protagonist whose battle for freedom, for restored health, for self-comprehension—in short, for salvation from his self-induced mortal plight—is the action of the play. In Antony, Dryden found a hero whose very brilliance in excess had more or less legitimatized itself through its grandeur, and whose faults, looking upon this man of action's pathetic and helpless efforts at conscious appraisal of his moral responsibilities, others are more ready to forgive than he is himself. For Antony has meant much to many others. He has seemed less subject to human limit than they themselves are, and, for each of them, some part of his mighty and varied self has been an "all," an idealized whole. He has been generous with his courage, his virility, his high spirits, his goods, even with his innermost feelings. But his life has been a constant dynamic moving onward, and now he is stopped and all the wideflung "lives" his potent nature has generated with and for others gather round him and are given voice.

Here, then, is an identity crisis, not in adolescence but at the end. Cleopatra, Ventidius, Octavia, Dolabella—all—*know* him and try to recall him to his true self. Each one has a claim that is morally substantial and theatrically potent. This multiple invitation to renewal forms the confusing *agon*, the central struggle, of the play. The fact that all the lines of appeal run to a common center and that each one, while dignified in itself, is at odds with every other is part of the watchlike economy of this beautifully built play. One's sympathies are not easily brought to rest, evasive romantic identification with any one character is forestalled, but there are heavy risks, too, in this type of dramatic structure. The neat externalizing of Antony's emotional commitments makes the contests *very* clear but it makes him seem weak. There are almost no inner issues, no looming but obscure emotional dubieties. This accounts somewhat for the talky, artificial quality of the play. It isn't the conflicts themselves which are trivial, far from it, but that the conflicts seem to exist independently like disease entities—Antony doesn't seem to generate the conflicts out of himself but instead he contracts them one after another like maladies. These conflicts are classified according to the expert emotional taxonomy of the period. Each confusion is to be got through, so that terminal immunity in the form of peace of mind can be achieved. Life, in this view, becomes a disagreeable means to an ulterior status. Hence, our vantage point is not—as it is in Shakespeare—from the midst of life outwards but from a hypothetical, musing eminence beyond the action from which we look on these struggles of one who must remain forever in the past, circumscribed in death by his own errors.

This sense of condescension to Antony is a symptom of an exhausted tragic vision. It is intensified by Dryden's immense inflation of the role of the eunuch, Alexas, from the "atmospheric" bit player he was in *Antony and Cleopatra* to the magnitude of a stagemaster like Jonson's Mosca, manipulating the feelings and actions of his betters in *All for Love*. It is symbolically appropriate that in Dryden's revisionist view of tragic behavior the fate of the great lovers, themselves personifications of dedicated sexual passion, should be determined by the nonman, the eunuch Alexas, who represents, perhaps, the ingenious and metallic quality of reason unimpeded by any animal passion. Alexas, as developed by Dryden, shows both the resourcefulness of cold reason and its insufficiency. Alexas is bloodless and his tidy and wholly selfish concern for his own literally sterile future is in deliberate contrast to the super-abundant generosity of Antony, who "grows rich by giving," and the fecundity of Cleopatra's protean nature. It is, perhaps, too much to say that the world to come after such mighty figures of olden times, the great lovers and the soldiers who didn't count the cost, is to be a world dominated by the spiritual eunuchry of bureaucratic compromise and of prudence and intrigue, but it should be stressed that the most indicative change Dryden made in his reimagining of Shakespeare's play is the total exclusion of Octavius Caesar from the direct action.

Octavius's power is felt; he hovers over the action like Nemesis. The future belongs to him. By contrast Antony seems quixotic, obsolescent, tied to noble and unduly personalized confusions about the nature of historical reality.

Part of the poignancy of Dryden's analysis derives from Antony's complete inability to grasp the nature of his opponent. The secure pragmatism of Octavius, his indifference to the opinion of others so long as his ends are served and his interests are unthreatened, combined with his freedom from any need to prove himself showily, his physical coldness and his instinct for the most economical way, make him virtually of another species from Antony. Dryden was wise not to put Octavius on the stage, for he is formidable as a representative of the inevitable future closing in upon and rejecting the Antonys of the world, but he would have been so colorless and unsympathetic on the stage as to have muddied Dryden's thematic intentions.

Dryden's Cleopatra is as far beyond standard stage portraiture as she is below Shakespeare's marvelous female. Dryden's Cleopatra reasons well enough to dislodge convictions far better anchored than Antony's, and the role should attract most good actresses within whose reach it readily falls. The scene between the wronged Octavia and the threatened Cleopatra is a model of the efficient staging of language. Dryden, whose own prudent marriage to Lady Ann Howard was visited by little happiness, had a practiced ear for female argument, and I think few modern readers will subscribe to Dryden's judgment in his preface that "The greatest error in contrivance seems to be in the person of Octavia." For, though she must move compassion as he notes, there is no need in the staging that her claim on Antony should seem any more exclusively valid than those of the other competitors for his terminal energies: Ventidius, Dolabella, or Cleopatra herself. Only if we completely disregard the possibility of nondomestic virtue, not to say greatness, do we need to regret the telling use of Octavia.

We must speak, too, of the healthy clarity and controlled flow of Dryden's blank verse. It is a very social poetry, full of succinct opinions to be shared and resting on the rationalist's fiction that passions which agitate can be concurrently discussed by those they are agitating. In the play's first speech there is a magnificent compression in the priest, Serapion's accurate cataloguing of the play's basic imagery and a systematic prefiguration of the central theme: the overflowing Nile has left great, antediluvian creatures panting on the shore. These "monstrous phocae" are doomed survivals thrown up by the "fruitful Nile's" torrent. They are fine imagistic equivalents for Antony and Cleopatra whose o'erswelling passion and great nature are equally outmoded and equally doomed. The play is close-wrought, the imagery and the action qualify each other as they should in a poetic drama. Dryden is the last great English poet who brought his mature skill to bear as a working playwright in the professional theater. In his rehandling of Antony's story, he brought to a circumscribed perfection what the heroic tragedy could do.

In *All for Love,* Antony starts with all that other heroes seek—fame, honor, access to beauty and power. He is a symbol; like a god he contains and guarantees meaning for others. In a very precise sense the play measures the mortality of his godhead and little by little, by matching his multiform meanings in the minds of his followers against the mutable facts of his declining being, strips him of divinity and of oversimple meaning and restores him to that special nobility which tragedy alone can give us—the felt essence of a man suffering enlightenment, thinking and dying. This *recovery* of Antony's humanity is an imaginative feat. It brings with it a poignant realization; a hero with sufficient brilliancy of character and achievement to embody otherwise inaccessible ideals becomes necessarily the disillusioner of others who are betrayed by the seeming permanence of this seeming marriage in his person of the two realms of ideal and fact which are otherwise separate. Here is a deeper, more moving meaning for "The best is enemy of the good," a meaning which resolves the deepest conflict in Dryden's artistic character. If one can believe that men of Antony's heroic stature are dead, that they are obsolete, that nature no longer gives us such mirage-like creatures, then we can subside and there is a kind of peace—of rest from struggle; the two realms are separate. What the artist can do is to rejoin them retrospectively, and portray the time of sacramental communication in that vanished world in fixed works of art. He need no longer seek for it in fact. He can elegize virtue, but he need not explain it or discern its workings in the fallen world. This explains the "storied" quality of Dryden's plays; his many techniques of distancing, of abstracting. Such is the special quality of Dryden's divided vision, such the characteristics of this terminal tragedy, *All for Love.*

Tragedy and the Heroic Play

by Moody E. Prior

Dryden's *All for Love; or, The World Well Lost* is generally acknowledged as his best play, and without much question it is the best tragedy of its age. In the Preface to the play Dryden expresses his dissatisfaction with French tragedy and his enthusiasm for Shakespeare, on whose *Antony and Cleopatra* he modeled this play. The subject was a favorite, as Dryden tells us in his Preface:

> The death of Antony and Cleopatra is a subject which has been treated by the greatest wits of our nation, after Shakespeare; and by all so variously, that their example has given me the confidence to try myself in this bow of Ulysses amongst the crowd of suitors; and, withal, to take my own measures, in aiming at the mark. I doubt not but the same motive has prevailed with all of us in this attempt; I mean the excellency of the moral: for the chief persons represented were famous patterns of unlawful love; and their end accordingly was unfortunate.

It may be that Dryden was directed to this play among the rest of Shakespeare's tragedies because of the excellency of the moral, in which case the choice artistically was a lucky one. No other of Shakespeare's plays lent itself so readily to the typical Restoration plot structure or could have submitted to its characteristic schemes and patterns without some fatal distortion. Conflicts of love and honor, decisions that held empire and joy in the balance, great personages, undying loyalties—all these were present in a story certified by history and glorified by Shakespeare. Dryden worked out the plot in such a way as to accentuate those features which lent themselves to the prevailing methods of heroic drama, and it is in this and not merely in the general tidying up, nor in the imposition of the unities of time and place onto the expansive scheme of Shakespeare's play, that the important modifications are to be found.

"Tragedy and the Heroic Play." From *The Language of Tragedy* (New York: Columbia University Press, 1947) by Moody E. Prior, pp. 192-211. Copyright 1947 by Columbia University Press. Reprinted by permission of the author and Columbia University Press.

Dryden's play begins with Antony in utter despair, shut off from the world in the temple of Isis. Actium is a bitter memory; Caesar is at the gates of Alexandria. At this juncture Ventidius arrives, interrupts Antony's gloomy meditations, upbraids him for his blind infatuation, and urges him to go to Syria and take personal charge of twelve veteran legions which he had marched up from Parthia and which will give him an advantage with which to defeat Caesar. Antony's hopes as Emperor and his pride as a soldier triumph, and he resolves to leave at once without so much as taking the risk of bidding farewell to Cleopatra. As he is departing with his officers, Alexas, the queen's eunuch, persuades him by clever stratagem to see Cleopatra once more. He attempts sternly to justify his departure from her, but she convinces him of her loyalty and love, and Antony gives up all thoughts of leaving. In the enthusiasm of the moment, he executes a successful surprise attack with his few local troops on Caesar's army, and returns triumphant to Cleopatra. Once more Ventidius intrudes, urging the impossibility of further military successes and the wisdom of using the momentary advantage to make favorable terms with Caesar. To clinch his argument, he confronts Antony first with his friend Dollabella from Caesar's forces, and then with Octavia, Antony's wife and Caesar's sister, and with their children. The combined appeal of these attacks on his better nature wins out, and he again abandons Cleopatra. In desperation, Cleopatra listens to Alexas' advice that she should arouse Antony's jealousy by working on the susceptibilities of Dollabella, once himself infatuated with her, who has been sent by Antony to give his farewell to the queen. The stratagem proves fatal. Ventidius had overheard Dollabella talking to himself and weighing the possibility of stating Antony's case in such a way as to recommend his own love to the queen, and he witnesses Cleopatra's efforts to arouse Dollabella's interest—efforts which failed because her own faithfulness would not permit her to go on with a distasteful ruse. Ventidius returns, moreover, with Octavia just in time to misinterpret Dollabella's kissing of Cleopatra's hand. Confronted by Ventidius and Octavia, Antony finally believes after Alexas falsely corroborates their evidence. In his utter despair he offends Octavia, who leaves him for good, and he refuses to believe Cleopatra and Dollabella. He is now completely alone. And the last blow is the news that the Egyptian navy has abandoned him and gone over to Caesar. In his mind Cleopatra is now doubly condemned. To shield her from his anger, the high priest Serapion sends her to her monument, and Alexas is placed to meet Antony and repair the damage done by his stupid machinations. But Alexas can only scheme. To soften Antony he tells him that Cleopatra has taken her own life. The news shatters Antony, and he falls on his sword. Cleopatra, fearing the event when she hears of Alexas' falsehood, comes in time to see Antony dying. Faithful to the end, she too takes her own life.

As the plot is managed, Antony oscillates from one allegiance to another as the two opposing sides win him over by one appeal or another. Granted this basic design, the development is ingenious. Each fluctuation makes more permanent his separation from Cleopatra or more difficult his saving of the empire. Ventidius succeeds by appealing to the emperor and warrior. Cleopatra matches this with a proof of her complete devotion and faithfulness. Ventidius overcomes this with the ties of friendship and family. Devotion being not enough, Cleopatra reluctantly tries jealousy, and this destroys both sides. As a last desperate ruse Alexas uses death, and this succeeds all too well. Each probability inherent in the situation is explored and eliminated. At the end, death is the only scheme left for Alexas to try, but death is also the only way out now for the defeated emperor. Only the treachery of the navy remains an unexplained and unpredictable factor in the scheme of forces which drive Antony first one way and then another. This manipulation of the plot has nevertheless one serious disadvantage in that Antony, presumably the protagonist, becomes the battle ground for contending forces, or rather the prize for which they contend. The strategy on one side is managed by Ventidius, on the other by Alexas. The latter is doubly necessary since, to maintain the equal balance between love and honor, Cleopatra is made unswerving in her devotion, with nothing of the coquette about her, and nothing equivocal about her motives; hence the stratagems by which Antony is enticed cannot originate with her: " 'Twas thy design brought all this ruin on us," she tells Alexas shortly before the catastrophe. To permit the conflict to proceed by a series of skirmishes, Antony is made open to the claims of the lover (Cleopatra), of the warrior and emperor (Ventidius), the friend (Dollabella), the husband (Octavia), and the father (his two children). The presentation of the conflicting claims appears with least subtlety in the third act, when Ventidius first shows the folly of further attempts at victory, then produces Dollabella, and finally Octavia and the two children. The high point is reached when Octavia sends the children to the wavering Antony; and as the children obey, all the forces are turned on him:

> *Ventidius.* Was ever sight so moving! Emperor!
> *Dollabella.* Friend!
> *Octavia.* Husband!
> *Both Children.* Father!
> *Antony.* I am vanquished. . . .   (3.406-10)[1]

It is as though each one calls out his card as he lays it down, and Antony realizes that he has nothing to beat the combination. No other episode in the play is as coldly deliberate as this, but the method in

---

[1] Line references are to Bonamy Dobrée's edition of *All for Love* in *Five Restoration Tragedies* (World's Classics).

most of them is the same. And the position of Antony as an almost helpless victim of these operations is intensified by such remarks as Alexas'
"He melts; we conquer," or Ventidius' "He moves as I would wish him,"
or Antony's own "Oh, my distracted soul."

It was perhaps inevitable that Dryden should have introduced jealousy among the possibilities for producing further complications in the
play, but it is somewhat unfortunate that he should have used it as the
critical issue on which the play turns to its final conclusion; for in order
to bring it about he had to resort to a number of dramatic contrivances
among which the sudden betrayal of a long friendship by Dollabella is
the least questionable. This episode made possible a love-honor conflict
of a secondary order, since Dollabella must choose between the rival
claims of friendship and love; and the play is thus brought closer to the
pattern of heroic drama, though not with too great a loss in concentration since, with this exception, the other important conflicts center entirely in Antony. More important in their effect on the play are the
other devices, typical of the heroic play, employed to set the stage for
Antony's jealousy. It becomes necessary for Ventidius to overhear Dollabella weighing the claims of friendship and love, thus using the dramatic
convention of the soliloquy as a talking out loud. It requires Ventidius
to leave off his spying on the interview between Dollabella and Cleopatra one moment too soon, and to return to it with Octavia, also one
moment too soon—a double coincidence of misunderstandings. To rest
the critical turn of affairs on such trifling dramatic tricks tends to weaken
an action that in so many other more probable ways predicates a tragic
conclusion. Such things might pass in the general atmosphere of the
heroic play, but they seem less acceptable here. For the important thing
about *All for Love* is that it involves such radical alterations in the
characterization and particularly in the language that the total result is
quite different from such works as *Aureng-Zebe* or even such blank verse
drama as *The Rival Queens*.

The blank verse of *All for Love* is not the heroic couplet gone flabby
for want of rhyme, nor is it an uncontrolled instrument for rant and
gaudy rhetoric. It is remarkable, in view of the similarities in plot with
the heroic play, that there should be so few traces of those brisk para-
doxes and tight antitheses which seemed so inseparable a complement of
the situation in the language. Occasionally in such a phrase as Ventidius'
"You speak a hero, and you move a god," traces of the couplet style appear, and something of the antithetical pointing up of a dilemma occasionally survives in a speech like that of Dollabella when he considers
betraying his friend:

> O friendship! friendship!
> Ill canst thou answer this; and reason, worse:
> Unfaithful in th' attempt; hopeless to win;
> And, if I win, undone: mere madness all.   (4.62-65)

More often such phrasing has the effect of Octavia's departing words—

> . . . for I despair
> To have you whole, and scorn to take you half.   (4.491-92)

which add an accent of finality to a beautifully modulated speech. It is no problem to illustrate the admirable virtues of this verse, for almost any speech will do. The following is Cleopatra's reply to Octavia's accusation that all of Antony's woes can be traced to Cleopatra:

> Yet she who loves him best is Cleopatra.
> If you have suffered, I have suffered more.
> You bear the specious title of a wife,
> To gild your cause, and draw the pitying world
> To favor it: the world contemns poor me;
> For I have lost my honour, lost my fame,
> And stained the glory of my royal house,
> And all to bear the branded name of mistress.
> There wants but life, and that too I would lose
> For him I love.   (3.522-31)

To appreciate further the transformation in style which this play represents, it should be noted that this speech occurs in the only interview between Octavia and Cleopatra, one of those contentions between rival interests which customarily called forth the fullest display of rhetorical brilliance in the heroic play. This verse has the clarity which training in the couplet might have produced, and the discipline; but it has ease and suppleness as well. It is a fine medium capable of absorbing the strain that any dramatic necessity can place upon it.

This style moves with such ease that its effects frequently come off with an almost deceptive simplicity. Consider, for example, the following speech of Antony:

> How I loved
> Witness ye days and nights, and all your hours,
> That danced away with down upon your feet,
> As all your business were to count my passion.
> One day passed by, and nothing saw but love;
> Another came, and still 'twas only love:
> The suns were wearied out with looking on,
> And I untired with loving.
> I saw you every day, and all the day;
> And every day was still but as the first:
> So eager was I still to see you more.   (2.327-37)

The opening, rather studied, image conveys an impression of trivial gaiety, but the whole passage gives an effect quite other than triviality. The imagery of the passage is derived from units of time—hours, days, nights, diurnal suns—all symbols of earthly flux and change reinforced by "one," "another," "wearied"; yet the statement in the passage is of permanence and constancy, so that the speech has an air of paradox about it. And in addition the phrase "suns were wearied out," the repetitions of "day" convey also the notions of majesty and immutability of cosmic cycles. This is by no means one of the more arresting passages in the play, but it serves to illustrate how the style combines something of the ease of unstudied discourse with all the studied complexity of poetry. Some of the Elizabethan freedom and daring in handling of images has been sacrificed, but the intimate relationship between the possibilities of the language and the demands of the form has been preserved.

The development of the action proceeds, as we have seen, by a series of oscillations on the part of Antony, between his love for Cleopatra and the claims of empire, family, and friendship represented by his Roman loyalties. This opposition of forces working on Antony is represented in the diction by a scheme of images which represent the appeal to Antony of these contrasting attractions. The two appear mutually antagonistic throughout. Thus Ventidius tells Alexas:

> Go tell thy queen,
> Ventidius is arrived, to end her charms.
> Let your Egyptian timbrels play alone;
> Nor mix effeminate sounds with Roman trumpets.   (1.209-12)

This simple opposition of timbrels and trumpets, with its suggestion of decadent pleasure on the one hand and vigorous strength on the other, contains the germ of an elaborate development in the diction. Traces of it appear widely diffused. When Serapion expresses his fears concerning the outcome of a Roman victory—

> . . . our plenteous harvests
> Must then redeem the scarceness of their soil.   (1.71-72)

—he is talking about the political consequences of such a victory, but the diction also balances suggestions of richness and fecundity against those of sternness and privation. In a more direct way, the opposition is implied in the images which are directed toward Ventidius and Alexas, the two leading machinators in the struggle for Antony. Alexas, giving the devil his due, says of Ventidius:

> Firm to his prince; but, as a friend, not slave.
> He ne'r was of his pleasures; but presides
> O'er all his cooler hours and morning counsels.   (1.111-13)

Ventidius, on the other hand, to whom Alexas is Cleopatra's "darling mischief, her chief engine," and "Antony's other fate," says to him:

> You are of Cleopatra's private counsel,
> Of her bed-counsel, her lascivious hours;
> Are conscious of each nightly change she makes,
> And watch her, as Chaldeans do the moon,
> Can tell what signs she passes through, what day.   (4.378-82)

Words like cool and morning define Ventidius; Alexas is associated with images of night and passion. The particular bias which a given image in this scheme receives is dependent in large part on the position of Antony at any given point in the play. Ventidius finds him under Cleopatra's spell "unbent, unsinewed, made a woman's toy" (1.193); after his resolve to fight, Antony tells his general,

> Thou shalt behold me once again in iron,   (1.497)

and Charmian reports to Cleopatra that she found him

> Incompassed round, I think, with iron statues.   (2.57)

On the other side, centering in Cleopatra and all she represents in contrast to Rome, the images are more elaborately and frequently developed, sometimes implying wantonness and malevolence when spoken by Ventidius or Octavia, or even by Antony when he determines to break from his toils, and at times implying pleasure, gaiety and allurement, as when spoken, for instance, by Antony in his resolve to lose the world for his love. The speeches of Ventidius contain many impressions of the first sort. He tells Alexas:

> Does the mute sacrifice upbraid the priest?
> He knows him not his executioner:
> O, she has decked his ruin with her love,
> Led him in golden bands to gaudy slaughter,
> And made perdition pleasing.   (1.184-88)

All the allurements of Cleopatra and the East are deadly in his eyes; he warns Antony when Alexas brings gifts from her for his departure:

> Now, my best Lord, in honor's name, I ask you,
> For manhood's sake, and for your own dear safety,
> Touch not these poisoned gifts,
> Infected by the sender, touch 'em not,
> Miriads of bluest plagues lie underneath 'em,
> And more than aconite has dipt the silk.   (2.232-37)

In his description of Cleopatra's flight from Actium, intended to call attention to the cowardice which he repeatedly assigns to the East, he nevertheless touches also on the colorful grandeur:

> What haste she made to hoist her purple sails!
> And to appear magnificent in flight.   (2.363-64)

Most of his speeches glance somehow on the combination of color and evil with which he associates Cleopatra and what Octavia calls her "black endearments." Only in Antony's speeches do the attractions of Cleopatra appear in imagery freed from suggestions of taint. Even during his moment of resolve to leave with Ventidius, he can recall his pleasure in terms cleared of reproach:

> How I loved
> Witness ye days and nights, and all your hours,
> That danced away with down upon your feet.   (2.327-29)

Though a few lines further he can state the consequences of his passion in words that convey impression of ruin and decay:

> While within your arms I lay,
> The world fell mouldring from my hands each hour,
> And left me scarce a grasp (I thank your love for't). (2.344-46)

During the period when he has returned to Cleopatra and before Ventidius' second triumph over him, Antony's speeches create an unsullied impression of her appeal. He speaks of his love in images that symbolize once more the paradox of her ever-fresh charms:

> There's no satiety of love in thee;
> Enjoyed, thou still art new; perpetual spring
> Is in thy arms; the ripened fruit but falls,

> And blossoms rise to fill its empty place;
> And I grow rich by giving. (3.25-29)

He gives full expression to the high-colored splendor of her attractions in his speech to Dollabella reminding him of their first view of Cleopatra:

> Her galley down the silver Cydnos rowed,
> The tackling silk, the streamers waved with gold,
> The gentle winds were lodged in purple sails;
> Her nymphs, like Nereids, round her couch, were placed;
> Where she another sea-born Venus lay. . . .
> She lay, and leant her cheek upon her hand,
> And cast a look so languishingly sweet,
> As if secure of all beholders' hearts,
> Neglecting she could take 'em. Boys, like Cupids,
> Stood fanning, with their painted wings, the winds
> That played about her face; but if she smiled,
> A darting glory seemed to blaze abroad,
> That men's desiring eyes were never wearied,
> But hung upon the object. To soft flutes
> The silver oars kept time; and while they played
> The hearing gave new pleasure to the sight,
> And both to thought. 'Twas heav'n or somewhat more;
> For she so charmed all hearts, that gazing crowds
> Stood panting on the shore, and wanted breath
> To give their welcome voice. (3.181-202)

This is the most elaborate presentation of those images which color the impression of Cleopatra's claims in the contending forces which divide the allegiance of Antony. With it must be compared Ventidius' speech to Octavia, in which, though confessing her charms, he dyes his speech with suggestions of her malevolence:

> Her eyes have power beyond Thessalian charms
> To draw the moon from heav'n; for eloquence,
> The sea-green sirens taught her voice their flattery;
> And, while she speaks, night steals upon the day,
> Unmarked of those that hear. Then she's so charming,
> Age buds at sight of her, and swells to youth:
> The holy priests gaze on her when she smiles;
> And with heaved hands forgetting gravity,
> They bless her wanton eyes. Even I who hate her,
> With a malignant joy behold such beauty;
> And, while I curse, desire it. (4.267-77)

The extreme expression of the malignant side of the opposition appears
in the speeches of Ventidius and Antony after they have witnessed the
treachery of the Egyptian fleet. Ventidius:

> Curse on this treach'rous train!
> Their soil and heav'n infect 'em all with baseness;
> And their young souls come tainted to the world
> With the first breath they draw.   (5.170-73)

And in the full tide of his despair, Antony speaks now the language
of his general, and Cleopatra is not even mentioned in his condemnation
of the deadly infection of the East:

> Th' original villain sure no god created;
> He was a bastard of the sun, by Nile.
> Aped into man, with all his mother's mud
> Crusted about his soul.   (5.174-77)

Shortly after these speeches, Alexas brings the false report of Cleopatra's
death. The conflict in Antony between love and empire ceases, and this
interplay of images representing Antony's divided soul comes to an end.
To follow the course of the diction through the close of the play, it is
necessary to trace other threads.

This scheme of opposed images reflects indirectly on the conflicting
demands of Antony's spirit. Of images that bear directly on his character, there are on the whole comparatively few and those usually of a
general sort, perhaps because the nature of the action is such as to re-
quire him to be open to a number of separate loyalties The problem is
largely simplified by introducing a wide variety of images divided between what might be termed Roman and Egyptian qualities. Two
speeches of Ventidius early in the play are designed to set the impression of greatness and weakness in Antony:

> Virtue's his path; but sometimes 'tis too narrow
> For his vast soul, and then he starts out wide,
> And bounds into a vice that bears him far
> From his first course, and plunges him in ills:
> But, when his danger makes him find his fault,
> Quick to observe, and full of sharp remorse,
> He censures eagerly his own misdeeds,
> Judging himself with malice to himself,
> And not forgiving what as man he did,
> Because his other parts are more than man.   (1.137-46)

This is a straightforward analysis for the most part, in which the language aims at sharp definition. Ventidius' other speech on Antony leans toward over-elaborateness:

> But you, ere love misled your wand'ring eyes,
> Were sure the chief and best of human race,
> Framed in the very pride and boast of nature,
> So perfect, that the gods who formed you, wondered
> At their own skill, and cried, "A lucky hit
> Has mended our design." Their envy hindered,
> Else you had been immortal, and a pattern,
> When heav'n would work for ostentation sake,
> To copy out again. (1.468-76)

Scattered phrases, such as his own reference to his "eagle's wings," Cleopatra's "my greater Mars," and the like, keep up the suggestions of greatness, but not in any consistently developed scheme, and the numerous signs of the glory of his empire are only indirectly related to impressions of Antony and play another role. A few images touch on his simplicity and honesty. When he has lost Octavia and suspects Cleopatra, Antony says:

> But I am made a shallow-forded stream,
> Seen to the bottom: all my clearness scorned,
> And all my faults exposed! (4.502-4)

In the same mood he tells the apparently faithless Dollabella:

> How could you betray
> This tender heart, which with an infant-fondness
> Lay lulled betwixt your bosoms, and there slept
> Secure of injured faith? (4.563-66)

If the character of Antony emerges from the play as something less than heroic and impressive, the difficulty is to be found partly in the management of the action and partly in the diction: it is the limitations of the man that appear in the vacillating character speaking and acting, and the diction does not do a great deal to add a compensating aura of magnitude.

In an indirect way, the character of Antony gains from the treatment which Octavius Caesar receives. The latter does not appear in the play at all, and thus the conflict of Antony is kept sharp within the limits defined by the other characters, and his defeat is not made a triumph

of some other military hero. At the end of the play Antony is able to
say:

> O happy Caesar! Thou hast men to lead:
> Think not 'tis thou hast conquered Antony;
> But Rome has conquered Egypt.   (5.167-69)

Throughout the play, moreover, the imagery helps to maintain an impression of Caesar as inferior to Antony. He refers to Caesar as "the
boy," and in his speeches the images suggest guile rather than heroism:

> Let Caesar spread his subtle nets, like Vulcan.   (3.18)
>   Nature meant him for an usurer;
> He's fit indeed to buy, not conquer kingdoms.   (3.241-42)

In their rise to fame, Antony's is the grander flight:

> Fool that I was, upon my eagle's wings
> I bore this wren, till I was tired with soaring,
> And now he mounts above me.   (2.162-64)

The treatment of Caesar thus places the fall of Antony primarily within
himself at the same time that it introduces a source of imagery which
directly adds to Antony's stature.

In keeping with a scheme which requires a rather clear-cut opposition
of issues, Cleopatra is preserved throughout sincerely loyal. It is true, she
has twice to prove her love—once, at the beginning when she reveals
that she refused favorable terms from Caesar and preferred to be ruined
with Antony, and again when she convinces Antony that she had no interest in Dollabella. But at no time can any action of Cleopatra's in the
play be interpreted as a sign of disloyalty except by those who oppose
her. Moreover, the images which build up suggestions of evil and malevolence around her reflect rather on Antony, since in almost every case
they are pointed toward the consequences of his affection on his sterner
and more strictly Roman virtues. Such a phrase as Antony's "Took you
into my bosom, stained by Caesar" (2.321) is spoken during one of his
moments of self-reproach; and the following figure of perfidy is uttered
by him in the depth of spirits brought on by the treachery of the Egyptian navy:

> Ingrateful woman!
> Who followed me but as the swallow summer,
> Hatching her young ones in my kindly beams,
> Singing her flatt'ries to my morning wake;

> But, now my winter comes, she spreads her wings
> And seeks the spring of Caesar. (5.236-41)

Other images tend to cancel these impressions: the "household dove" in the following passage, for instance:

> Nature meant me
> A wife, a silly harmless household dove,
> Fond without art, and kind without deceit;
> But Fortune, that has made a mistress of me,
> Has thrust me out to the wide world, unfurnished
> Of falsehood to be happy. (4.99-104)

Other images suggest her simplicity and innocence:

> There I till death will his unkindness weep:
> As harmless infants moan themselves to sleep. (3.550-51)

And still others her sincerity. Thus Dollabella says after he receives convincing demonstration of her devotion to Antony:

> I find your breast fenced round from human reach,
> Transparent as a rock of solid crystal;
> Seen through, but never pierced. My friend, my friend!
> What endless treasure hast thou thrown away,
> And scattered, like an infant, in the Ocean,
> Vast sums of wealth which none can gather thence. (4.228-33)

Neither in the action nor in the imagery is this Cleopatra a serpent of old Nile. At the same time the imagery of the play, if it does not have the effect of destroying these impressions of loyalty and simplicity, does have the effect of identifying her with all the allurements and pleasures of the civilization of which she appears as the most attractive embodiment. Cleopatra gains in stature and impressiveness thereby, so that when Serapion announces his dire news—

> O horror, horror!
> Egypt has been; our latest hour is come:
> The Queen of Nations from her ancient seat,
> Is sunk forever in the dark abyss:
> Time has unrolled her glories to the last,
> And now closed up the volume. (5.77-82)

—his words seem to convey not so much predictions of the fall of an empire, but the fall of its queen.

The tragic catastrophe is anticipated and prepared for in the images throughout the play, and there is everywhere a close paralleling of the diction with the development of the situations. The portents and supernatural sights announced by Serapion at the outset may be dismissed as a concession to a tragic convention; the supernatural plays no real part, as it does in *Macbeth*, for instance. The important development is begun by the somber impressions indicative of the situation: Antony is at the low ebb in his fortunes and has isolated himself with his own gloomy reflections. We are told by Alexas,

> All southern, from yon hills, the Roman camp
> Hangs o'er us black and threatening, like a storm
> Just breaking on our heads.   (1.45-47)

Antony "makes his heart a prey to black despair" (1.66); he will keep his birthday "with double pomp of sadness" (1.222). His failures haunt him. He tells Ventidius of the disgraceful defeat at Actium, which becomes a symbol of his great decline,

> Here, here it lies; a lump of lead by day,
> And, in my short distracted nightly slumbers,
> The hag that rides my dreams.   (1.313-15)

There are practically no images which give to his downfall suggestions of brilliance except that of the meteor:

> Why was I raised the meteor of the world,
> Hung in the skies, and blazing as I travelled
> Till all my fires were spent; and then cast downward
> To be trod out by Caesar?   (1.224-27)

For the most part they are dreary. Caesar, Antony says,

> . . . drives me before him
> To the world's ridge, and sweeps me off like rubbish.   (2.166-67)

Ventidius describes Antony as

> Shrunk from the vast extent of all his honors,
> And cramped within a corner of the world.   (1.194-95)

Antony tells Dollabella,

> Thou find'st me at my lowest water-mark.
> The rivers that ran in and raised my fortunes

> Are all dried up, or take another course.
> What I have left is from my native spring;
> I've still a heart that swells, in scorn of fate,
> And lifts me to my banks.   (3.145-50)

Only the last lines imply some measure of contrast to those impressions of aridity and gloom which crowd the first two acts.

Though the concentration of such images occurs in the earlier portions of the play, figures indicative of the collapse of Antony's might extend through the entire fabric. Cleopatra, says Alexas, "winds herself about his mighty ruins" (1.85). Ventidius, observing Antony in his passion, remarks,

> . . . the tempest tears him up by th' roots,
> And on the ground extends the noble ruin.   (1.235-36)

Antony does indeed cast himself down and give himself over to melancholy thoughts:

> Lie there, thou shadow of an Emperor;
> The place thou pressest on thy mother-earth
> Is all thy empire now: now it contains thee;
> Some few days hence, and then 'twill be too large,
> When thou'rt contracted in thy narrow urn,
> Shrunk to a few cold ashes.   (1.237-42)

He tells Cleopatra, "The world fell mould'ring from my hands each hour" (2.346); and when she tries to dissuade him from departure, he asks,

> . . . would you multiply more ruins on me?
> This honest man has gathered up the shipwreck of my fortunes.
>   (2.367-68)

"Ruin," in fact, is the most persistent single word in the play, a recurrent note running throughout.

Heightening these impressions are the references to the fallen empire, invariably introduced to point the magnitude of Antony's decline, and suggestive of activity and greatness. Antony tells Ventidius:

> Fortune came smiling to my youth, and wooed it,
> And purple greatness met my ripened years.
> When first I came to empire, I was borne
> On tides of people, crowding to my triumphs;

The wish of nations; and the willing world
Received me as its pledge of future peace.
I was so great, so happy, so beloved,
Fate could not ruin me; till I took pains
And worked against my fortune, chid her from me,
And turned her loose; yet still she came again.
My careless days and my luxurious nights
At length have wearied her, and now she's gone,
Gone, gone, divorced forever.   (1.337-49)

In a similar vein he talks to Dollabella:

Thou hast beheld me other than I am.
Hast thou not seen my morning chambers filled
With sceptered slaves, who waited to salute me;
With eastern monarchs, who forgot the sun
To worship my uprising? Menial kings
Ran coursing up and down my palace-yard
Stood silent in my presence, watched my eyes,
And, at my least command, all started out
Like racers to the goal.   (3.156-64)

In both instances mention is made of fortune. When Antony comments
at the close of this speech, "Fortune is Caesar's now; and what am I?"
Ventidius replies, "What you have made your self." In each case the
reference is such as to eliminate the possibility that Antony is the victim of fate. These particular references to empire thus help to center
the cause of his decline in Antony, and accentuate the drabness of the
present. The contrast which these passages bring out deliberately is often implied, as when Antony asks Ventidius,

Why dost thou drive me from myself, to search
For foreign aids? to hunt my memory,
And range all o'er a waste and barren place
To find a friend? The wretched have no friends.   (3.88-91)

Against the background of this elaborate scheme of images, there is a
fine appropriateness to Antony's speech when he has heard of the loss
of his navy and the death of Cleopatra:

My torch is out; and the world stands before me
Like a black desert at the approach of night:
I'll lay me down and stray no further on.   (5.324-26)

The images thus anticipate and sustain an action which is concerned with the loss of the world and the fall of its hero. But if the world is well lost, there should properly be some resolution of these prevailing images of darkness, decay, and barrenness into terms that will convey the shift which the action involves from uncertainty and misery to certainty and peace. Early in the play Ventidius is told that Antony has been heard to say in scorn,

> Take all,
> The world's not worth my care. (1.134-35)

And Ventidius hears these words from Antony himself:

> No, when I found all lost
> Beyond repair, I hid me from the world,
> And learned to scorn it here; which now I do
> So heartily, I think it is not worth
> The cost of keeping. (1.370-74)

These, however, are words of defeat. The accent changes when he tells Ventidius that Cleopatra "deserves/More worlds than I can lose" (1.424-25); and the sentiment becomes not one of defeat but of triumph when he resolves to stay with her:

> Give, you gods,
> Give to your boy, your Caesar,
> This rattle of a globe to play withal
> This gu-gau world, and put him cheaply off:
> I'll not be pleased with less than Cleopatra. (2.508-12)

The bravado of this image represents the height of Antony's optimism, and it is not again repeated. For the world and Cleopatra are not separable; he cannot so readily choose between them. The conditions of the play impose a hard choice on him. If he loses the empire to Caesar, he loses Cleopatra; if he tries to save the empire, he must leave her forever. Yet his empire is meaningless to him without her. His half of the globe he had given her "in dowry with my heart" (4.560). And when he expresses for the last time his willingness to give up the world, after he believes Cleopatra to be dead, it is with all these considerations in mind —and the figure for the world is a ring:

> My Queen is dead.
> I was but great for her; my power, my empire,
> Were but my merchandise to buy her love;

And conquered kings my factors. Now she's dead,
Let Caesar take the world—
An empty circle, since the jewel's gone
Which made it worth my strife: my being's nauseous;
For all the bribes of life are gone away.   (5.306-13)

This speech has the air of resignation, and is almost immediately followed by the somber image of the extinguished torch. After he has wounded himself, he sees Cleopatra once more, "The one dear jewel that his haste forgot," and receives final reassurance of her love. In the speech which follows, spoken just before his death, the somber and brilliant suggestions are interwoven:

But grieve not, while thou stay'st,
My last disastrous times:
Think we have had a clear and glorious day;
And heav'n did kindly to delay the storm
Just till our close of evening.   (5.447-51)

The image breathes reconciliation. It recalls vaguely the bright images which are associated with Cleopatra in the play. And the grimness of the extinguished torch and the dark desert is replaced by the quiet of evening. This impression is recalled by Cleopatra's speech over his body before she too takes her own life:

Hail you dear relics
Of my immortal love!
O let no impious hand remove you hence;
But rest forever here: let Egypt give
His death that peace, which it denied his life.   (5.536-40)

The resolution of the somber images in the case of Cleopatra is on the whole more brilliant. There is something of the triumphal about Cleopatra's death that contrasts vividly with Antony's. It finds its expression in a series of images that are of the nature of paradox—in their death the lovers conquer Caesar and win the world:

Now seat me by my lord. I claim this place;
For I must conquer Caesar too, like him,
And win my share of the world.   (5.534-36)

Where in Antony's case, darkness comes as the quiet end of day, in Cleopatra's, darkness itself becomes desirable.

> 'Tis sweet to die, when they would force life on me,
> To rush into the dark abode of death,
> And seize him first; if he be like my love,
> He is not frightful sure. (5.509-12)

Antony has described death as a friend (5.388ff); Cleopatra as a lover. And her death is not a separation, but a permanent union at last:

> Let dull Octavia
> Survive to mourn him dead: my nobler fate
> Shall knit our spousals with a tie too strong
> For Roman laws to break. (5.477-80)

When Charmian asks the reason for her regal attire, she replies:

> Dull that thou art! why 'tis to meet my love,
> As when I saw him first, on Cydnos bank,
> All sparkling, like a goddess; so adorned,
> I'll find him once again: my second spousals
> Shall match my first in glory. Haste, haste, both,
> And dress the bride of Antony. (5.527-32)

The words of Serapion at the end are a kind of quiet benediction on this final security of death:

> Sleep, blest pair,
> Secure from human chance, long ages out,
> While all the storms of fate fly o'er your tomb. (5.590-92)

But it is in the death of Cleopatra that the action and the diction justify the title in its fullest sense—*All for Love; or, The World Well Lost.*

It is apparent at times that the scheme of the action created problems in diction which Dryden was not always able to solve happily. There is an occasional thinness and lack of concentration in the images. The role of Antony in the action was in some ways a handicap, and it is significant that in the fifth act, when there is neither need nor opportunity for further choice or change of mind, the language finally builds up into a sustained and cumulative climax. The need to give Dollabella equal place with the rest in the heart of Antony leads to some obvious heightening of the diction—the amatory images, for example, which help to disturb the larger scheme of figures in the play—and in fact one gets the impression that the language is less well managed where Dollabella is concerned than almost anywhere else. These and other similar criticisms would be trivial, except that they help to show the handicaps which the conventions of the heroic drama placed in Dryden's way. The really important fact, however, is that Dryden succeeded in finding a particular modification of the traditions of heroic drama which permitted a use of language quite different from that which prevailed in the parent form. He adopted a rhythmic scheme that, while imposing a formalizing restraint, was nevertheless flexible enough to be adaptable to any possible dramatic needs. And he gave his language imaginative weight without losing the clarity and poise which he had mastered in the couplet. *All for Love* was his one moment of liberation from some Octavia among the muses who had kept him within bounds of artistic respectability and frustration. It was his great achievement that he accomplished once more, on somewhat new and limited terms, the union of the poetical resources of language and the requirements of dramatic form. How fine his accomplishment was may be realized by comparing *All for Love* with any representative heroic play, and then with any of the efforts of his fellow dramatists to escape its pattern.

Some Characteristics of
Dryden's Use of Metaphor

by Earl Miner

I used to seek and find out grand lines and stanzas; but my delight
has been far greater since it has consisted more in tracing the leading thought thro'out the whole.

(Coleridge, *Lectures*, 1818)

In doing full justice for perhaps the first time to one of our major
groups of poets, the revival of the Metaphysical poets a generation ago
also set the history of English literature into better perspective. The
events following this major change in our taste have made it impossible
to regard English poetry as a tradition with the twin peaks of Elizabethan and Romantic accomplishment. The change in taste led to the
challenging of Milton, the revaluation of Pope, and to renewed appreciation of seventeenth century poetry. We need not congratulate ourselves too heartily, however, for what has been primarily a Romantic
rejection of Romanticism. If the change had been sounder—if it had
not entailed a rejection of Romanticism—Wordsworth, Shelley, and Ten-
nyson would not have had to undergo the drubbing of recent times. (As
many have observed, both the "Classicism" and the anti-Romanticism of
T. E. Hulme and others were less Classical than Romantic.) Donne and
the other Metaphysicals were first given justice because they shared with
the Romantic poets the essential characteristic of poetry since 1800: the
private mode. The shift in taste was easy, from a private poetry rich in
emotional texture to another private poetry tough in intellectual fiber.

The subsequent events lead us toward the present renewed interest in
Dryden. Obeying few laws but his own, Milton was certain to be ques-
tioned; and being Milton, he was equally certain to silence his accusers.
Then F. R. Leavis and others set about to march forward toward the
Romantics, to follow the "line of wit," the continuation of qualities
esteemed in Donne on to Pope. Since Pope if any poet is witty, and since

"Some Characteristics of Dryden's Use of Metaphor" by Earl Miner. From *Studies
in English Literature* (Summer 1962), 309-320. Reprinted by permission of the author
and Rice University Press.

he often echoes Donne, it was easy to make out a case which raised him once again in general esteem. As more than one person has pointed out, however, appreciating Pope as another Donne does not take us very far. Yet when once Pope had been praised for labors not his own, it was easier to re-examine his real practice; and sooner or later Dryden was sure to benefit from the study of Pope—especially since T. S. Eliot's measured praise and Mark Van Doren's careful examination of Dryden had already brought attention to him as the last of the great poets between the Elizabethans and the Romantics to have been dispraised or ignored. Grierson wisely observed of Van Doren's book, however, that it only "writ large" Arnold's strictures against Dryden and Pope. Subtle and helpful as they are, Eliot and Van Doren leave us feeling that Dryden, if not Pope, is a classic of our prose rather than of our poetry.

The notion is derived either from a lack of sympathy with, or understanding of, Dryden's values, his conception of the place of man in time and eternity, and the cast of his mind. Such large matters defy treatment in a short essay, but it is possible to analyze in brief some aspects of his style which have also been misunderstood, I feel, and which have certainly prevented appreciation. For if Donne's private mode produced a poetry fundamentally like that of the Romantics, it has been possible to set aside the public mode Pope shares with Dryden and to turn attention rather to Pope's extraordinarily rich verse texture, which has its own resemblance to Romantic imagery: imagistically *The Rape of the Lock* is in some respects more like *Tintern Abbey* or *The Wasteland* than is Dryden's Anne Killigrew *Ode*. There is a danger, and an inherent injustice to both poets, in the expectation that Dryden's use of imagery should be the same as Pope's.

There appear to be four characteristics assigned to Dryden's poetry today which are held to be detrimental. He mistakenly tries to *say* something; he sets too high a premium on clarity; he uses the heroic couplet too exclusively; and his Augustan rhetoric is somehow unpoetic. Now the fact is that such "faults" more nearly describe the poetry of Pope than that of Dryden; and of the last three it may be said that what Dryden made good Pope perfected. We must search for Dryden's special genius elsewhere. He is not primarily a poet of striking passages or of noble fragments, but a creator of poetic wholes articulated with great skill and beauty throughout many parts. To appreciate him, we must seek poetic delight—in a poet whose learning is only now being appreciated—as Coleridge came to, by "tracing the leading thought thro'out the whole." One of his characteristic metaphors for poetry is music, another architecture; and in his poetry no more than in these arts can we understand the design of the whole by seeking to admire a single phrase or column. The way to appreciative understanding is through a poet's special strengths; since one of Dryden's great strengths is metaphor, al-

beit of a kind different in essential respects from most other poets', I
shall use it as the center of discussion, beginning with the small and
going on to larger wholes.

Two isolated lines of striking application to our experience today provide a useful beginning—useful in allowing us to make distinctions,
since one is but ordinary, the other superior Dryden.

> Yet still war seems on either side to sleep.
>
> *(All for Love,* I.i)

> And peace itself is war in masquerade.
>
> *(Absalom and Achitophel,* 1.752)

Both lines do *say* something about specific situations in their contexts,
as also about human experience. The first is weaker, however, because
its rhetoric is misleading. There is little reason for the alliteration of
"seems . . . side . . . sleep" or for the assonance of "seems . . . sleeps"
—no inevitability of the kind which raises rhetoric into high poetry. An
actor might make something of the line by bearing down on "still" or
"seems," but I doubt that the audience would much notice. There is in
addition a metaphoric fuzziness to the line. War is personified, but can
a personification sleep "on either side"? It may indeed do so in Elizabethan and other kinds of poetry where incantation is a major resource,
but in the context of Dryden's style the metaphor is less pleasing. The
second line gives us Dryden's true energy, that combination of strength
in unobtrusive rhetoric and syntactic motion which carries us forcefully
onward. The metaphor is a perfect example of *discordia concors,* since
peace cannot possibly be war unless one of the two is somehow changed.
The logic of the line is of course that war, or warlike men, artfully take
on the disguise of peace; but the predication of the line is rather that
peace is war: we have not a new war but a new, fearful kind of peace.
The metaphor is at once clear, rich, and striking—the clarity alone allowing for the exciting force.

With the proper function of saying something and of clarity in mind,
we must go on to longer passages and whole works. Since they are apt
to present greater problems, it is advisable to avoid those we can by
reminding ourselves of what we mean by "metaphor." The simplest definition to win agreement is "an assertion of likeness or identity." I. A.
Richards' well-known analysis of the constituents of metaphor into the
tenor and the vehicle betrays, however, certain subsidiary assumptions
which must be brought into the open. In Burns's line "O my luve's like
a red, red rose," the vehicle is "rose" which stands for (by assertion of
likeness) "luve," or the woman loved. In practice the distinction has
implied that the vehicle must be a single image or a phrase comprising

an image ("war in masquerade"). That the unspoken assumption is too limited can be understood by referring back to the definition, to a host of poems or, more to the purpose, to the opening of *Absalom and Achitophel.*

> In pious times, ere priestcraft did begin,
> Before polygamy was made a sin;
> When man on many multiplied his kind,
> Ere one to one was cursedly confin'd;
> When nature prompted, and no law denied
> Promiscuous use of concubine and bride;
> Then Israel's monarch after Heaven's own heart,
> His vigorous warmth did variously impart
> To wives and slaves; and, wide as his command,
> Scatter'd his Maker's image thro' the land.

All would agree that the first six lines have few if any images, that they deal with ideas rather than with sensuous details. Yet they make up a tissue of temporal states likened to each other (and therefore metaphors) in a complex development. If the lines are diagrammed, we can see how Dryden wittily equates certain conditions at a specific historical moment. Each unit becomes a metaphor for the rest, since different as many of them are, all are bound together by the shared idea of a blessed past. Just as the idea controls the passage, so the rhetoric of alliteration joins the units from point to point, now saying the alliterated words are alike in meaning, now that they are different. (I shall capitalize important alliterated words, italicize words of temporal significance, and break the passage into its constituent units.)

> *In* Pious times
> *ere* Priestcraft did begin
> *before* Polygamy was made a sin
> *when* Man on Many Multiplied his kind
> *ere* One to One was Cursedly Confin'd
> *when* nature Prompted and no law denied Promiscuous
>   use of concubine and bride.

Each of the units begins with a temporal preposition or adverb, each advances in units of increasing length. The alliteration of Pious/Priestcraft follows the usual connotations, but the other words ironically deny the force of such sense (the metaphor is witty in that it is made to deny the "stock response"); for it is really Pious/Polygamy which are equated by the initial rhyme. The succeeding couplet is built upon the antithesis reflected in the first of its lines by the alliteration of Man/Many/Multiplied—words of increasing length; while the next, opposed line is rigorously balanced by One/One . . . Cursedly/Confin'd. The third couplet makes up one unit with Prompted/Promiscuous joining halves of a brilliant subdued parallelism of ideas:

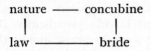

The succeeding lines explore the logic of the initial temporal metaphors (*"Then* Israel's monarch . . . "*) and are, if less schematic, even more complex. In their lack of images, the metaphors of the opening six lines are not characteristic of Dryden; they are an extreme case and must be presented as such, but their handling is in every other respect typical of the poet. I need not demonstrate the intellectual clarity of the lines: Dryden has something to say and says it. If he is at fault for saying something, then poetry has no business in employing language. It cannot be that his poetry lacks complexity, or we should have understood him long ago. The truth of the matter is that he is in the highest (if also in a special) degree rich, complex, and, in a word, difficult. The difficulty can be understood by considering what our austere, relatively simple passage from *Absalom* does in addition to what has been described.

At the outset we must understand that the witty opening is not founded on that erotic daydreaming with which our hypocritically prurient age likes to dismiss the Restoration. Dryden's lines embody a concept taken from a long tradition of biblical scholarship (the poem, after all, speaks of David, Absalom, and Achitophel: II Samuel) in which the figure of David was central. The concept—one related to "Christian liberty"—is that progressively since the Fall of Man mankind has lost a measure of its freedom. A crucial issue in this tradition was polygamy, for how else might scholars who read the Bible for its historical accuracy explain that the great patriarchs were allowed several wives and concubines although men of later ages were "cursedly confin'd" to one? The matter is very complex, but the debate over polygamy (as well as the many mistresses of Charles) inspired writers to renew the issue, and David—the second king of Israel, long after the age of the patriarchs—was carefully discussed. Dryden could count on his age to recognize the subject at once.

It is not so much the subject which is significant, however, as its treatment. The rhetoricians from ancient to modern times were agreed that the function of metaphor is amplification (including diminution). Metaphor consequently raises questions of tone—of elevation or lowering, of praise or blame. The opening of *Absalom* raises the question of the metaphors' tonal function: what attitude toward Charles are we meant to take? Are we to take them as amplifying figures redounding to his credit? If so, he is strangely damned with very sly praise. Are we to take them as diminishing figures critical of his immorality? If so, then matters are even stranger in a poem designed, among other things, to support him and which repeatedly, as implicitly here, imputes Godlike qualities to him. Dryden has clearly produced a tonal masterpiece in which irony is the solvent of opposed attitudes. He blames Charles by pretending to praise his/David's promiscuity. But the ironic praise-become-blame turns once more to praise amidst the laughter: for David/ Charles is creative, imitative of God, as the contrast with Achitophel/ Shaftesbury's near sterility shows (170-172). The passage provides a well-nigh miraculous solution of the problem Dryden faced:—of allowing for Charles' faults in such a way that they *almost* seem virtues. Almost— because anything further would have been evasion or bombast. He finds his solution by translating the historical issues of polygamy into metaphors of temporal states with particular focus upon David.[1]

To mention David again is to suggest the final function of the initial metaphors, as also to give Drydenic point to Coleridge's statement that poetic wholes give more pleasure than poetic parts. Certainly we are meant to take pleasure in the witty opening lines, yet for every such passage or brilliant line in Dryden one could find several in Pope. What one seldom finds in Pope is Dryden's ability to create wholes in which structure, ideas, values, tone, and metaphors are but aspects of each other. This is what constitutes his distinctive genius, what accounts for his difficulty and, the difficulty dealt with, what conveys his characteristic pleasure. For the passage with which *Absalom* begins takes us step by step into the allegory of the poem. The allegory is historical, in particular a biblical metaphor handled with astonishing ease through a maze of details. I have observed that the figure of David is at the center of metaphors of temporal states (the blessed past of liberty) at the outset of the poem, but the point works in reverse as well. The metaphors are employed to shape the structure of the poem as they fuse the biblical details: the metaphorical details combine into a grand metaphor of the whole (biblical history reveals the meaning of modern events). Values as well as structure are involved. Charles is lent David's anointed kingship and divine qualities: David was long identified as one of the Old Testament prototypes of Christ. And the metaphor gives meaning to the experience represented by the tenor: the confusion following the Popish Plot. The richness of the metaphor can be most readily illustrated by a

[1] The opening lines of the poem have long been appreciated and glossed in numerous ways. In his extensive study of the poem—*Dryden and the Conservative Myth* (New Haven, 1961)—Bernard N. Schilling emphasizes two functions of the opening passage other than those discussed in this essay: the insistence upon Absalom's illegitimacy (and therefore his ineligibility to succeed to the throne), pp. 147-148; and an initial focus upon Charles as a fallible human being, enabling Dryden gradually to build up to Charles as "a majestic ruler . . . bringing order to the world," p. 281.

pair of later passages. From time to time within his allegory of biblical history he has his characters themselves use biblical history metaphorically, as when David/Charles says of himself and Absalom/Monmouth:

> Kings are the public pillars of the State,
> Born to sustain and prop the nation's weight;
> If my young Samson will pretend a call
> To shake the column, let him share the fall.   (953-956)

It appears that David can create biblical metaphors as easily as John Dryden. There are many such instances, but nothing testifies to Dryden's complete assurance in his control over the allegory so much as his willingness to take such a witty risk with it as he does for a moment to become deliberately anachronistic in speaking of the Catholic plotters: "Some thought they God's anointed meant to slay/By guns, *invented since full many a day*" (130-131).

Dryden's use of larger metaphors, which are only rarely (*Absalom, The Hind and the Panther*) allegories, represents a technique which has not been given a satisfactory name. The common phrase, "the Augustan metaphor," cannot properly be made to apply to the biblical, pastoral, musical, and other metaphors he employs. Maynard Mack's phrase for the technique in Pope's poetry, "the metaphor of tone" (" 'Wit and Poetry and Pope': Some Observations on his Imagery" in *Pope and his Contemporaries* [London, 1949], p. 36) comes closer, but he binds it too narrowly to the mock-heroic. Moreover, we have seen that such larger metaphors involve structure, subject matter, and thematic values as well. Perhaps "controlling metaphor" will do as a term, since in poem after poem his individual metaphors fall into place as part of a vast design which is itself metaphorical.[2] How such a technique functions may readily be seen by inspecting *Mac Flecknoe*, which is especially useful in that it is familiar and also because it shows that we must often recognize in Dryden's poems that several controlling metaphors fuse into one.

Mac Flecknoe is usually called a mock-heroic poem, which in a very loose sense it is. Its satire functions by pretending to be praise. But if we compare it with Pope's *Dunciad*, where all the heroic, which is to say epic, devices are in full mock-action, then we must conclude that Dryden's poem is not mock-heroic in any strict or throughgoing sense. Its slight plot concerns, not heroic action, but a coronation; and Shadwell is hilariously praised as Mac Flecknoe for being a dull writer. (Dryden's

---

[2] Insofar as the controlling metaphors express and lend coherence to a body of thought, they are clearly related to the "conservative myth" discussed in great detail by Schilling, *op. cit.* Yet such an intellectual myth can function without controlling metaphors, as *The Medall* shows; and Dryden often creates "myths" of another sort: e.g., the descent of the angel in the two St. Cecilia Day poems or the Venus-Mars meeting of Cleopatra and Antony in *All for Love,* the beginning of Act III.

assurance in his satire was to become Pope's sorrow in *The Dunciad*.)
The basic subject of the poem is, then, literature, which is somehow
bound up with pervasive imagery of coronation. In fact, we see that
monarchy becomes a controlling metaphor for literature:

> Thro' all the realms of *Nonsense*, absolute . . .   (6)

> That in this pile should reign a mighty prince,
> Born for a scourge of wit, and flail of sense,
> To whom true dulness should some *Psyches* [a Shadwell play] owe . . .
>
> (88-90)

> Leave writing plays, and choose for thy command
> Some peaceful province in acrostic land.   (205-206)

Such passages might be greatly multiplied, but in reading for them one
ought also to discover another element: religion. The religious thread
sometimes shows clearly when entwined with such another as monarchy
—"As king by office, and as priest by trade"—but more often it is buried
in allusion, another characteristic form of metaphor with Dryden.

There are, then, three elements in the poem: monarchy, religion, and
art (to take literature into its broader class). Each element grows from
innumerable details, images, and specific metaphors into a controlling
metaphor; each represents a major subject in the poem. The metaphor
of monarchy is most important to the structure of the poem, whose
situation is a coronation. Art—architecture, music, and especially literature—is most important as the subject of the poem and touches Shadwell where it most hurts—his musical and literary pretentions. Religion,
both classical and Christian, is most important in controlling the tone.
But the really significant thing is that all three are constantly relevant in
the poem and to each other; it is indeed no exaggeration to say that the
three metaphors function as metaphors for each other as well as for other
tenors. Two examples will make this unusual technique clear.

> The hoary prince in majesty appear'd,
> High on a throne of his own labors rear'd.
>
> (106-107)

> (High on a Throne of Royal State, which far
> Outshone the wealth of *Ormus* and of *Ind* . . .
> Satan exalted sat. . . .
>
> [*Paradise Lost*, II.1-5])

> Heywood and Shirley were but types of thee,
> Thou last great prophet of tautology:
> Even I, a dunce of more renown than they,
> Was sent before but to prepare thy way.
>
> (29-32)

The echo of Milton combines the three metaphors: monarchy (Satan; "Prince . . . Majesty . . . throne"); art (the epic; "His own labors," i.e., Flecknoe's poetry published at his own expense); and religion (the subject of the work alluded to, *Paradise Lost*). The second passage is more typical in combining but two of the metaphors: art (Heywood and Shirley, the earlier dramatists, "dunce") and religion ("prophet"). The religious metaphor dominates here, although it is largely submerged, the four lines suggesting obliquely that the early dramatists are to Shadwell as the Old Testament prototypes of Christ were to Christ, "the last great prophet," for whom Flecknoe is the John the Baptist preparing the way. Throughout the poem the controlling metaphors shift in such fashion from their own to each other's roles. (The fact was well recognized by the publisher or whoever gave the poem its subtitle: "A Satire upon the True-Blue/Protestant Poet T. S.," with its sure sense of the poem's intent.)

Nowhere in the poem does their interrelatedness function more brilliantly than at the ending, which is appropriately anticlimactic. Since the long-winded King Flecknoe seems unwilling to finish his abdication speech with its praise of his successor, his newly anointed son, Mac Flecknoe, sends "the yet declaiming *bard*" down what is clearly a stage trapdoor: just as two characters in one of Shadwell's plays had treated another. The king's cloak is blown upwards as he falls: "The mantle fell to the young *prophet's* part/With double portion of his father's art" (216-217). The allusion to Elisha, who received the mantle of Elijah (from above) with but half the older prophet's "art," shows how much luckier Shadwell is: in other words he is twice as dull as Flecknoe, four times curst to Elisha's blessing. Dryden's control is perfect. Shadwell's progress is regress, and everything he represents is sterile or perverted.

The controlling metaphors of *Absalom* and *Mac Flecknoe* are alike in certain crucial respects. In both poems the most minute particulars rise to form a vast design for the whole. In both the metaphors control the structure, tone, and values of the poem. They differ, however, in other important respects. The metaphor in *Absalom* is primarily biblical—the complex of historical and heroic metaphor is subdued. *Mac Flecknoe,* on the other hand, has three controlling metaphors functioning, each sufficiently important to act as a metaphor of another at any moment. More importantly, the metaphor of *Absalom* functions affirmatively, while those of *Mac Flecknoe* are ironic. The whole point of the latter poem depends upon a recognition of the fact that fat, bibulous, dull Shadwell is not a prince, a prophet, or a real artist; the metaphors simply fail at each crucial juncture to work in the terms ironically presented. Shadwell is judged by the standards they represent and found wanting. To this point another of like significance must be added. In the ironic failure of the metaphors to hold (the tenor is never what the vehicle would have it be), it is not the values represented by the metaphors, but

Shadwell, that is questioned. They are affirmed; he is mocked. Some people may yet assume that a "mock-heroic" mocks the heroic, as it obviously does not. In *Absalom,* on the other hand, however complex the irony becomes, both the characters of the poem and the values represented by the metaphor are amplified. Shadwell ends looking ridiculously foolish, but Shaftesbury/Achitophel is dangerous precisely because he is so great.

Much more needs to be said upon the score of Dryden's imagery, if only because other poems show it used in other ways; and for a full understanding we shall need to relate it to other aspects of his style and to other fundamental qualities of his thought and practice. The application of the obvious if too seldom honored principle that each poet must be understood in terms of his own practice should show at least that although his imagery may give pleasure apart from the total structure of his poems and plays, the true pleasure, as also the true understanding, must be sought by a grasp of the whole. Yet if in so doing we come to give Dryden his full justice as one of the greatest "classics" of our poetry, it would betray the spirit of this writer, who is also a classic of our prose, if we were to fail to follow its example and bring to our own criticism an equally catholic appreciation and understanding of our other great English poets.

Dryden and the Atoms of Epicurus

by Edward N. Hooker

My starting point is a single poem, John Dryden's *Religio Laici*. The Latin title of this English poem might be rendered as The Faith, or Beliefs, of a Layman. *Religio Laici* is a fine poem; one critic, in fact, described it as the finest didactic poem in the English language. Of its art and beauty, however, I shall refrain from speaking. What I propose to do is to show, first, that the poem was a political act, a bold stroke delivered at a time of political crisis; and, second, that it manages to raise the curtain for us, revealing a dramatic upsurge of intellectual forces—philosophic systems, beliefs, assumptions, dogmas—that gave a special meaning and flavor to the moment of history.

That moment of history was the period from 1678 to 1682, in which occurred the events described by a recent historian as "The Attempted Whig Revolution"—the period near the end of which, in November, 1682, *Religio Laici* appeared. Trouble had been brewing before 1678, but in September of that year two perjured rascals uncovered a sham plot against the King and the Protestant religion; and when, shortly afterwards, the justice of the peace before whom they had sworn out their "informations" was found in a ditch, murdered (or slain by his own hands), the tide of fear, hatred, and hysteria was let loose. At that fearful instant the architects of the revolution began actively to direct the course of popular passions, some in the hope of overthrowing the monarchy, some with the intention of excluding James, the King's successor, from the throne, some out of a simple craving for personal power. Whatever the mixture of motives, the grand designers appear to have had as their object an abrupt and rather drastic change in the mode of government. Among the chiefs of the conspiracy were the Duke of Buckingham and the Earl of Shaftesbury, two extraordinarily brilliant, ambitious, and frustrated men.

Dryden had thrown himself into the controversy from the start, in 1678, taking the side of the King because in his eyes that was the side of stable, constitutional government. He wrote two plays with a strong

"Dryden and the Atoms of Epicurus" by E. N. Hooker. From *ELH*, XXIV (1957), 177-190. Reprinted by permission of The Johns Hopkins Press.

political undercurrent. In addition, he composed a series of brilliant political poems, including *Mac Flecknoe* and the astonishing, rollicking *Absalom and Achitophel,* and the razor-sharp satire, *The Medall.* It was in *The Medall* that Dryden recalled a memorable piece of Shaftesbury's past, when he had engaged his talents in the service of Cromwell and the Puritan "saints":

> Next this (how wildly will ambition steer!)
> A vermin wriggling in th' usurper's ear.
> Bart'ring his venal wit for sums of gold,
> He cast himself into the saintlike mold:
> Groan'd, sigh'd, and pray'd, while godliness was gain,
> The loudest bagpipe of the squeaking train.

All of Dryden's work published at this time shows a dominating political motive, and reflects the urgency of the political crisis. All, that is, until we come to *Religio Laici.* Dryden's critics and editors have been bothered by the fact that in the midst of wild political controversy, Dryden seems to pause cheerfully to give us a leisurely account of his religious beliefs. The oddity of the thing has been neatly expressed by George Saintsbury:

> That a man who had never previously displayed any particular interest in theological questions, and who had reached the age of 51, with a reputation derived, until quite recently, in the main from the composition of loose plays, should appear before his public of pleasure-seekers with a serious argument in verse on the credibility of the Christian religion, and the merits of the Anglican form of doctrine and church-government, would nowadays be something more than a nine days' wonder.

To a modern reader with even a small acquaintance with Dryden there is another oddity about the poem which smites one as soon as he commences reading it. The beginning, which is a rather stately and magnificent overture, suggests in a crowd of images that human reason, while it is sufficient for our ordinary, practical needs, is grotesquely inadequate to solve the ultimate problems of man's destiny, his relationship to the world in which he lives, and the sources and means of happiness or frustration. This is the way the poem opens:

> Dim as the borrw'd beams of moon and star
> To lonely, weary, wand'ring travelers,
> Is Reason to the soul; and, as on high
> Those rolling fires discover but the sky,
> Not light us here, so Reason's glimmering ray
> Was lent, not to assure our doubtful way,

> But guide us upward to a better day.
> And as those nightly tapers disappear,
> When day's bright lord ascends our hemisphere;
> So pale grows Reason at Religion's sight;
> So dies, and so dissolves in supernatural light.

That reason should be described as a pale, glimmering light is a bit of a shock, coming from a chronic rationalist, a poet who had argued, debated, reasoned, and butted his way through verse and drama for twenty years. It is doubly shocking, coming from an early member of the Royal Society and a man who prided himself on being modern. Only a few years before *Religio Laici* Dryden had committed an act of—well, I will let you name the crime. He had not only rewritten John Milton's *Paradise Lost*; he had converted the old Puritan's epic into a rhymed opera entitled *The State of Innocence*. A comparison of the two is instructive. In *Paradise Lost* the angel Raphael, questioned eagerly by our forefather Adam, intimates gently that there are some questions into which man was not supposed to probe:

> Solicit not thy thoughts with matters hid;
> Leave them to God above; Him serve, and fear!

Shortly thereafter Adam began to question Raphael about the sex life of angels. The questioning drew from the angel a blush "celestial rosy red," but remarkably little scientific information. In Dryden's opera things are different. Questions are raised and debated, and one is left with the impression that Dryden would gladly have answered them *all* if the end of the last act had not rolled around too soon.

Of course a man so habitually ratiocinative as Dryden would not write a poem to repudiate reason. It becomes apparent upon reading it that *Religio Laici,* instead of rejecting reason, has something to say about the scope and limits of reason, about its abuse, and about the social consequences of an irresponsible exploitation of it.

Some years ago I had the notion that *Religio Laici* was part of a political and philosophical controversy, and that in writing the poem Dryden was supporting one side of a fierce debate which was agitating men of that time. One afternoon in 1951, as I was reading in the British Museum, I discovered two books that formed part of the controversy. Both were composed as replies to another work which had previously been published, a work which they both regarded as crammed with errors of a particularly sinister breed. With a little more hunting I succeeded in finding the book they referred to, the irritating substance which set off a series of angry reactions by way of reply and counter-reply for about eight years.

The book which precipitated the trouble bore on its front the imposing title of *A Treatise of Humane Reason*. It was published somewhere
around August 1674. There was no author's name attached to it, either
then or when it was reprinted the following year. But the excitement
stirred up curiosity, and it was not long before the identity of the author
was discovered. He turned out to be one Martin Clifford, who at that
time served as Master of the Charterhouse in London. The sober article
about him in the *Dictionary of National Biography* notes simply that he
was distinguished in those days for his licentious tastes and his powers of
buffoonery. Nothing in the records of Martin Clifford suggests a philosophical bent or an interest in religion. Rather the contrary. But we *do*
know that he was a protégé of the feckless Duke of Buckingham, a
worthy whom Dryden was to describe, in 1681, in these lines:

> A man so various, that he seem'd to be
> Not one, but all mankind's epitome:
> Stiff in opinions, always in the wrong;
> Was everything by starts, and nothing long;
> But in the course of one revolving moon
> Was chymist, fiddler, statesman, and buffoon. . . .

Clifford's treatise is a rather remarkable performance, so deft and
shrewd as to arouse the suspicion that a greater talent than Clifford's had
a share in the writing. On the surface a plea for toleration, it managed
to assure nonconformists of all types that they were the real champions
of truth. The underlying attitude of the writer (or writers) emerges in
the assumption that apart from the knowledge of physical nature, truth
is so uncertain that every man's reason is valid; where all may possibly
be mistaken, each is equally right. Learning inherited from the past is
likely to be error or deceit; each man is qualified to decide for himself,
with or without knowledge. Perhaps the most revealing feature of the
treatise is the notion that dissent and divergence are in themselves ultimate values, regardless of what they stand for or what they diverge from.

By 1675 the replies to Clifford had begun to appear in print. There
were probably a number of answers which directly or indirectly tried to
counteract the effects of Clifford, but at least two still survive from 1675
which on their very title pages proclaim their intention. Both of these
are anonymous, as if they feared to reveal themselves to foes who were
powerful and dangerous. The more interesting of the two answers was
a book called *Plain-Dealing*, published by a Cambridge bookseller,
Henry Dickinson, whose shop was located on Trinity Street (on a site
now occupied by Bowes and Bowes), and only a stone's throw from the
gatehouse of Trinity College, which was Dryden's college. Whether it
was the product of a Cambridge scholar or a group of Cambridge men,
Plain-Dealing in several respects anticipates the position which Dryden

took a few years later in *Religio Laici.* What *Plain-Dealing* objected to most vigorously in Clifford's treatise was its complete Pyrrhonism (or full-blown skepticism), its tendency to Socinian subtlety, and its subservience to the philosophy of Thomas Hobbes, who, it asserted, was Clifford's "old master."

The only defense of Clifford's *Treatise of Humane Reason* which I have been able to find is a book called *An Apology for the Discourse of Humane Reason,* published anonymously but written by a friend of Clifford's named Albertus Warren, a devout admirer—and one of the few admirers—of Thomas Hobbes. Warren had written the *Apology* in 1677-1678. Two years later, in 1680, he added a supplement and published the whole work, with a dedication to the Earl of Shaftesbury, who, he tells us, had been a most valued friend and patron to Clifford. Why Albertus Warren failed to publish in 1678 what he had written in behalf of Clifford, is any man's guess; but there was a cogent reason for its publication in 1680, for by that time Shaftesbury was exerting all of his astonishing energies to bring dissension to a climax.

In the replies to Clifford which were written from 1675 to 1682, one of the main concerns of the writers was that the principles advocated in the *Treatise of Humane Reason* tended to the fragmentation of human society rather than its unity. In 1681 a young man entered the lists with arguments against dissension and factionalism. ". . . in our poor Island," he wrote, "there are as many different Passions and Affections, Plots and Agitations, Factions and Fashions, Opinions and Religions, almost as [there are] men." This particular plea for moderation and unity was written from the standpoint of a clergyman, and it was entitled *Religio Clerici.* One can see a kind of inevitability in the fact that Dryden's poem, coming one year later and supplementing the arguments from a secular point of view, was given the title of *Religio Laici.*

Dryden's *Religio Laici,* then, is primarily neither a religious poem nor a poem about religion. There are various bits of evidence, besides what I have suggested, to support the conclusion that it was composed as part of a specific controversy, and intended to counter a set of ideas that had been cherished and fostered by the Duke of Buckingham and the Earl of Shaftesbury. Shaftesbury and Buckingham had used the ideas as a convenient instrument in the political battle which culminated during the years 1678-1682 in what we have called the Attempted Whig Revolution.

Thus far I have attempted to outline the immediate occasion of Dryden's poem. But the poem deals with the scope and limits of human reason, and therefore has implications beyond the immediate occasion. To explore these implications, to sketch in Dryden's position, and to cast at least a little light upon the complex of ideas and attitudes against which he was reacting, is the task to which I shall set myself.

In *Religio Laici* we find four modes of thinking specified in which,

Dryden is convinced, human reason has failed. First of all, the great philosophic systems, constructed with the utmost of human ingenuity, fall short of religion in accounting for the origin of the world and of the life in it; the best of the philosophers merely guessed, and his guess was no better than that of Epicurus, whose world consisted of an infinity of atoms whirling, bumping in infinite space until some of them, by merest chance, leap into a common rhythm and an intelligible form. Philosophic systems, again, have failed in defining the way to happiness, for they have all attempted to comprehend the *summum bonum* in a formula for adjustment, instead of recognizing that, except on a purely bovine level, men are incapable of happiness unless their imagination and faith are touched and informed.

The second abuse of human reason is represented by the Deists, to whose position Dryden devotes much of the first half of the poem. The summary of the Deists' tenets is given in terms which make it clear that the poet is thinking of Lord Herbert of Cherbury's five common notions. He has no objections to the beliefs of Deism; he merely intimates that unaided reason is given rather too much credit. The error of the Deist is the belief that nothing of unique value is embedded in tradition or history, that it is possible to wipe the slate clean (as Descartes did) and start all over again, and by the pure exercise of reason to discover "all ye know, and all ye need to know."

The third abuse of reason involves an excessive reliance on tradition, combined with the assumption that under certain circumstances reason may determine infallibly which elements in tradition are valid. The error consists in dogmatic certainty in an area in which certainty is inadmissible.

The fourth abuse of reason occurs in what Dryden describes as the operations of "the private spirit." The error grows, first, out of the assumption that the conclusions of individual reason, even when it is exercised without training and without knowledge, are precious discoveries; and, secondly, out of the belief that in areas where mathematical certainty is not to be expected, there is no real knowledge and that, therefore, one man's conviction is bound to be as valid as anyone else's.

If it seems strange that these thoughts can be elicited from a poem on the Faith of a Layman, I must point out that Dryden himself, in the prose preface to the poem, carefully informs us that he is following a particular philosophic tradition. "Being naturally inclin'd to scepticism in philosophy," he wrote, "I have no reason to impose my opinions in a subject which is above it. . . ."

Dryden's skepticism, the frame of reference within which *Religio Laici* was composed, has been widely misunderstood—and quite needlessly. By the time *Religio Laici* was published at the end of November, 1682, he was already at work on another literary project, and within four months of the poem's appearance the first volume of *Plutarch's*

Lives was in the hands of the printer. Plutarch was a prime favorite of Dryden's, a sage with whom he was likely to identify himself. He described Plutarch's skepticism in much the same way as he described his own: each was content "only to propound and weigh opinions, leaving the judgment of his readers free, without presuming to decide dogmatically." In this position of moderation, Plutarch found himself opposed to two philosophical extremes. First, that of the dogmatic system-makers, the Stoics and Epicureans, who "pretend" too much to certainty in their dogmas, and to impose them with too great arrogance." And, second, the other extreme, the wholesale skeptics, or the Pyrrhonists, who "bring *all* certainty in question," and, with a peculiar kind of dogmatism, insist that nothing is more likely than anything else. Plutarch, as a skeptic of the later academy, though he recognized little certainty in human knowledge, yet had the wisdom to see that knowledge and experience will incline "the balance to that hand where the most weighty reasons, and probability of truth, were visible." There are areas in our lives, such as moral philosophy, which admit of so few doubts that the dogmatic skepticism of "the private spirit" is an untenable position. Such, in brief, was Plutarch's—and Dryden's—philosophic skepticism.

After the opening of the poem, as we have seen, Dryden proceeds to examine the inadequacies of the rational systems, with specific allusion to the Stoic and Epicurean philosophies. Apart from his reference to Epicurus, and to the dance of the atoms, which miraculously leap into form, there are abundant clues as to which system Dryden had primarily in mind; for the early part of the poem is sprinkled with phrases and images taken from the great Latin poem by Lucretius, expounding the atomistic philosophy of Epicurus. The fact is scarcely surprising in view of Dryden's intense interest in—and even obsession with—the atomistic theory. Twenty-two years before *Religio Laici* he had written a poem to Sir Robert Howard, in which he referred to a work by Sir Robert in the following words:

> . . . this is a piece too fair
> To be the child of chance, and not of care.
> No atoms casually together hurl'd
> Could e'er produce so beautiful a world.

And in the intervening twenty-two years the jarring atoms of Epicurus appear in a variety of Dryden's works, and in a variety of forms: through analogy, in the field of politics by reference to the jarring factions, and in the field of religion by reference to the jarring sects.

The deep concern over the effects of the atomistic theory was not confined to John Dryden. Scientists found it a highly useful working hypothesis in their investigations in physical nature. But by 1660 the working hypothesis had been blown up into a very different shape, and in its altered shape was being peddled as the final truth concerning nature, man, and human society. The new monster had a wide appeal. In 1662 Edward Stillingfleet wrote in *Origines Sacrae* that of all theories the Epicurean at that time was making the greatest noise in the world. A few years later John Wilkins, the remarkable Bishop of Chester who had been for years the leading spirit in that amazing group of scientists laboring at Oxford (a group which became the nucleus of the Royal Society), commented on the extravagant and irrational opinions then afloat, inspired by Epicurus and his atoms. A little later Ralph Cudworth, probably the most learned member of the Cambridge Platonists, remarked that of late there had been an extraordinary enthusiasm for Epicurus. From all sides came testimony to the effect that Epicurus had indeed risen from the dead, and that the atomistic theory had burst its seams.

Of course no ancient philosopher is revived on whim or impulses; he is revived only if his ideas serve to give coherence and meaning to drifts, attitudes, tendencies already existing in another age. And the reason why Epicurus became "guide, philosopher, and friend" to so many in the two decades before *Religio Laici* is apparent in a remark made by Samuel Parker in 1681. Parker, a rather hard-headed individual who had an overriding contempt for Platonic mysteries and airy notions, said plaintively that the very craftsmen and mechanics of his time had philosophized themselves into an atomistic atheism. "And," he complained, "they are able to demonstrate out of [Hobbes's] *Leviathan* . . . that all things come to pass by an eternal Chain of natural Causes" and that human nature is a mere machine! Parker had a feud with Descartes as well, but his chief *bête noir* was Thomas Hobbes, the champion of what Parker called the "folly and nonsense of meer mechanism."

Hobbes, as we know, chiefly by the publication in 1651 of his *Leviathan* had become the foremost English champion of atomism and mechanism, reducing all things to matter in motion. Opponents, who rose by the score to refute him, had little success, partly because they met him on his own grounds and fought with weapons of Hobbes's choice; while Hobbes, sitting within the security of his tight little system, from which all strictly human experience was excluded, could outchop logic with any competitor. But Hobbes was formidable partly because the intellectual climate favored the dogmatists and systemmakers who had already made the brilliant discovery that you can hope to find a simple, inclusive formula to describe nature and man—*if* you assume that man is a machine. Strip man of his history, strip him of civilization, strip him of his critical and creative powers, of his imagination and his aspiration, and your formula may apply even to him.

Hobbes was formidable, as I intimated, because he was in the swim. He was soon reinforced by an abler, more subtle mind—that of Spinoza, whose *Tractatus Theologico-Politicus* was published in 1670. That

Spinoza's work threatened religion seemed apparent at once to theologians; among others, to Richard Simon, whose *Critical History* Dryden was reading just before or during the days when he was composing *Religio Laici*. But religion was not the circumference of Spinoza's intention or influence. James Tyrrell, who was a lawyer, historian, and personal friend of John Locke, placed Spinoza and Hobbes in the same tub: both sages maintaining that man's actions and thoughts are bound up in an inexorable chain of determinism, which obliterates the power of choice and, therefore, the human distinction between good and evil.

It is extremely difficult to determine precisely how much effect Spinoza's *Tractatus* had in England between 1670 and 1682. It is difficult because there are many twanging the same string of the harp. One of these, strangely enough, was La Rochefoucauld, whose *Maxims* were published in France in 1665, and first translated into English in 1670. Though there are vaguenesses and ambiguities in La Rochefoucauld's intentions, the reader will find a clear inclination on the part of the author to view man's action and choices as the result of the condition of his body. One of the maxims puts the matter baldly: "Force of character and weakness of character are misnomers; they are in fact nothing but good or bad physique." The import of his doctrine was recognized by the eighteenth century philosopher Francis Hutcheson, who complained that the old Epicurean notions had been revived in the seventeenth century by Hobbes, La Rochefoucauld, and others.

La Rochefoucauld's position and prestige insured him a hearing in England. One of his followers (who probably drew upon the ideas of Hobbes as well) was the famous wit, courtier, rake, and poet John Wilmot, Earl of Rochester, who admitted to Gilbert Burnet that at one period of his life he had been drunk for five years uninterruptedly. Somewhere between 1674 and 1679 Rochester gave vent to a poem entitled *A Satyr against Mankind,* in which human beings appear as "reas'ning engines," reason as a pretentious futility, and the criterion of good and evil as the power of a thing to titillate our senses. The glittering example of such men as Rochester was fresh in Dryden's memory when he remarked of the political wildmen among Shaftesbury's followers: They "are generally men of atheistic principles, nominal Christians, who are beholding to the front only, that they are so called; otherwise Hobbists in their politics and morals."

By 1680 the spread of Epicurean atomistic doctrine had washed up so many monsters that one of the great men of the age, Robert Boyle, known to us as the father of modern chemistry, felt impelled to take up the cudgels against it. This he did, in a book called *A Discourse of Things above Reason . . . By a Fellow of the Royal Society.* Boyle's discourse is tactful, deft, and ingratiating—quite worthy of a brilliant and a humble mind. His general position is a philosophical skepticism roughly similar to that of Plutarch and Dryden; a position Baconian rather than Cartesian. From this vantage point he delivers his blows at the dogmatic systems of rationalism and atomism. To the philosophers who deny the existence of everything which cannot be weighed or measured, or of which they have no clear and adequate idea, Boyle observes quietly that it is no easy matter to perceive, or to have clear and adequate ideas of the world of infinite space inhabited by infinite multitudes of whirling atoms—the world which Epicurus, Gassendi, and their atomistic followers have offered us.

I cannot examine all of the abuses of reason which Dryden analyses in *Religio Laici*; but in what has been said, I hope I have come close to the core of his meaning. He was not a philosopher. He was a playwright and a poet with an acute and comprehensive mind, who joined battle against dogmatist and atomist because their ideas appeared to threaten the values of human society and to menace the stability of the state—especially as Shaftesbury and Buckingham had corralled and harnessed them for their own purposes.

In writing a poem about the scope and limits of human reason Dryden was no anti-rationalist or anti-intellectualist. Part of what he had to say was expressed in our time by Austin Warren in an essay on the novelist E. M. Forster. Said Warren: "Complete rationalism, like glaring sunlights dries up the vegetation." The comment which this statement demands is that when rationalism narrows and hardens to the point of denying the special powers of the human mind and the special qualities of civilized experience, it is no longer rationalism; it is the offspring of dogma out of fantasy.

I am tempted to illustrate; and the illustration that comes to hand is from a popular work on biology published within the past few years, and written by a rather distinguished mathematician and theoretical physicist, who is arguing for the mechanistic school of thought. I quote:

> According to this point of view, basic manifestations of life like growth, motion, reproduction, and even thinking depend entirely on the complexity of the molecular structures forming living organisms, and can be accounted for, at least in principle, by the same basic laws of physics which determine ordinary inorganic processes.

It would undoubtedly be highly convenient to have the processes of thinking reduced to a simple formula of physics—but I am afraid that we shall have to face the problems of human nature and human society with tools and insights other than those supplied by cybernetics.

One trouble with such expressions of rambunctious rationalism as that which I have quoted is that they drive men of a different temperament to another extreme, an extreme of anti-rationalism like that adopted by Mark Rampion, a character in one of the most brilliant novels of our century. Rampion remarks in a diatribe against the rationalists:

By torturing their brains they can get a faint notion of the universe as it would seem if looked at through non-human eyes. . . . The results of . . . all these famous theories about the cosmos and their practical applications —they've got nothing whatever to do with the only truth that matters. And the non-human truth isn't merely irrelevant; its dangerous. It distracts people's attention from the important human truth. It makes them falsify their experience in order that lived reality may fit in with abstract theory.

Both extremes of view flourished in Dryden's age, and he held no brief for either. He was aware that man is a strange and complex creature,— as Alexander Pope felicitously put it, a being darkly wise and rudely great—a child of nature who refuses to thrive on a formula—a creature whose mind is fit to inhabit two worlds and is dwarfed and distorted if it is confined to one. To shrink in distaste, as Dryden did, from the over-reaching usurpations of constricting dogma and corroding skepticism is another way of affirming one's conviction that our good depends on the realization of all man's powers and capacities in mutual aid and support. Our age has reason to understand the ancient secret: that there is no quick and easy road to the New Jerusalem.

Ode on Anne Killigrew

by E. M. W. Tillyard

I

Henryson's *Testament of Cresseid* is a beautiful and moving poem of one good minor poet; Davies' *Orchestra* a beautiful and exhilirating poem of another. Dryden's *Ode on Anne Killigrew* is a masterpiece of a major poet. We need not like it best, but, if we do compare, it makes the other two look a little amateurish. One reason for this is the high proportion of our attention which, at first sight, the purely formal qualities of the *Ode* usurp. Henryson's tragic story, the setting of *Orchestra* and the world picture and the politics set forth in it, count for more than the purely prose content of the *Ode*. Dryden does indeed tell us things about Anne Killigrew: that she was virtuous and gifted; that she wrote verse and painted landscapes and royal portraits; and that she died of smallpox. But the two hundred lines spent in saying this are, as information, nearly all padding, while what astonishes and delights is the wealth of imaginative invention and the glory of the verbal music. Here, if anywhere, Arnold's attribution of the prosaic to Augustan verse is refuted, while the raptures into which his contemporaries fell over one kind of musical verse are perfectly appropriate to the excellence if not to the kind of Dryden's.

The form of the *Ode* is inherited directly from Cowley, but further ancestry included Spenser's *Epithalamion* and Ben Jonson, while the accent of majesty owes much to Milton and particularly to his short pieces *On Time, Upon the Circumcision,* and *At a Solemn Music.* Compare for instance this from Dryden's *Ode*

> Hear then a mortal Muse thy praise rehearse
> In no ignoble verse

with this from *On Time*

> Then long Eternity shall greet our bliss
> With an individual kiss.

"*Ode on Anne Killigrew.*" From *Five Poems* (London: Chatto & Windus, 1948) by E. M. W. Tillyard, pp. 49-65. Reprinted by permission of Chatto & Windus, Ltd.

The invention and music are not equally brilliant throughout, but I cannot agree with Mark Van Doren that the *Ode* is "sadly uneven" and that apart from three great stanzas the rest are at the most equal to Cowley. In general the tone of solemn rapture is sustained, and the ebbings form the preparations, necessary in a long lyric, for the full flood of music. There may however be isolated lapses. It is hard to feel warmly about the political metaphor in stanza six: the idea that through the descriptive passages in her poetry she had staked out claims in the adjacent province of painting, as an ambitious ruler forms seditious groups in the country he means to invade.

> To the next realm she stretched her sway,
> For Painture near adjoining lay,
> A plenteous province and alluring prey.
> A Chamber of Dependences was framed
> (As conquerors will never want pretence,
> When armed, to justify the offence),
> And the whole fief in right of Poetry she claimed.

And at the end of stanza seven the line

> What next she had designed, Heaven only knows

is not impressive in sound even if we can forget the absurdity which a modern does, and a contemporary did not, find in it.[1]

After the music the construction calls for admiration. The poem is an elegy on a poetess and like the Dido poem in Spenser's *Shepherd's Calendar*, like *Lycidas*, and like *Adonais* it presupposes the happy fate of the deceased. It is built on the two themes of earth and heaven, which themselves are linked by the commonplace that earthly poetry partakes of the divine; and it evolves as follows. The first stanza gives the three main themes: poetry, for Anne Killigrew is even now singing; heaven and earth, for she sings in some heavenly region, while her earthly songs served as prelude and probation for the heavenly music. The second stanza has the same mixture of theme but with the emphasis on earth and her prenatal poetical antecedents. By immediate heredity she comes of poetical stock, by reincarnation from Sappho. The stanza ends with heaven. Anne Killigrew's is too pure a soul to suffer further incarnation: when she has ceased listening to the poem now addressed to her she must return to the quire of heavenly singers. The third stanza again contains all three themes but with the emphasis on heaven, which celebrated her

---

[1] "Heaven only knows" means in the context that heaven, having heard her songs there, does know, as mortals cannot, what her next artistic efforts would have been, had she survived.

birth with joy. This pure heavenly rejoicing suggests its contrary in stanza four, the general impurity of contemporary poetry; and the pessimistic satirical and urgent tone contrasts finely with the serene static tone of the first three stanzas. It comes to rest on Anne Killigrew and the thought that she was both an exception and an atonement. In so doing it introduces the body of the ode, stanzas five to eight, which deal with the lady's attainments on earth. Heaven is kept in the background, and we hear of her successes in poetry and in painting and of her untimely death. Death leads to mourning, and in stanza nine her brother's sorrow when he learns the news is conjectured. But he is at sea and has no news. Only, if sailorlike he scans the stars, he might notice a new bright member of the Pleiades—the star which is his sister's soul. This mention of the stars is the return of the theme of heaven; and it leads to the last stanza, where poetry, heaven, and earth are brought together in the description of the opening graves and the Last Judgment with Anne Killigrew leading the poets, the first souls to join their resurrected bodies, to their heavenly mansion. The poem's evolution is perfect, and it is the greatest pity that in the *Oxford Book of English Verse,* the chief recent means of access, it should have been truncated.

So far I have dealt with matters of forms, and it may now be asked of what feelings, opinions, or states of mind are the poem's music and formal perfection the index.

The states of mind poems express stand at varying distances from the subjects these poems purport to treat. Dryden's subject, Anne Killigrew's premature death, has no close connection with the things he was really saying. He must have known that her poems and pictures were the indifferent stuff which posterity has decided them to be. Nevertheless he used the conventional grief and extravagant adulation to convey certain strongly held opinions and feelings.

One of these is a heartfelt enthusiasm for the arts, the same enthusiasm that animates Dryden's literary criticism. When he praises Anne Killigrew's accomplishment, he is speaking not for her but for poetry and painting in their entirety; and when at the end he makes the earth lie more lightly on the poets than on other men, he is paying a sincere tribute to the poetic sensibility: a tribute not less sincere for the outrageous assertion that Anne Killigrew will lead the poetic throng to heaven. There is no piety in his references to heavenly music, yet through them he demonstrates how sincerely he prizes the practice of the arts on this earth.

Next, by attributing to Anne Killigrew many excellences which she did not possess and by putting that attribution into a shapely form Dryden expressed his belief in manners and decorum. Decorum is connected with what should be, not with what is. We regulate the opening and the end of our letters on that principle. And Dryden attributed to the object of his elegy the qualities it was proper for her to have, whether or not she did in fact have them.

Both the above beliefs belong to a more general one which we can call a belief in civilization and which includes the beliefs in solid craft against empty ingenuity, in reason against fanaticism, in order against disorder, in monarchy against mob-rule, in established religion against arbitrary and undisciplined nonconformity. Some of these beliefs could be substantiated from the details of the poem. For instance the single line in stanza five

> Each test and every light her Muse will bear

testifies to the belief in solid craft. But the most powerful expression is of the general principle, and it is given by the very movement and composition of the poem: by the controlled yet enthusiastic movement, by the masterly formal and logical shape, and by the nobly pompous circumlocutions.

> Born to the spacious empire of the Nine—

the accent of that implies social and political order.

If even a portion of the above claims is accepted the *Ode* is found to possess a substance that answers worthily to those formal and musical qualities that first strike us. It takes its rank among the major elaborate lyrics such as the opening odes in the third book of Horace.

II

Most of the matters just enumerated have a direct bearing on the general thought of the age. I therefore can now pass easily from speaking of Dryden's *Ode* as a work of art to the ideas which it embodies.

THE WORLD PICTURE

Many of the things which I said Dryden stood for would have been accepted by other ages. Certainly, Henryson and Davies believed in order and decorum. What then distinguishes Dryden's belief from theirs? It is not a question of mere knowledge. Dryden knows all about order and degree and the "vast chain of being"; he still inherits the medieval scheme of the universe. His account of the various regions of the eternal heavens where the soul of Anne Killigrew might inhabit is as precise as anything in *Orchestra*. She has left the regions of mutability below the moon; she may be in a planet (comparatively close to the earth); she may be in the region of the fixed stars and circle with the great host of heaven; or she may be called to "more superior bliss," farther from earth and nearer to God, in the empyrean. Similarly with the stars: he knows about their conjunctions and horoscopes. He uses the technical term *in trine* when he says that the more malicious stars (like Saturn and Mars) were in a benign mood at Anne Killigrew's birth. Along with this correctness is the orthodoxy of the last stanza. Anne Killigrew, now in heaven, will reassume her body on the Day of Judgment and reascend to her final heavenly home. It looks as if the old material were there; and yet the emphasis has altered, being now on man and off the rest of creation in a new way. In other words the humanism of the Renaissance, which in Davies was still truly combined with the inherited world picture, has been carried much further and has destroyed the old proportions. Dryden really believes in the social virtues of human civilization, but he does not really believe in astrology (as the "advanced" men of his age did not believe in it) nor in the angels. In fact he uses both stars and angels primarily as ornaments. The address of Anne Killigrew as a "young probationer and candidate of heaven" is charming, even impressive, in its context but it is an ornamental conceit, not a conceit containing the genuine belief that she was in the act of ascending the ladder of creation into the angelic state. Walton in his biography of Hooker describes him on his deathbed

> meditating the number and nature of the angels and their blest obedience and order, without which peace would not be in heaven; and oh that it might be so on earth.

Of course Hooker was a divine, but even so he lived in a different world from Dryden's. His vision of cosmic order is a grander if stranger imagining than Dryden's eminently human principle of ornamental decorum. Then take the lower end of the chain of being: the animals and inanimate nature. One of Anne Killigrew's pictures takes these in.

> The sylvan scenes of herds and flocks
> And fruitful plains and barren rocks;
> Of shallow brooks that flowed so clear,
> The bottom did the top appear;
> Of deeper too and ampler floods,
> Which as in mirrors show'd the woods;
> Of lofty trees, with sacred shades
> And perspectives of pleasant glades,
> Where nymphs of brightest form appear
> And shaggy satyrs standing near,
> Which them at once admire and fear.

This is purely descriptive and ornamental. There is not the least sense of any of the things pictured being a part of a cosmic as against a decorative scene. Nymphs and satyrs are simple Classical ornament, they are not the Classical equivalent of "real" supernatural beings with their necessary place in the chain. The same is true of the herds and flocks. Nor is there any sense of the landscape being emblematic or of corresponding to any other cosmic plane. Anything that is not purely pictorial is realistic, looking forward to the nature poetry of Thompson, to the age of science and away from the age of theology.

It could not be otherwise. The doubts about the world order, present yet pending in the age of Elizabeth, had been realized. The heavens had proved to be not immutable, the earth was no longer the center of creation, and the political stability of the Tudors, which had done so much to conserve the framework of the old order, had given way to a less popular house and to civil war. With the beginnings of science it was the facts and not the supposed perfect organization of the physical world that excited men's imaginations. And the exploitation of those facts was man's affair and not God's. A new adjustment was necessary, and it was at the expense of the two extremes of the chain of being.

The theological effects of this change in the scale came out in the next century. Dryden's age was one of great nominal piety. In believing less in the angels it did not intend to believe less in God. But by believing more exclusively in man it did prepare for a theological change. When there was a continuous chain of existence up to the foot of God's throne, God, though inconceivably remote, was directly linked with man. When the intervening links were snapped, there might remain other means of access, yet the suggestion arose that God was somehow less concerned with his creation than before. Those who had no very lively sense of the single soul's direct communication with its God would tend to sever communication altogether. Hence the Deism of the eighteenth century with its idea of a God, perfectly benevolent indeed, but who had created once and for all a world so satisfactory that further interference by him was unnecessary. Dryden would have repudiated such heresy, but by his accent when he writes of the angels and the lower creation he was really preparing the way for it.

DECORUM

Dryden's *Ode* implies a strong agreement with the contemporary estimation of manners and decorum. It offers a splendid pompous façade and in so doing protests that a good outward show is self-valuable. In stanza seven the king and queen are described in terms of what ideally they should be, not as they were, and Dryden has perfect assurance that he is right to speak thus. We may perceive this assurance the better if, in contrast, we speculate on the state of mind of the *Times* reporter who in describing the coronation of Edward VII wrote quite blatantly and in cool prose that the noblest looking figure in the Abbey was the King. It was surely very different from Dryden's when he wrote

> In beauty foremost, as in rank, the queen.

Given the times he lived in, Dryden really had no choice but to write like that: anything else, in a formal ode, would be scandalously ill-mannered. Any compulsion the *Times* reporter experienced was a smaller and more commercial matter; and we can hope that as he wrote he felt a sinking of the heart or a touch of nausea. For a second example of decorum take the landscape in stanza six. Though it may be vivid and though some of the details may recall actual nature, it is above all what a landscape should be: a staged piece after the manner of Claude; decorous above everything. . . .

This emphasis on manners must have gained strength from the recent contacts with France. The French have felt and still do feel more strongly than the Anglo-Saxons about the value of manners irrespectively of what they express or conceal. The contrasted tempers are well brought out in Henry James's *American* in the episode where the hero's French friend is hanging between life and death after a duel. The preparations—physical, sentimental, and spiritual—for death have been made with perfect completeness and propriety, and a second Frenchman is made to remark that with everything so well arranged it would be a pity if death did not ensue. Henry James's American does not sympathize, but a contemporary of Dryden would have understood. The American thought the Frenchman insincere and heartless, the Frenchman thought the American barbaric. Similarly modern readers dislike Restoration literature for being merely formal, a façade with no true feeling behind it, while Restoration readers were shocked by any display of naked feeling. Such displays were found in the Miracle Plays and in the medieval ballad and were thought uncivilized or, as they put it, Gothic. It should be possible to admit the claims of both habits of mind: to admire both the emotional sincerity of *Clerk Saunders* and the genuine moral discipline which any high standard of decorum cannot fail to imply.

There is another form of decorum. When Dryden says he is praising the reception of Anne Killigrew to heaven "in no ignoble verse," he implies the doctrine of decorum governing the different literary kinds. There was an appropriate style for the various subjects. The heavenly theme must be answered by a high manner. It is a principle that explains why Milton used so rough a meter in writing on Hobson and why in *Paradise Lost* he cultivated a sustained manner of writing remote from the chatter of fireside or marketplace. The whole principle is well illustrated by Dryden's last paragraph of his preface to *Religio Laici,* in which he explains why he writes in the style he has chosen.

> The expression of a poem designed purely for instruction ought to be plain and natural and yet majestic; for here the poet is presumed to be a kind of lawgiver, and those three qualities I have named are proper to the legislative style. The florid elevated and figurative way is for the passions.

The same notion of decorum extended to the portrayal of character. Just as Dryden's queen *must* be the most beautiful lady present at the coronation, so any person represented must bear the ideal qualities of his station or profession. Rymer in his *Tragedies of the Last Age* attacked Evadne (in Beaumont and Fletcher's *Maid's Tragedy*) for her immodesty. The play was a tragedy and it is decorous that all women in tragedy, whatever their conduct, should be naturally modest.

> Tragedy cannot represent a woman without modesty as natural and essential to her. If a woman has got any accidental historical impudence, if, documented in the school of Nanna or Heloisa, she is furnished with some stock of acquired impudence, she is no longer to stalk in tragedy on her high shoes but must rub off and pack down with the carriers into the province of comedy, there to be kicked about and exposed to laughter.

Similarly in his *Short View of Tragedy* Rymer attacked Shakespeare's Iago.

> But what is most intolerable is Iago. He is no blackamoor soldier, so we may be sure he should be like other soldiers of our acquaintance. Yet never in tragedy, nor in comedy, nor in nature, was a soldier with his character. Take it in the author's own words:

> > EM.   . . . some eternal villain,
> > Some busy and insinuating rogue,
> > Some cogging, cozening slave, to get some office.

> Horace describes a soldier otherwise:

> > Impiger, iracundus, inexorabilis, acer.

> Shakespeare knew his character of Iago was inconsistent . . . but to entertain the audience with something new and surprising, against common sense and nature, he would pass upon us a close, dissembling, false, insinuating rascal instead of an open-hearted frank, plain-dealing soldier, a character constantly worn by them for some thousands of years in the world.

Rymer was an extremist, but the things he pushed to extremes were the things the whole age accepted.

CLASSICISM

Dryden's poem is highly civilized in a certain way, and it was natural for his contemporaries to look for support to those epochs of history which seemed to be civilized in the same way and to turn against those which seemed hardly civilized at all. In Athens between the times of Pericles and Aristotle and especially in the Rome of Caesar and Augustus human nature and society seemed to be properly prized, superstition properly suppressed, and decorum properly observed, while in the Middle Ages human nature was twisted by asceticism, superstition was rampant, and a fanatical enthusiasm made decorum impossible. Dryden's age knew very much less history than our own. It judged the Periclean and Augustan ages by the acts and opinions of a tiny minority, and it knew nothing of the turn toward humanism about the twelfth century. This ignorance was not all loss, for it enabled the educated class to master a limited area of literature and to get the pleasure that comes from such mastery. This class attained an enviable coherence and uniformity of culture through the assurance that a limited body of knowledge was genuinely common property. Dryden knew that, when in the first stanza of his *Ode* he speculated on the heavenly region where Anne Killigrew's soul might inhabit, every educated reader would know that he was recalling, though in Christian terms, Virgil's speculations at the beginning of the *Georgics* on where the apotheosized Augustus would have his heavenly seat. And it is partly because he is so sure he will be understood that Dryden can take this most daring flight with such steady nerves.

The same passage fulfills too an actual obligation to imitate the Classical authors. It was necessary to seek ratification in Classical precedent. When Ben Jonson, the first Neoclassic critic in England, enjoined *imitation* he meant by it the borrowing and then the molding of a Classical prototype to your own use: in fact what Pope did later in his imitations of Horace. Dryden not only obeys the injunction in the passage just mentioned but by a single touch shows how entirely he approves of it. At the beginning of stanza five he discusses the relation of art and nature in Anne Killigrew's verse.

> Art she had none, yet wanted none,
> For Nature did that want supply;
> So rich in treasures of her own
> She might our boasted stores defy.
> Such noble vigour did her verse adorn
> That it seemed borrowed, where 'twas only born.

Anne Killigrew's originality, far from being a virtue, needed Dryden's defense. She should have been derivative but luckily she had such native energy that she gave the impression of having borrowed from the classics. The passage is a rough parallel to Pope's elegant fiction in his *Essay on Criticism* of "Young Maro" or Virgil having so strong a native genius as to rely on nature alone. He then turns to Homer (whom he should have copied deliberately) and finds that he has produced something which after all has the appearance of being derived from Homer —and all is well in the end.

THE STATUS OF THE ARTS

When in the last stanza Dryden speaks of the poets being the first to leave their graves at the Day of Judgment and calls them sacred, he does so in an accent of serene assurance: an assurance lacking in similar pronouncements on the sanctity of poets in Shelley's *Defence of Poetry* and Carlyle's section on the Hero as Poet. Shelley's and Carlyle's protests have the shrillness induced by the knowledge of powerful opposition; Dryden is confident that his words will pass. In an age when scientific truth was threatening the realms of the imagination it is strange that the status of the arts was so high. Yet there is no question that it was so and that it remained so for some years after Dryden's death. One manifestation was the superlative status of the epic among human activities and of epic poets among mortal men. The Earl of Mulgrave in his *Essay upon Poetry,* a poem in couplets published in 1682, was doing nothing unusual when he called Heroic Poems the "chief effort of human sense," and Heroic Poets "gigantic souls" as far above other human beings as an ordinary man is above a changeling. Earlier in the century (1641) in *Reason of Church Government* Milton had said that poetic abilities

> are the inspired gift of God rarely bestowed but yet to some in every nation; and are of power, beside the office of a pulpit, to inbreed and cherish in a great people the seeds of virtue and public civility, to allay the perturbations of the mind and set the affections in right tune:

and Dryden's contemporaries would not have gainsaid him. To recognize that the status of poetry remained high beyond the age of Dryden one can read the list of subscribers prefixed to the first edition of Pope's *Iliad* and recall the stories of people pointing him out to their children as the great poet.

How such a state of things was possible is not difficult to perceive. In the Middle Ages poetry had its place either as the handmaiden of religion or as legitimate amusement, but when the hold of the Church over all departments of life was relaxed, some of the awe and glamour possessed by the Church was transferred elsewhere. A part went to the monarchy, a part went to the arts. What had been a craft turned into a fine art; and a craftsman turned into an inspired artist. The process continued into the age of science and actually reached its height in spite of the birth and spread of ideas which, unchecked, would be fatal to the arts. Taken by themselves the ideas animating the newly founded Royal Society were hostile to poetry. Yet Dryden could let his poetic imagination expatiate in his *Ode on Anne Killigrew,* while approving the new scientific activities of the age: a situation not unlike Davies' when he cheerfully included in *Orchestra* his stanza on the Copernican theory, a theory which was destined to destroy the main tenets of the poem.

THE HEROIC CONVENTION

The principles hitherto discussed went beyond the Restoration period, but there is another that applies to it alone. The gigantic proportions to which Dryden inflates Anne Killigrew is one of many examples of the gigantic inflation of human nature common at the time. In the Heroic Plays the characters are all excessive and the sentiments extreme. Lovers are violently amorous, young soldiers excessively audacious, duty piti-lessly exacting and certain to conflict with the claims of love. In *Annus Mirabilis* the English naval commanders show a more than human stature and courage:

> Our dreaded admiral from far they threat,
> Whose batter'd rigging their whole war receives;
> All bare, like some old oak which tempests beat,
> He stands, and sees below his scatter'd leaves.
>
> Heroes of old, when wounded, shelter sought;
> But he, who meets all danger with disdain,
> Ev'n in their face his ship to anchor brought
> And steeple-high stood propt upon the main.
>
> At this excess of courage all amaz'd,
> The foremost of his foes a while withdraw;
> With such respect in enter'd Rome they gaz'd
> Who on high chairs the godlike fathers saw.

In the *Conquest of Granada* Almanzor is a character excessive in cour-age, contempt of death, and power of command. The comment on him after the first episode of the play is

> How much of virtue lies in one great soul,
> Whose single force can multitudes control.

Near the end of his life in the story of Sigismonda and Guiscardo, included in the *Fables*, Dryden gave his finest picture of heroic characters, a picture so convincing that we forget the convention to which they belong. These are Tancred, Duke of Salerno, and his daughter Sigismonda. Tancred discovers his daughter's secret marriage with a man of lower rank, Guiscardo, and in the ensuing quarrel between father and daughter neither will yield in the least to the other. They are towering, uncompromising characters: the father willful and tyrannical, the daughter calculatingly passionate and entirely certain of herself. We are reminded less of Dryden's earlier heroic characters than of York and Queen Margaret in the third part of Shakespeare's *Henry VI*. A second magnificent transformation of the heroic principle is in Congreve's *Way of the World*, where Mirabel and Millamant are great characters, sharply distinguished from the smaller folk that surround them. And in nothing does Congreve show greater art than in masking this sharp distinction during the actual experience of the play. As we watch, Mirabel and Millamant are two of a number of comic characters; it is only on later reflection that we recall their heroic proportions.

Sigismonda and Guiscardo and the *Way of the World* are exceptional. What we are now considering is a habit of mind so widespread at this time that it must mean something. Part of the meaning is the belief in decorum, mentioned above. Appearances were at the time unusually important. Even if the reality behind the appearance is defective, the appearance is better than nothing and must be maintained. Hence convention agreed to portray commanders as coming up to an ideal and superhuman standard of audacity. But decorum does not account for a thrasonical tone peculiar to the Restoration heroes. There had been heroes of other ages, whose deeds were as exaggerated as any of Almanzor's; and it is instructive to compare them in other respects. Malory's Launcelot is excessive in knightly prowess but he is anything but a boastful self-sufficient man. When in a specific test he had proved himself the greatest knight in the world, he "wept as he had been a child that had been beaten." Compare this with Almanzor's protest:

> But know that I alone am king of me.

The Elizabethans had their boasters and their arrogantly self-sufficient men, Tamburlaine and Bussy, but though they were attracted they condemned them. Christian humility, not stoical self-sufficiency, was still believed in. But the narrower humanism of Dryden's day and the Baconian arrogance of the new science inflated the human pretensions; and to these the practice of the heroic convention was partly due. But the pe-

culiar thrasonical tone of this convention arose, I conjecture, not from
a belief in this more exclusive humanism but in the doubts that beset it.
Was man really up to these pretensions? Did the English political record
really correspond to the sublime characters given to the royal rulers? Yet
these pretensions were persisted in, and the very stridency of tone in
which they were made expressed the uneasy conscience that lay behind
them. The next century asked the same questions and gave a different
answer. Pope has a very different version of human nature and he can
be bitterly satirical on the qualities and exploits of an English king.
And, as a whole, the eighteenth century, while believing in the unaided
human reason, was modest in its claims for humanity.

Luckily Dryden's *Ode on Anne Killigrew* escapes the offensiveness of
some heroic writing. Dryden's claims for his heroine are so patently ridiculous that we do not take them seriously, and they are conventionally
extravagant rather than thrasonical. They thus turn our minds to those
general matters of faith in which Dryden sincerely believed and of whose
value no reasonable person can have any doubt: to the faith in the value
of good manners and of an ordered way of life.

The Odes to Music

by John Hollander

Dryden's First Ode: The Cantata of Musical Genesis

Any critical reading of John Dryden's 1687 St. Cecilia's Day ode would do well to keep in mind both the literary convention of the musical ode in praise of music and the general fate of the poetic applications of *musica speculativa* after the Restoration. In general, one would want to conclude with Dr. Johnson that, although the first of the two odes seems "lost in the splendour of the second," it nevertheless contains "passages which would have dignified any other poet." [1] But its particular success can perhaps be measured only against the resounding failure of Neoclassic poetry to versify musical doctrine in any but the most pedestrian fashion, on the one hand, and, on the other, against the relatively flabby way in which Dryden's predecessors had adapted the celebration of singing to the singing of that celebration, as it were, to the exigencies of a good cantata text.

On the first of these questions, we might turn for a moment to a prior case of Dryden's treatment of a theme of speculative music. Taken out of context, the opening of the third stanza of his great ode "To the Pious Memory of the Accomplisht Young Lady Mrs. Anne Killigrew, Excellent in the Two Sister-Arts of Poesie and Painting" (1686) might be thought to resemble some of the complimentary epigrams treated previously:

> May we presume to say, that at thy *Birth*,
> New joy was sprung in HEAV'N as well as here on *Earth*?
> For sure the Milder Planets did combine
> On thy *Auspicious* Horoscope to shine,
> And ev'n the most malicious were in Trine.

"The Odes to Music." Part of the chapter, "The Sky Untuned," from *The Untuning of the Sky* (Princeton, N.J.: Princeton University Press, 1961) by John Hollander, pp. 401-422. Copyright © 1961 by Princeton University Press. Reprinted by permission of the Princeton University Press.

[1] *Lives of the English Poets*, II, 244.

> Thy *Brother-Angels* at thy *Birth*
>   Strung each his Lyre, and tun'd it high,
>   That all the people of the Skie
>   Might know a Poetess was born on Earth.
>   And then if ever, Mortal Ears
>   Had heard the Musick of the Spheres! . . .[2]

(ll. 39-49)

But this superficial resemblance pales into insignificance before the poem's splendid elaboration of the theme of the angelic, the strict correspondence of poetry and music throughout, and the final commendation of earthly art itself toward which the whole elegiac structure moves. The "Musick of the Spheres" is no mere mechanical, intruded gesture of praise here, but has been prepared for in the first stanza's closing supplication:

> Hear then a Mortal Muse thy praise rehearse
>   In no ignoble Verse;
> But such as thy own voice did practise here,
> When thy first Fruits of Poesie were given,
> To make thyself a welcome Inmate there;
>   While yet a young Probationer,
>   And Candidate of Heav'n.

(ll. 16-22)

The traditional relationship between *musica instrumentalis*, practical music at its most specific, and the *musica mundana* of celestial generality, is here applied to Anne Killigrew's life of art ("practise" seems to have the weight of both meanings here). The whole poem employs angels, earth, heaven, the traditional angelic activity of singing, etc., in substitution, in a way, for the conventions of pastoral elegy; and if the conceit of the "heavenly quire" is deemed overly conventional, it is because of its conventionality that it can be employed in such a way as it is here. Professor Tillyard has raised the issue of sincerity with respect to just this point about the angelic singing, but he sees quite rightly, I think, how if "there is no piety in his (Dryden's) references to heavenly music, yet through them he demonstrates how sincerely he prizes the practice of the arts on this earth." [3] The point is that Dryden is able to make use of such references precisely because they are unbelieved, and precisely because music can function consistently as a surrogate for both painting and poetry, with none of the engagement of questions of belief that are

---

[2] Text from the second edition of 1693. Unless otherwise noted, I have used the texts of the poems in the edition of John Sargeaunt (Oxford, 1945).

[3] E. M. W. Tillyard, *Five Poems* (London, 1948), p. 52.

occasioned by praising an actual singer by equating her music with that of the Universe.

Dryden is, of course, also capable, in his verses "On the Death of Mr. Purcell" (written one year before his "Alexander's Feast"), of employing the music of the spheres in a fairly traditional, complimentary way. The lines were set to music by Dr. John Blow ("Master to the famous Mr. H. Purcell" as his tomb in Westminster Abbey rightfully attests), and it is interesting to note that, at the end of the first stanza, Dryden was preparing some of his techniques for the "Alexander's Feast." We shall see shortly how the elaborate repetitions of phrase in the latter were contrived to meet the exigencies of the kind of setting that the text would receive; the line "And list'ning and silent, and silent and list'ning, and list'ning and silent obey" (l. 9) prefigures this sort of repetition in a way in which nothing in the first ode does. The conventionalities of perfect musicianship enter at the middle of the second stanza, and although they are rather nicely tied to an Orphean conceit which operates through the comparison of Hell and Earth, rather than of Earth and Heaven, the old device of the practical musician outdoing the heavenly choir is unmistakably at work here:

> We beg not Hell our *Orpheus* to restore;
> Had He been there,
> Their Sovereigns fear
> Had sent Him back before.
> The pow'r of Harmony too well they knew;
> He long e'er this had Tun'd their jarring Sphere,
> And left no Hell below.

3.

> The Heav'nly Quire, who heard his Notes from high,
> Let down the Scale of Musick from the Sky:
> They handed him along,
> And all the way He taught, and all the way they Sung. . . .

There is undoubtedly an increment of dramatic power produced by the use of the Underworld motif, and tuning "their jarring Sphere" has more literary plausibility, in a sense, than the customary silencing of the sweet, heavenly one would have. The image at the beginning of the final stanza suggests what Professor Tillyard characterizes as "the outrageous assertion that Anne Killigrew will lead the poetic throng to heaven." [4] But the notion that the quasi-deified Purcell will ascend to heaven along a ladder of perfection that is so named as to suggest at once the musical

[4] *Ibid.*, p. 52.

gamut (in the Greek sense, the *harmonia*) and the *gradus ad Parnassum* of diligent practice and devoted effort, is extremely effective and moving.

The problems that Dryden faced in the composition of the 1687 "Song for St. Cecilia's Day" were virtually the same as those faced by Oldham and the other writers of the texts who had preceded him. But other impulses were at work in his case. There was his marvelous gift of exposition, particularly of summarizing, that triumphed in the dismissive conclusion of "The Secular Masque" (1700), wherein Diana, Mars, and Venus, representing the three Stuart courts, are appropriately and schematically rebuked:

> All, all of a piece throughout:
> Thy Chase had a Beast in View;
> Thy Wars brought nothing about;
> Thy Lovers were all untrue.
> 'Tis well an Old Age is out,
> And time to begin a New.

And there was that happy faculty of Dryden's which took so well to the irregular versification of the so-called "Pindarick ode," that faculty invoked by Mark Van Doren in his observation that Dryden "was constitutionally adapted to a form of exalted utterance which progressed by the alternate accumulation and discharge of metrical energy." [5] In the first ode, these two talents combine to produce an admirable celebration of the power of music.

The ode falls into three main sections, commencing with an introductory narrative of the role played by music, treated as abstract Harmony at the beginning, in the Creation (ll. 1-15). A second section, comprising the next five strophes (ll. 16-47), poses the question "What Passion cannot MUSICK raise and quell?" (l. 16); and after a celebration of some original performance by Jubal upon "the chorded Shell," the original *testudo* or tortoise-shell thought to have been the first lyre, successive strophes go on to celebrate the particular affective and passion-eliciting qualities of trumpet, drum, flute, lute, violin, and organ. The last section (final strophe and added "Grand Chorus") introduces St. Cecilia, in comparison with whom Orpheus comes off unfavorably, and proceeds to complete the cycle whose commencement is invoked in the opening lines. Music, this time treated as the sounds of the ultimate trumpet, blown by the archangel to announce the end of that second of eternity containing all of human history, is seen as playing an equally effective role in the Destruction as it played in the Creation.

[5] Mark Van Doren, *John Dryden, A Study of his Poetry,* third ed. (New York, 1946), p. 189.

From the very beginning of the piece, the exposition is activated by a kind of narrative excitement:

> From Harmony, from heav'nly Harmony
> This universal Frame began;
> When Nature underneath a heap
> Of jarring Atomes lay,
> And cou'd not heave her Head,
> The tuneful Voice was heard from high,
> Arise, ye more than dead.
> Then cold and hot and moist and dry
> In order to their Stations leap,
> And MUSICK'S pow'r obey. . . .
>
> (ll. 1-10)

What jars here is not "disproportion'd sin," as in "At a Solemn Musick," but rather the atoms of chaos, which associate themselves with their proper elemental status "in order to their Stations" under the organizing influence of Harmony. While this seems only barely reminiscent of Marvell's recounting of music's creation of a world along specifically political lines, it suggests much more his treatment of Cromwell as Amphion in "The First Anniversary of the Government under O. C.," where the creative, wall-building music accomplishes its ends by ordering what had been chaotic previously.[6] The conclusion of the opening strophe turns a connective "from" into a "to," and changes the meaning of "Harmony" slightly; what is meant now is a melody, an interval, or more probably a chord, instead of the abstract sense of harmony as order in the original and repeated lines:

> From Harmony, from heavenly Harmony
> This universal Frame began:
> From Harmony to Harmony
> Through all the Compass of the Notes it ran,
> The Diapason closing full in Man.
>
> (ll. 11-15)

The octave, that is, the perfect consonance (next to the unison, of course), is the proper "close" (or, in modern terminology, "cadence") for the actual musical composition of Creation, moving along, as Dryden probably meant specifically, over a thoroughbass, "From Harmony to Harmony." Man is that octave cadence, and his shaping crowned the whole act of Creation, and was followed only by the silences of the first Sabbath.

---

[6] Van Doren (*op. cit.*, p. 202) holds that stanza II of the "Song for St. Cecilia's Day" may have been influenced by "Musicks Empire."

The central portion of the ode, employing separate sections for the celebration of the virtues of each instrument, holds more to the pattern of some of the earlier cantata-texts. Obbligatos on the appropriate instruments would seem to have been the order of the day (although Handel's setting, first performed in 1739, makes much more elaborate use of these than Draghi's original one appears to have done). Dryden does not seem to have kept in mind, in composing his text, that clear distinctions would be drawn, in the setting, between passages of recitative, aria, duet, chorus, etc.; his "Grand Chorus" is the only indication of a textual division that was obviously planned to correspond to a musical one.[7] The vivid metrical variation in strophe 3 ("The TRUMPETS loud Clangor/Excites us to Arms," etc.) is much more effective (with its abrupt switch out of its quasi-dactylic scheme, into "The double double double beat/Of the thund'ring DRUM," and back again) on paper, than when set; although any late Baroque musical setting would set up rhythms of its own to correspond to the effects that Dryden's verse achieved. The second stanza does have the enrichment of the delicate second reference to the "Shell"-lyre:

> Less than a God they thought there could not dwell
> Within the hollow of that Shell,
> That spoke to sweetly, and so well. . . .
>
> (ll. 21-23)

where the overtones of the roaring sea-shell seem implicit, somehow, beneath the conventional epithet.

But it is the concluding strophes, along with the first, that are of most interest here. The last one before the chorus compliments St. Cecilia in some of the same terms in which countless "Fair Singers" during the preceding fifty years had been complimented:

> *Orpheus* cou'd lead the savage race,
> And trees unrooted left their Place,
>   Sequacious of the Lyre;
> But bright CECILIA rais'd the Wonder High'r:
> When to her Organ vocal Breath was given,
> An Angel heard, and straight appear'd
>   Mistaking Earth for Heav'n.
>
> (ll. 48-54)

Dryden has here combined the two elements of the St. Cecilia legend into his little dramatic climax: the angel that the historical saint's *praying* summoned is here treated as having appeared at the sound of the organ,

---

[7] Ernest H. Brennecke, Jr., in "Dryden's Odes and Draghi's Music," *PMLA*, XLIX (1934), pp. 1-36, deals admirably with just these questions of setting in the case of both odes.

her visible attribute. One cannot be sure whether Dryden was consciously suggesting that it was the "music," the affective beauty of her prayer, which "drew an Angel down," or whether this is merely a rather effective bit of wit. Dryden may also very well have appropriated Ben Jonson's line from "The Musical Strife," [8] but there is certainly sufficient tradition for the figure in the complimentary convention to have allowed him to come upon it himself, quite naturally.

The final chorus, which together with the opening brackets the whole ode, is of a more original stuff:

Grand CHORUS

As from the Pow'r of Sacred Lays
The Spheres began to move,
And sung the great Creator's Praise
To all the bless'd above;
So, when the last and dreadful Hour
This crumbling Pageant shall devour,
The TRUMPET shall be heard on high,
The dead shall live, the living die,
And MUSICK shall untune the Sky. (ll. 55-63)

Just as the trumpet of Gabriel and of the Koran's Israfel is completely separate from the purely martial trumpet celebrated earlier in the ode, the music that untunes the sky must be referred back to the opening lines: it is only as the dissolvent counterpart of the original ordering that we can make more than the most extravagent sense of the final line. Dr. Johnson wished that "the antithesis of *music untuning* had found some other place";[9] and he evidently found the penultimate line so "awful in itself" that he could not bring himself precisely to designate it. But I think that the music untuning the sky is more than merely a figure representing the transcendence of music, even across the dissolution of the universe. "This crumbling Pageant" is the cosmos, of course; but Professor Van Doren may be hinting at something else, in his remark that Dryden's "finale is the blare of a trumpet, and his last glimpse is of painted scenery crashing down on a darkened stage." [10] The conclusion of the ode seems quite close to some of the conventions of the masque at this point. We have observed the self-congratulatory tone and import of some of the earlier St. Cecilia's Day odes. Here, the "Pageant" is the musical meeting itself, in much the same way as, in a masque, the allegorical texture of

[8] Geoffrey Walton in *Metaphysical to Augustan* (London, 1955), p. 126, points out, *re* this possible borrowing, that "Jonson already has a declamatory note suggestive of the Restoration."

[9] *Lives*, II, 245. It may, of course, have been merely the voraciousness of the "hour" in eating a "crumbling Pageant" that bothered him.

[10] *John Dryden*, p. 203.

plot, dramaturgy, and theater come to equate the world of the masque's imagery with the parochial, but momentarily universal, world of the court in which it is presented.[11] The London music meetings had none of the masque conventions, of course, such as the identity of the masquers, the closing measures in which spectacle and audience unite, etc. But the marvelous finale quality of the chorus here is considerably enhanced by the fact that the whole cantata, starting up with the literal tuning of strings, should end with an "untuning"; by the fact that the text draws upon the conventional notion of psychic *tonus* (although rather for praise, than for *prayer*, here) in a kind of reversal, implying that, now that the praise of music has been completed, the souls of the singers and hearers will "untune," or "slacken," as have the strings of the actual instruments.

But whatever the force of the ultimate line, it cannot be denied that it is the first and last sections of the ode that are truly distinguished. They are devoted to the eternal subsistence of music, seen as both abstract *harmonia mundi* and final trump; but like the outraged angels and humbled spheres of the epigrams, that "music," a sophisticatedly wrought construction from the stock of *musica speculativa,* is employed in praise of a practical music that is *mundane* rather than *mundana*, worldly rather than universal. The second member of this pair has become merely a term with which to exalt the other.

"Alexander's Feast": The Drama of Musical Power

If the "opening" and "finale" of the first St. Cecilia's Day ode give evidence of a sense on Dryden's part of a kind of musical programmatic dramaturgy, however, it is to the "Alexander's Feast; Or, the Power of Musique" of ten years later that we must turn for the fulfillment of that promise. Questions ranging from that of over-all theme to those of more minute details of arrangement of line and repetition of word, raised by the musical setting of the first ode, were settled quite definitively in the execution of the second one. Draghi's setting of the closing line, for example, actually involved the singing of "And Musick shall untune the sky, untune, untune, and Musick shall, and Musick shall . . . ," etc.[12] Then there was the problem of adapting the vigorous and flexible strophic structure to the exigencies of the setting's alternation of chorus, solo, duet, etc., and the final crucial matter of theme, and of a move from the expository to the dramatic. As a solution of all these problems, "Alexander's Feast" must be considered as a true libretto, rather than merely as another in the series of commendatory odes.[13] It is almost proverbial

[11] See Rosemond Tuve, *Images and Themes in Five Poems by Milton,* pp. 113-121.
[12] Quoted by Brennecke, *op. cit.,* p. 29.
[13] *Ibid.,* pp. 34-35.

now how Dryden found the prospect of writing another ode "trouble-some, & no way beneficiall," [14] and how its actual composition was accompanied with great concern and some nervousness.[15] The original setting by Jeremiah Clarke (?1673-1707) was never published and no trace of it remains, so that we cannot know precisely the degree to which Dryden's efforts were successful in the case of some of the more technical matters which he faced as librettist. But the authority with which the ode celebrates its epoch's dominant myth of music is unimpeachable, and its brilliance as a poetic text completely apart from its musical setting has always been dazzling.

His search for a subject could not have taken him far. His dramatic libretto called for one of the old stories of affective music: Orpheus, Arion (rather than the more strictly political Amphion), the Sirens, and Ulysses. Less likely candidates were the stories of the musical martyrs of one sort or another: Orpheus' dismemberment, Herakles' murder of his teacher Linus with the man's own lyre, the punishment of Terpander for adding an extra string to the lyre, the ridicule of the historical Timotheus of Miletus for his innovations along similar lines, Marsyas and his unfortunate espousal of the hateful *aulos,* Midas and his grossly ridiculed lack of taste. All of these must have seemed either overly grotesque or patently ridiculous. Even the story of St. Cecilia herself was too bare of canonical and familiar musical incident. The *philomelamachia* ending in death was not only unsuitable because of its tragic conclusion, but because such a subject would seem better adapted to a chamber dialogue than to the expansion of a cantata.[16] But another Timotheus, a purely fictional Alexandrian *aulos*-player who became confused with the historical composer of *nomoi* mentioned above, had served from the very beginning as part of the Orpheus-figure, as a Baroque poet-musician-rhetorician-hero. Writers in English for the hundred years previous had used as an instance of the power of music the story of how Alexander the Great, in the version of John Case from *The Praise of Musicke* (1586), "sitting at a banquet amongst his friends, was nevertheles by the excelent skil of Timotheus a famous musician so inflamed with the fury of *Modus Orthius,* or as some say of *Dorius,* that he called for his spear & target as if he would presently have addressed himself to war." But immediately thereafter, Case remarks, "the same Timotheus seeing Alexander thus incensed, only with the changing of a note, pacified this moode of his, & as it were with a more

---

[14] See his letter of September 3, 1697, in *Letters,* ed. Charles E. Ward (Durham, N.C., 1942), p. 93.

[15] *John Dryden,* p. 204. Also see his letter to Tonson (in Ward's collection, pp. 96-97) about correcting his erroneous MS. substitution of *Lais* for *Thais, passim.* One cannot, of course, determine whether the former or the latter appeared as Alexander's distinguished camp-follower on his Persian campaign. Also Dr. Johnson in his "Life of Dryden," *op. cit.,* p. 255.

[16] J. S. Bach's *"Der Streit zwischen Phoebus und Pan"* (1731?), while a full cantata, may have been satiric in intent.

mild sound mollified & asswaged his former violence." [17] Aside from the
fact that Case has his "modes" mixed up here (Dorian, as well as Phrygian,
might be considered a "warlike" mode, but *"Modus Orthius"* is a purely
rhythmic term having nothing to do with melody), his account remains
pretty much the standard one in English. It has been observed how
Cowley, Burton, Playford, and Jeremy Collier, among others, all have
versions, of differing degrees of detail, of the Timotheus story;[18] as a
probable source, Collier's recounting of the story has its date of appearance (1697) and the liveliness of the scene it sketches on its side: "One
time, when *Alexander* was at Dinner, this man play'd him a *Phrygian*
Air: The Prince immediately rises, snatches up his Lance, and puts himself in a Posture of Fighting. And the Retreat was no sooner Sounded
by the Change of the Harmony, but his Arms were Grounded, and his
Fire extinct, and he sat down as orderly as if he had come from one
of *Aristotle's Lectures*. I warrant you *Demosthenes* would have been
Flourishing about such a Business a long Hour, and may not have done
it neither, But *Timotheus* had a nearer Cut to the Soul: He could Neck
a Passion at a Stroke, and lay it Asleep." [19] Here, as throughout this essay,
incidentally, Collier seems to have been motivated by common sense as
much as by his traditional modal *ethos*. "By altering the *Notes,* and the
Time," he carefully remarks, he could sweeten a hearer's "Humour at
a trice." [20] Any late seventeenth century audience would comprehend such
a notion that made no appeal to what had become the purely literary
schemata of the music of Antiquity.

But however it came to him, the story of Timotheus was Dryden's
program, as the ultimately persuasive powers of music were his theme.
The ode's unity keeps to the story, and it is only in the seventh strophe
that St. Cecilia is allowed to appear in a cadential, climactic way. As
far as the over-all structure of the ode is concerned, Dryden has not only
repeated the closing lines of each strophe as a chorus, but he had so arranged each stanza that the truncated section, brilliant and summary in
itself, would be no mere caudal appendage, but bound to the rest by

---

[17] Text quoted in M. C. Boyd, *Elizabethan Music and Musical Criticism*, p. 30.
Boyd (App. C, pp. 292-300) prints many relevant extracts from Case's book.

[18] See *John Dryden*, pp. 204-206. James Kinsley, "Dryden and the *Encomium Musicae*," *Review of English Studies*, New Series, IV (1952), p. 265, lists and quotes many
of these versions. Mr. Kinsley's article is otherwise, I am afraid, rather misleading in
its attempt to connect "Alexander's Feast" with the Renaissance tradition of the
praise of music that was first outlined so well by Prof. James Hutton ("Some English
Poems in Praise of Music," *English Miscellany*, II [1951], 1-59). But Mr. Kinsley seems
utterly to ignore the genre of the poem, its relationship to musical lore as doctine
and as mere decorative imagery, etc. etc. His expansion of the earlier tradition of the
encomium musicae so as to include the ode without any further needed qualification
seems at worst, *simpliste*, at best, Procrustean.

[19] Jeremy Collier, "Of Musick," in *Essays on Several Moral Subjects* (second ed.,
1698), II, 22.

[20] *Ibid.*, II, 22.

rhyme or metrical phrase. The end of the third strophe, for example, starts out with the announcement of the arrival of Bacchus:

> Now give the Hautboys breath; He comes,
>> He comes.
>> *Bacchus* ever Fair and Young
>>> Drinking Joys did first ordain;
>> *Bacchus* Blessings are a Treasure;
>> Drinking is the Soldiers Pleasure;
>>> Rich the Treasure;
>>> Sweet the Pleasure;
>> Sweet is Pleasure after Pain. (ll. 53-60)

The last five lines are repeated as a chorus, and the repetitions and echoing of short phrases attest here, as elsewhere throughout the poem, to Dryden's concern for the safety of his text during the process of setting. But the over-all scheme allows the various stanzas to contain, each within itself, a separate episode; a feeling appropriate to the action of each episode is exemplified throughout each strophe, and particularly in the chorus. Thus, in the first one, the scene is laid, and Alexander, "the lovely *Thais*" and "his valiant Peers" are shown feasting after the victory over Xerxes: "Their Brows with Roses and with Myrtles bound./(So should Desert in Arms be Crown'd:)" (ll. 7-8). The atmosphere is one of love following victory, the myrtle of Venus and the sensual rose, it is pointed out, are the proper guerdon of warlike prowess.[21] Alexander and Thais, "In Flow'r of Youth and Beauty's Pride," are invoked in the chorus:

> *Happy, happy, happy Pair!*
>> *None but the Brave,*
>> *None but the Brave,*
> *None but the Brave deserves the Fair.* (ll. 16-19)

And here is the first of many cases of that brilliant shift from iambic to trochaic measures to the catalectic dactyls such as those of *"None but the Brave,"* etc., which marks in particular the prosodical artistry of the whole poem.

The next section introduces "Timotheus plac'd on high/Amid the tuneful Quire," surely not complimented in these lines (although the cliché of praise seems to be in evidence here), but rather depicted as in the high choir-loft or musicians' gallery, under "the Vaulted Roofs" of a sumptuous

---

[21] James Kinsley, *op. cit.*, p. 266, points out a possibly relevant passage in Dryden's translation of Plutarch's life of Alexander, in which the burning of the palace is described as having been done by a garlanded Alexander. But I think that the implication about the relationship between heroic love and war is the principal point about this line.

palace. In contrast to this, however, his playing is elaborately praised, as we are told how he

> With flying Fingers touch'd the Lyre:
>   The trembling Notes ascend the Sky,
>   And Heav'nly Joys inspire.   (ll. 22-24)

And while "Heav'nly Joys" commends rather more than describes, the remainder of the second section is devoted to the treatment of the theme of the empyrean. The muse governing this stanza, and Timotheus' first song, is Clio:

> The Song began from *Jove;*
> Who left his blissful Seats above,
> (Such is the Pow'r of mighty Love.)
> A Dragon's fiery Form bely'd the God:
> Sublime on Radiant Spires He rode,
> When He to fair *Olympia* press'd:
> And while He sought her snowy Breast:
>   Then, round her slender Waist he curl'd,
> And stamp'd an Image of himself, a Sov'raign of the World.
>
>   (ll. 25-33)

But the muse has become the patroness of fiction, rather than of history. The story, recorded in Plutarch, of how Alexander's mother Olympias claimed to have been impregnated by some divine dragon, was one which Dryden had elsewhere condemned in no uncertain terms: "Ye Princes, rais'd by Poets to the Gods,/And Alexander'd up in lying Odes,/Believe not ev'ry flatt'ring Knave's report . . . ," [22] he warns the readers of his rewriting of Chaucer's *Nun's Priest's Tale*. But here the fiction is identified with the magic of the music, and is praised at the end when we are told that Timotheus "rais'd a Mortal to the Skies," almost as if the greatest triumph of his musicianship had been the creation of the noble fiction of Alexander's divine paternity. But it is as a God that Alexander is acclaimed by the crowd at the end of the strophe:

> A present Deity, they shout around:
> A present Deity, the vaulted Roofs rebound.
>   With ravish'd Ears
>   The Monarch hears,
>   Assumes the God,
>   Affects to nod,
> And seems to shake the Spheres   (ll. 35-41)

---

[22] "The Cock and the Fox," from *Fables* (1700), ll. 659-661. Kinsley, *op. cit.*, p. 266, calls attention to this, as well as to other material from Plutarch that Dryden seems to have employed, in one way or another, in filling out the scene of the poem.

If the Spheres are disturbed as a result of Timotheus' transcendent musicianship, it is only through the almost rabble-rousing effects of his music and his fictions that create a din, on the one hand, and half-convince all that the Monarch "Assumes the God," on the other. Only here, in the entire poem, is the heavenly apparatus in evidence. The myth of music throughout is the affective one in terms of which music activates feeling through the medium of sense, and from this point on, Timotheus' playing is to move by persuasion, rather than to affect through "lying."

The third stanza celebrates Bacchus, starting out with the report of what subject it was that "the sweet Musician" actually sang, and then moving almost imperceptibly into the invocation, itself, of Bacchus: "Now give the Hautboys breath; He comes, He comes," etc. We are not told here, as we are in the fifth section, which *harmonia* it actually was that Timotheus played; we may presume that it was the Ionian, which, with the Lydian that in section five becomes the erotic mode, was designated by Plato as one of the "soft or drinking harmonies." [23] Dryden has carefully allowed only wind instruments to occur in this section. The fourth section recounts Alexander's hallucinatory, perhaps drunken (but whether on wine, or music, or both is left deliberately vague) revelry ("Fought all his Battails o'er again;/And thrice He routed all his Foes, and thrice he slew the slain"). But then, we are told,

> The Master saw the Madness rise,
> His glowing Cheeks, his ardent Eyes;
> And while He Heav'n and Earth defy'd,
> Chang'd his Hand, and check'd his Pride.
> He chose a Mournful Muse,
> Soft pity to infuse. . . . (ll. 69-74)

This would have been a Mixolydian mode that Timotheus employed to chasten his King's exuberance by using it to accompany the reminder of the death of Darius, which had, according to Plutarch, moved Alexander deeply. His song of Darius, "Fallen, fallen, fallen, fallen,/Fallen from his high Estate," causes tears to come to the eyes of Alexander. But in the next strophe, we are told that the Musician sang in "*Lydian* measures" (l. 97), to soothe the king and turn him to amorous feelings. (It is interesting that Dryden should have called the Lydian melodic mode a metrical one, but the additional meanings of "dance" and "means," as well as the rhyme with "Pleasures," operate to enforce the equivalence, rather than the identity, of the two.)

> War, he sung, is Toil and Trouble;
> Honour but an empty Bubble.

[23] *Republic*, 398-399.

> Never ending, still beginning,
> Fighting still, and still destroying,
> If the World be worth thy Winning,
> Think, O think, it worth Enjoying.
> Lovely *Thais* sits beside thee,
> Take the Good the Gods provide thee.
> The Many rend the Skies, with loud applause;
> So Love was Crown'd, but Musique won the Cause. . . .
>
> (ll. 99-108)

Here again, the strophe moves into Timotheus' song itself. This time, it is as much moral argument as pure emotional exhortation; it is a little like a Cavalier lyric about Love and Arms inserted into the ode at this point. The theme of Mars and Venus, at any rate, served to introduce the whole scene, and the sixth strophe, the concluding one of the Timotheus story, ends itself with a comparison of Thais to the greatest heroine of war fought all for love. After the king had sunk in sleep upon the breast of his courtesan, Timotheus struck "the Golden Lyre" again, this time, we should guess, with Phrygian strains. Certainly the prosody of this stanza is the most varied and elaborate. "Revenge, revenge" is the musician's text, and a full complement of Furies, Snakes, ". . . a ghastly Band,/Each a Torch in his Hand!" conjured up in the minds of all by the ecstatic mode, incite the king to wreak that revenge upon the very palace in which he has been reveling:

> Behold how they toss their Torches on high,
>   How they point to the *Persian* Abodes,
> And glitt'ring Temples of their Hostile Gods.
> The Princes applaud with a furious Joy;
> And the King seized a Flambeau with Zeal to destroy;
>   *Thais* led the Way,
>   To light him to his Prey,
> And, like another *Hellen,* fir'd another *Troy.*   (ll. 142-150)

It is Love, then, which concludes the story, as it opened it. In the final strophe, we are given the climactic mention of Timotheus:

> Thus long ago,
> 'Ere heaving Bellows learn'd to blow,
>   While Organs yet were mute,
> *Timotheus,* to his breathing Flute
>   And sounding Lyre,
> Cou'd swell the Soul to rage, or kindle soft Desire. . . .
>
> (ll. 155-160)

The flute and lyre mentioned together may, of course, stem from the traditional confusion of the two Timotheus figures, the historical lyricist and the fictional *auletes;* but it also harks back to the opening theme of Love consummating the warrior's victory, with perhaps an overtone of Horace's second epode with its ". . . *bibam,/sonante mixtum tibiis carmen lyra,/hac Dorium, illis barbarum?"* wherein the battle of Actium was to be celebrated with mingled musics of a gravely victorious and a frenziedly celebratory nature.

But Timotheus is, finally, outdone, in a sudden intrusion of St. Cecilia that, on the surface, seems rather unconvincing. She is complimented as having "Enlarg'd the former narrow Bounds,/And added Length to solemn Sounds," that is, as combining the virtues of Classical measures and of the benefits of the music of Christian worship. It cannot be for this only that Dryden demands,

> Let old Timotheus yield the Prize,
> Or both divide the Crown:
> He raised a mortal to the Skies;
> She drew an Angel down. (ll. 167-170)

Dr. Johnson remarked that this "conclusion is vicious; the music of Timotheus, which *raised a mortal to the skies,* had only a metaphorical power; that of Cecilia, which *drew an angel down,* had a real effect: the crown therefore could not reasonably be divided." [24] To debate this conclusion might not necessarily entail an excursion into ontology to show that for Dryden the power was metaphorical in both cases, but such a debate should be avoided in any event. The final appearance of St. Cecilia as a peculiar sort of *deus ex machina* must be understood as operating within the convention of the St. Cecilia's Day music meetings, with which Dryden was of course familiar. She triumphs over Timotheus (or only meets his accomplishment; Dryden is significantly noncommittal) only through the antithesis of the final conceit, but the intention of this seems quite clear. The reference to her attraction of the angel is casually tossed off, as if to indicate that this story was an accepted part of what was almost a liturgy of these music meetings. The close of the ode is a conventional one, a ritual in itself, and the final piece of wit serves to tie the whole ode and its subject into its proper occasional function. But, in another sense, it is indeed St. Cecilia who has been unthroned.

For all of "Alexander's Feast" has gone to praise not only the power and glory of earthly, affective music, but it has gone to praise poetry as well. It is Timotheus the mythmaker, the forger of fictions, who is commended at the beginning of the poem and at the end; and throughout its course the ode seems to depend upon almost bootlegged poetic references,

[24] "Life of Dryden," in *Lives,* II, 255.

such as the "Measures" of line 97, and the argument about War and Love in the lines following. It is at any rate the "goddess PERSUASION," who, as Shaftesbury put it, "must have been in a manner the mother of poetry, rhetoric, music, and other kindred arts," [25] that triumphs at the conclusion of the celebration of music.

Both as a libretto and as a poem, "Alexander's Feast" commends the power of that goddess. The brilliant musical dramaturgy of the cantata text gives way, on reading, to the marvelous metrical effects, which not only serve themselves to excite, calm, chasten, etc., but to imitate in some way the actual musical setting that they would receive, and in which they would be immolated. The poem is a "musical ode" in many of the senses suggested by that compound: an ode set to, about, purporting to resemble, and even substituting for music. More than that, it implicitly stipulates for its own age and for successive ones as well what music is, and how it should be considered. It is to be *made* rather than, as in the first ode, to be expounded like doctrine, even if that doctrine puts down all the cosmological orthodoxies about the music of universe. In a very real sense, the 1687 ode contains a program for the later one, just as it sums up so succinctly, not the history of music in the lives of Western men, but the history of what those men have thought and felt and imagined that very music to be. Music itself, practical music, the music of opera and public concert, the music of the highly trained, status-seeking professional, is the hero (or, in its variousness, a hero-heroine) of "A Song for St. Cecilia's Day." It has untuned the sky in the sense that it has already rendered the notion of heavenly music, whether as an actuality or in any one of the many, active metaphorical versions which we have studied above, as trivial as it rendered silent the singing spheres. The untuned sky is the abandoned monochord of *musica speculativa,* and "Alexander's Feast" is no mere strand of *exemplum* from that ancient instrument, but a brilliant performance whose only lesson is its own worth.

[25] Third Earl of Shaftesbury, *Characteristics* (1711), ed. J. M. Robertson (New York, 1900), I, 154.

Various John Dryden:
"All, All, of a Piece Throughout"

by Arthur W. Hoffman

Dryden was, in a way, all his life a victim of occasions, public occasions in terms of which he cast up much of his poetic account. The last decade of his life was a public occasion too in its coincidence with the last decade of his century. In the 1690's many of the turbulent conflicts of the extraordinarily troubled century had been worn out by their own violence and wearied into a sort of peace; at the same time various John Dryden had sailed into his own port and could look back on the stormy seas he had traversed. Repeatedly in the prefaces and poems of this decade Dryden expresses himself as looking back, reviewing, summing up, imbued with the attitude of a captain at the end of a voyage. The personal attitude gains in symbolic resonance by its congruence with the end of the century.

The last turn in the infinite variety of Cleopatra was marble constancy, a turn which both completed and converted the cycle of her variousness. Some such paradox of variety and constancy applies in the case of Dryden and has bedeviled his critics; it is his fatal charm. In *The Hind and the Panther* he wrote:

> My thoughtless youth was wing'd with vain desires,
> My manhood, long misled by wandring fires,
> Follow'd false lights; and when their glimps was gone,
> My pride struck out new sparkles of her own.
> Such was I, such by nature still I am.

(Part I, ll. 72-76; II, 472K)[1]

"Various John Dryden: 'All, All, of a Piece Throughout.'" A slightly revised version of Chapter VI of *John Dryden's Imagery* (Gainesville: University of Florida Press, 1962) by Arthur W. Hoffman, pp. 130-147. Copyright © 1962 by The Board of Commissioners of State Institutions of Florida. Reprinted by permission of the University of Florida Press.

[1] All references to the text of Dryden's poetry are to *The Poems of John Dryden* (4 vols.), edited by James Kinsley (Oxford, 1958). The volume and page numbers in Professor Kinsley's edition are here given directly after the line numbers and with the symbol *K* attached.

He had, in the judgment of some, lackeyed the varying tide until he rotted himself with motion. Even in his final Roman choice he could be accused of time-serving, but his Roman choice survived the Roman king, a king whose actions Dryden did not much approve. Under William, the Protestant king, Dryden, as translator of the *Aeneid,* could be expected to dedicate the epic poem to the reigning monarch, but this time Dryden, very likely to the despair of his publisher, Tonson, would not dedicate to the king. Dryden had lost his official positions as poet laureate and historiographer royal, and the income that was important to a man at his age, and he was losing his health, yet never in his long career did he undertake so much or write so serenely well. If he had all his life courted favor, and favored courts, he seems to have been at his best last, when out of favor. He bravely showed the way toward authorship supported without patronage. To Dryden, in the last decade of his life, the king was nothing. He was, at the end of his career, more willing than ever before to leave the world to Caesar; he saw more clearly that Caesar was beguiled. The Hind had advised "a long farwell to worldly fame":

> And what thou didst, and do'st so dearly prize,
> That fame, that darling fame, make that thy sacrifice.
>
> (Part III, ll. 289-90; II, 510K)

There may be a quibble in the word "worldly," but Dryden did, at any rate, in important ways, sacrifice his worldly fame. Possibly there remained "that darling fame" which he, no more than Milton, could give up.

Dryden's imagery throughout his poetry discloses a great deal of evidence of almost unremitting preoccupation with the problem of authority. In praise and blame, in panegyric and satire, and in the modulated poems of discursive, reasonable argument, the heart of the matter is authority, a quest for the countenance that compels the term "master." A characteristic tension, a partial failure and a peculiar success in Dryden's poetry are produced by the persistent effort to locate authority *in* the world. The drama of this attempt centered upon the image of the king while the historical drama of the royal symbol moved in the other direction; Albert Camus, speaking of the end of this historical drama in France, summarized its significance thus:

> . . . the fact remains that, by its results and consequences, the condemnation of the king is at the crux of our contemporary history. It symbolizes the secularization of our history and the dematerialization of the Christian God. Up to now God played a part in history through the medium of the kings. But His representative in history has been killed, for there is no longer a king. Therefore there is nothing but a semblance of God, relegated to the heaven of principles.[2]

[2] Albert Camus, *The Rebel,* translated by Anthony Bower (New York, 1954), p. 92.

It may well be that Dryden's effort was, in Santayana's phrase, a belated masquerade. Since Dryden's age was in the process of transmuting the king into "an idol monarch, which their hands had made," the king image and its ambiguity threatened to change and dissolve on Dryden's hands. So far as Dryden's late verse is concerned, the secular monarch seems almost to have resigned his part in what is "immortal and unchang'd."

The poetry of Dryden's last decade is filled with memorable images expressive of an enlarged sense of the world and a reduced sense of the world's importance; the images are vivid, firm, comprehensive, and judicial:

> Theirs was the Gyant Race, before the Flood.
> The second Temple was not like the first.
>
> > (*To . . . Mr. Congreve,* l. 5 and l. 14; II, 852K)
>
> *All, all, of a piece throughout;*
> *Thy Chase had a Beast in View;*
> *Thy Wars brought nothing about;*
> *Thy Lovers were all untrue.*
>
> > (*The Secular Masque,* ll. 92-95; IV, 1765K)

Dryden had contended for wit against dullness, for stability against the whirl of fashion, for reason above passion, for the poet-maker against the facile imitator, for learning against obscurantism, for the true fire against random enthusiasm, for political authority above popular whim. In all of these contentions he had appealed to and for the image of the king. In his last poems he has not abandoned—he could not abandon—his habitual images, but the scale of meaning has altered under the influence of his new total perspective. There is a world that he has been disburdened of, a public world. The political sanction or pseudosanction of his laureateship has been lifted from his shoulders and he holds the office of poet unofficially—unofficially but perhaps religiously, the sacredness without the solemnity. In the Prologue to *Love Triumphant* (late 1693 or early 1694) Dryden presents himself in the image of one resigning the symbols of office. In his new freedom he practices a set of pieties toward a fellow poet and dramatist, toward a gracious lady, and toward a kinsman and namesake. His finest powers are shown in these poems, without straining, genially and surely.

Two poems of this last decade are the finest examples of Dryden's mastery of a middle style; they are the epistles *To my Dear Friend Mr. Congreve, On His COMEDY, call'd The Double-Dealer* and *To my Honour'd Kinsman, JOHN DRIDEN, OF CHESTERTON IN THE COUNTY OF HUNTINGDON, ESQUIRE.* Of these two poems I shall discuss the former, which illustrates very well the special virtues of a style that means not colorless compromise but a balanced prospect of conversational informality and dignified elevation. The middle style reigns by a smooth alternation and intermingling, by laying under contribution both lords and commons in language and imagery. The tone restricts and smiles at the dignity imported by imagery. Consider the manner of the beginning in this epistle:

> Well then; the promis'd hour is come at last;
> The present Age of Wit obscures the past.   (ll. 1-2; II, 852K)

The language of this couplet puts forward suggestions full of dignity and elevation; the moment of the fulfillment of prophecy is, after long expectation, at hand, and its coming marks a significant revolution of time. It is midway in the second line that *wit* is established as the subject under discussion. Thus the aura of suggestion is, in one continuous motion, powerfully developed and cleanly restricted; the falcon is flown and then called, a fiction is indulged and then modified. If the fiction were offered only to be withdrawn, the proceeding would be as barren as a magician's trick in which an offered object vanishes in a convenient sleeve. There is, however, true wit in the stylistic maneuver because the fiction leaves its impress upon the statement, the solemn suggestions have been made smilingly, and their true seriousness will emerge in the course of the poem. The wit, in fact, is in the beginning; "Well then," says the speaker, as preface to the solemn statement, a sort of small type for the second coming. "Well then," says the speaker, implying that the solemnity that follows is the enforced consequence of something that has gone before. The something that has gone before is Congreve's play, and with the advent of such wit, who can but prophesy? The prophet is a little reluctant, surprised by fulfillment, ironic at his own expense. The prophet sees himself ousted as he welcomes one greater than the prophets—"Well then. . . ." It is in this matrix that the solemnities of the couplet are to be entertained.

With such an attitude a great deal of dignity can be supported, as this poem proceeds to prove. As the triumph of the new age is proclaimed, a perspective is achieved on the past age and a summary view of history presented. The Elizabethans are "the Gyant Race, before the Flood." The Restoration writers tamed and cultivated the sheer strength of wit that they inherited, but the process of refinement and polishing sapped the original strength:

> Our Builders were, with want of Genius, curst;
> The second Temple was not like the first.
>
> (ll. 13-14; II, 852K)

Thus Dryden continues to write the history of wit with the dignity of biblical history and symbols. Wit has had its period when there were giants in the earth, has had its obliterating flood, has had its peerless temple destroyed and has built a second temple that is no match for the first. And now wit has, in Congreve, its architect of genius whom Dryden dignifies with Roman honors:

> Till You, the best *Vitruvius,* come at length;
> Our Beauties equal; but excel our strength.
>
> (ll. 15-16; II, 852K)

But the prophetic background to the symbolic templebuilding also points to the founder and builder in the biblical tradition, the Messiah whose pronouncement about destroying and building the temple was so bold and so misunderstood.

Possibly the templebuilding image as Dryden carries it out is actually threefold in its suggestions:

> Firm *Dorique* Pillars found Your solid Base:
> The Fair *Corinthian* Crowns the higher Space;
> Thus all below is Strength, and all above is Grace.
>
> (ll. 17-19; II, 852K)

Besides the naming of Vitruvius, the Roman architect, and the tacit suggestion of the Messianic templebuilder, the style of the building might suggest to Dryden's audience some features of the style of St. Paul's restored by Sir Christopher Wren after the London fire of 1666. As though conscious of the heavy load thus laid on, Dryden expands to a triplet and concludes with an Alexandrine. He is no mean templebuilder himself, and he knows how to found grace in strength. Moreover, he is for the moment done with the expansive structures which imagery can build, and the triplet and Alexandrine have the effect of summarizing and concluding a movement rehearsed in the terms which the opening lines so smilingly and ironically licensed.

Having explored, on the one hand, within significantly qualifying limits the dignity and elevation that are within the grasp of the middle style, the poem turns directly to a nearly prosaic statement of Congreve's qualities and literary lineage so that formal dignity is quickly counterbalanced by simplicity of diction:

> In easie Dialogue is Fletcher's Praise.   (l. 20; II, 852K)

For ten lines the poem moves in an easy, flowing, conversational style, and the symbolic figure of the temple with its strength and grace is done over in nonfigurative simplicity in a summarizing enumeration of qualities of strength and grace found in Etherege and Southerne and Wycherley and combined in Congreve's work. This prosaic summation, like the earlier figurative one, rests on a triplet with final Alexandrine.

The first major section of the poem (the first "paragraph" of forty lines) concludes with a renewed Roman and Renaissance allusiveness in which the drama of the speaker's relationship to Congreve, so brilliantly hinted in the opening line, is more explicitly presented. Essentially it is the drama of the old master and the bright and shadowing surprise of young genius; the poem mixes dignified allusion with informal directness, honoring the young man with names like Scipio and Raphael, and qualifying with a word like "beardless." The colors of the picture are so mixed that virtue appears on both sides, in the young man whose grace attracts consent and in the older man who graciously offers his homage and submission. Tensions and animosities latent in the situation are recognized and overcome.

The second major section of the poem begins with a significant change in tone, and the imagery that is employed alters the aspect of the situation. Heretofore the speaker has spoken collectively of himself and his age as though they were at one in their attitudes and recognitions, as though the age were as ready as he to recognize the new master in the kingdom of wit. The shadow of actuality now falls upon the prophet and forerunner, and Dryden's archetypal image of his age, the image of the king deposed, appears:

> Oh that your Brows my Lawrel had sustain'd,
> Well had I been Depos'd, if You had reign'd!
> The Father had descended for the Son;
> For only You are lineal to the Throne.
> Thus when the State one *Edward* did depose;
> A Greater *Edward* in his room arose.   (ll. 41-46; II, 853K)

In this drama the speaker and Congreve are at one, king and prince, father and son, their tensions dissolved in relationship; now the tension of conflict is between them and the actually reigning powers of the age. As poets, both are victims of a usurpation:

> But now, not I, but Poetry is curs'd;
> For *Tom* the Second reigns like *Tom* the first.
>
> (ll. 47-48; II, 853K)

The speaker's tone ranges from lament to indignation. He confronts facts, he denounces, but then he lifts his eyes to the future and prophesies with renewed confidence. The accent of the languages employed at the beginning of the poem returns with its overtones of solemnity, but qualified by wit, an enacting and mimetic wit in the versification, the signature of the speaker's and Congreve's legitimate claim to the throne:

> Yet this I Prophesy; Thou shalt be seen,
> (Tho' with some short Parenthesis between:)
> High on the Throne of Wit; and seated there,
> Not mine (that's little) but thy Lawrel wear.
>
> (ll. 51-54; II, 853K)

The first parenthetic expression here is the formal equivalent of the stated meaning. This witty consorting together, this quick dancing movement in which form and content visibly strike hands, characterizes the conclusion of this second section which renews the affirmation of Congreve's genius:

> So bold, yet so judiciously you dare,
> That Your least Praise, is to be Regular.   (ll. 57-58; II, 853K)

Regularity is the least praise of such a couplet. Unevenness of stress and boldness of rhyme enact the qualities described. In the next couplet the statement is of genius exceeding the measure of what can be laboriously learned or taught, and the couplet exceeds the measure with an Alexandrine. The next three lines are the third crescendo in the poem's praise of Congreve, the third summation of his powers, and they match the others, they are a formal return, as the verse expands to a triplet and concludes with an Alexandrine:

> To *Shakespeare* gave as much; she cou'd not give him more.
>
> (l. 63; II, 853K)

The verse extends itself to its farthest reach; it cannot give more.

The final verse paragraph moves to a new aspect of the speaker's relationship to Congreve; the speaker appeals to Congreve to be the guardian and preserver of his fame. A final development in the imaged character of both the speaker and Congreve occurs in this last act of the poem's drama of their relationship. The appeal casts Congreve in a role like that of savior, a diminished form of that role because the speaker's seriousness goes beyond the fiction to "Heav'n" and "Providence," and also in the role of strong, young hero in battle, and in the plain simplicity of the part of friend. The speaker appears as prophet, as king, as abdicating playwright, as man worn with age, as vanquished warrior, and as friend. Most of these roles have appeared before, so that the last paragraph resumes established motifs; they are all brought together to be resolved

in a concluding harmony, and rather than the motifs themselves, it is this
harmony that remains to be described. Both persons of the drama have,
in the last act, two general modes of existence; these two modes are perhaps most clearly developed as they apply to the suppliant speaker. First,
there is his existence as man, and second, his existence as name, the former
the thin-spun life to be slit by the abhorred shears of the blind Fury,
but the second to be preserved, the life beyond life, the surviving fame.
On the one hand, the speaker bequeathes nothing; he is poor and in debt.
On the other hand, he is rich with honors and bequeathes his laurels to
his descendant. His poverty is the care of providence:

> Unprofitably kept at Heav'ns expence,
> I live a Rent-charge on his Providence.   (ll. 68-69; II, 853K)

His wealth of fame is a hero's care:

> Let not the Insulting Foe my Fame pursue;
> But shade those Lawrels which descend to You.
>   (ll. 74-75; II, 854K)

Very generally these two modes may be designated as Christian and
Classical; the speaker exists as an aged prophet, a Simeon, a dying sinner,
and as a vanquished hero, and Congreve as a good man, and as a surviving
hero. The blending of these two notions animates all of the language.
The departure of man-victim and artist-hero doubles the significance of
"th' Ungrateful Stage." The blending produces such a fine result as the
doubled reverberation in "the Insulting Foe." Surely *the Insulting Foe* is
"*Tom* the First" and "*Tom* the Second" and all their tom-cat progeny to
the last literary generation. Dullness, however, is the *Dunciad* counterfeit
of death. The language of this passage holds also the deeper suggestion
that death is "the Insulting Foe" who crumbles the body and must be
kept from dominion over the fame.

The most important achievement in this poem is brought about by
skillful control of tone. Tone, of course, voices the various stages in the
movement of the poem's dramatic action, but in this poem the tones
gradually sharpen the image of the speaker, causing the *persona* of the
elder poet to emerge and distinctly play its part. That part has its own
strategy of movement from the opening irony to the final moving appeal.
The wryness of the opening compliment, the speaker's suggested disadvantage, his gradual rise to the throne on which he seats Congreve, his
bestowal of his laurels upon the younger man, his claim of obligation
exerted upon his friend and heir—this sequence of tones constitutes the
skillful and reticent drama of the older poet's retained pride, a drama
which enhances the integrity of the tribute to Congreve. Dryden's development and strategic employment of a *persona* as a culminating effect of

tone look forward to Pope's great successes in the use of masks in his satiric poems.

The judgment of Scott, Van Doren, and other critics that Dryden was an improving poet to the last would certainly have pleased Dryden, because he thought so himself. He was, in the poem to Congreve, the artful master of a *persona* representing the old poet, and this artful mastery appears more directly as self-mastery in the letters and prefatory comments which are related to his last volume, called *Fables,* published in March of 1700. He managed to deprecate himself and the ills of old age with a fine irony while retaining the image of pride in his latest achievements; in February of 1699 he wrote to his relative, Mrs. Steward:

> In the mean time, betwixt my intervalls of physique and other remedies which I am using for my gravell, I am still drudging on: always a Poet, and never a good one. I pass my time sometimes with Ovid, and sometimes with our old English poet, Chaucer; translating such stories as best please my fancy; and intend besides them to add somewhat of my own: so that it is not impossible, but ere the summer be pass'd, I may come down to you with a volume in my hand, like a dog out of the water, with a duck in his mouth.[3]

In November of 1699, in another letter to Mrs. Steward, Dryden is clearly pleased that the Earl of Dorset and Charles Montague, having seen two poems to be included in the *Fables* volume, one to the Duchess of Ormond and the other to his cousin, John Driden, are of the opinion that he has never written better. In his Preface to the *Fables* Dryden expresses his own judgment of the state of his abilities in the work of this last volume:

> I think myself as vigorous as ever in the faculties of my soul, excepting only my memory, which is not impair'd to any great degree. . . . What judgment I had, increases rather than diminishes; and thoughts, such as they are, come crowding in so fast upon me, that my only difficulty is to choose or to reject; to run them into verse, or to give them the other harmony of prose: I have so long studied and practised both, that they are grown into a habit, and become familiar to me.[4]

The poem to the Duchess of Ormond provides an example of what these latest developments, especially the still increasing judgment, mean when applied to the poem of compliment, and it is fortunate that in this poem we have a late instance of Dryden at work in the extended and soaring kind of compliment.

In general the images in this poem are images that have become habitual to Dryden. It seems desirable, however, to attempt to describe the special qualities of this imagery as it is here managed and to find appropri-

---

[3] *The Letters of John Dryden*, ed. Charles E. Ward (Durham, N.C., 1942), p. 109.
[4] *Essays of John Dryden*, ed. W. P. Ker (Oxford, 1926), Vol. II, p. 249.

ate terms to designate and define the facility of manner that this poem
achieves. It seems to me that in this poem Dryden has done something
special to cast all of the imagery in high relief. Along with the occasion
of compliment he has made imagery itself and the poetic process of
imaging an overt subject of his poem. The result is that images are not
simply presented but are subjected to a philosophical consideration as
they appear; the process of imaging is being scrutinized as the images are
put forward. As the full title of the poem suggests, Dryden's topic here
is not simply the Duchess of Ormond and what can be made of her as
an object of compliment, but it is the presentation of a poem to one who
is herself the subject of poetry, and what we get is a poetic consideration
of the relations between the subject matter of poetry and the poem, the
center and the concentric circles of poetic statement at varying radial
distances, the thing itself and what may be poetically predicated of it.
Dryden performs an act of praise, an act that he has performed over and
over in the course of his career as a poet, but this time, as part of his
general concern to sum up and review, he gives an added dimension to
his poem; this dimension is achieved by a luminous displayed consciousness of what it is like and what it means to write poetry.

Dryden begins with a bold tribute to Chaucer, a tribute that sets
Chaucer in the company of Homer and Virgil. The accommodation in
time is really double because Chaucer is praised in a couplet which
suggests very well the whole characteristic activity of English Classicism:

> The Bard who first adorn'd our Native Tongue
> Tun'd to his *British* Lyre this ancient Song. (ll. 1-2; IV, 1463K)

Dryden himself undertakes, in succeeding lines, to tune an ancient compliment to his modern purposes; Juvenal had written that Virgil's poetry
put Homer's palm in doubt, and Dryden now adapts the remark to
Chaucer's entrance into the company of the masters. Here we have a
handsome instance of the readiness and even eagerness with which English
Classicism at its best could accept great figures of the native tradition
and award them rank with the greatest figures in its literary pantheon.
Dryden's judgment of Chaucer is an early example of the splendid flexi-
bility which put the stamp of classic upon Milton's epic and accepted
Milton as the equal and even the superior of Homer and Virgil. At its
best English Classicism is alert to discern through veils of style and place
and time the form of the classic.

Dryden's poem conveys the timeless equivalence of the great poets in
language that is not of one poet or one time but an easy composition of
ancient and modern. Homer, Virgil, and Chaucer are ranged together
around central themes which they have all undertaken, and the circle
from past to present is completed with the inclusion of Dryden who is

entering upon a subject dealt with by Chaucer before him. Dryden proceeds to argue and to explain this equivalence, working up to his images by hypothesis and a sequence of logic, a method adapted and modified from the Metaphysical poets; as Dryden employs the method, the argument leads to the images rather than following them, in the manner of Donne, as justification of an initial shock and elaborated demonstration of the validity of an opening surprise. Dryden's premise here is Platonic —that Chaucer and he, working from different instances, have been both creating from the same idea of beauty—and he caps the argument with the Platonic myth of cyclical return of all things to their original conditions and relationships. The poets stand on the same plane, always and everywhere, and their subjects are the same. These general propositions seem, in turn, to govern the handling of imagery in this poem, images being the various poetic predications, the subject in its imaginative diversity; the outlines of a particular theory and method of imagery have been implied once the fundamental oneness of the major poetic subjects is asserted. The proper image is not the unique or merely original image, but the image which, however new in itself or new by infusion from a new context, continues the link with the past and brings the past to bear in the present. Thus the voices of great poets may continue to speak.

It should be observed that besides drawing the thread of time into a circle from which the major poets face a common center, the first section of Dryden's poem entertains the idea that the occasions of poetry are at times equivalent; it is suggested that the line of creative development leading from a noblewoman of the fourteenth century to the character of Emily in Chaucer's *Knight's Tale* may be entered upon again by a seventeenth century poet who, beginning with a woman in many ways analogous to Chaucer's original, arrives at the same character. To the poetic imagination two points of actuality may entail the same idea and lead to the same character realized in a work of art. There is a dancing continuity of movement between the actual and the ideal, between the subject and the poetic images of the subject which the poem emphasizes by a series of free transpositions asserting the indifference of names:

> O true *Plantagenet,* O Race Divine,
> (For Beauty still is fatal to the Line,)
> Had *Chaucer* liv'd that Angel-Face to view,
> Sure he had drawn his *Emily* from You:
> Or had You liv'd, to judge the doubtful Right,
> Your Noble *Palamon* had been the Knight:
> And Conqu'ring *Theseus* from his Side had sent
> Your Gen'rous Lord, to guide the *Theban* Government.
>   Time shall accomplish that; and I shall see
> A *Palamon* in Him, in You an *Emily.*   (ll. 30-39; IV, 1464K)

Chaucer draws the character of Emily from the Duchess of Ormond; the Duke and Duchess of Ormond become Palamon and Emily and in their lives enact the poem. All change; all remain. In the words of Yeats, "All things remain in God," and:

> Birth is heaped on birth
> That such cannonade
> May thunder time away,
> Birth-hour and death-hour meet,
> Or, as great sages say
> Men dance on deathless feet.[5]

Thus far Dryden's poem has circled its center with the primary purpose of establishing the recurrence of Chaucerian subject and Chaucerian poetic result. From this point on, however, other circles of predication are drawn around the poetic center and the initial suggestion of the affinity of major poets and major poetic themes is amply illustrated. The poem moves around its center in paths of imagery widened into highways by the greatest movements of poetry. The Chaucerian images are not lost but continued and extended; the recurrence is not only with Chaucer and his *Knight's Tale* but also with Virgil's and Homer's epics, with Virgil's *Pollio,* and with the Old and New Testaments, creation, paradise, flood, and second coming. The simplicity of the act of making a poem to the Duchess of Ormond becomes, in the luminous consciousness of this poem, the recurrent and manifold act of poetry, and the single subject radiates light through a whole universe of poetic images. The poem has many ways of saying this, but the universality is most clearly asserted in astronomical imagery; Ormond and Emily, at the center, are repeatedly compared to the sun, and Dryden's use of this imagery is a recurrence, with a difference, of Chaucer's imagery.[6] The Platonic myth states in astronomical terms the theme of universal recurrence:

> As when the Stars, in their Etherial Race, ⎫
> At length have roll'd around the Liquid Space, ⎬
> At certain Periods they resume their Place, ⎭
> From the same Point of Heav'n their Course advance,
> And move in Measures of their former Dance.   (ll. 21-25; IV, 1464K)

We are prepared, then, for the full sweep of the poem's orbit, prepared for recurrences that lie along the orbit, prepared for inclusiveness and reminiscence in the method of the imagery.

[5] W. B. Yeats, *Collected Poems,* "Mohini Chatterjee."
[6] E.g. "Up rose the sun, and up rose Emilye," etc.

The two principal circuits of imagery are Classical and biblical, and as circles drawn about a common center, the analogy of these poetic predications is implied. The first cycle of Classical imagery is drawn from epic, primarily from Virgil's *Aeneid,* and it presents a miniature of the full epic voyage:

> Already have the Fates your Path prepar'd,
> And sure Presage your future Sway declar'd:
> When Westward, like the Sun, you took your Way,
> And from benighted *Britain* bore the Day,
> Blue *Triton* gave the Signal from the Shore,
> The ready *Nereids* heard, and swam before
> To smooth the Seas; a soft *Etesian* Gale
> But just inspir'd, and gently swell'd the Sail;
> *Portunus* took his Turn, whose ample Hand
> Heav'd up the lighten'd Keel, and sunk the Sand,
> And steer'd the sacred Vessel safe to Land.   (ll. 40-50; IV, 1464K)

Within this image of the epic voyage, with its suggestion of the full cycle of the movement from Troy to Italy, from the darkened past to the bright future, Dryden's poem includes the daily cycle of the sun's voyage through the heavens, and along with the pronounced epic features, there is, possibly, a glancing reminiscence of Desdemona's passage to Cyprus, the guiltless keel subduing the elements, beauty as a sacred symbol of harmony, an ordering principle. The poem takes advantage of the fact that, as governors, the Ormonds have once voyaged to Ireland, and the voyage that is "presaged" repeats a previous voyage; the future is a prepared path leading into the past, a new movement renewing an old cycle.

Virgil's epic of government served for the image of the first voyage to Ireland, and Virgil's *Pollio,* the eclogue of prophecy, is the image of the voyage to come:

> When at Your second Coming You appear,
> (For I foretell that Millenary Year)
> The sharpen'd Share shall vex the Soil no more,
> But Earth unbidden shall produce her Store:
> The Land shall laugh, the circling Ocean smile,
> And Heav'ns Indulgence bless the Holy Isle.
>
> Heav'n from all Ages has reserv'd for You
> That happy Clyme, which Venom never knew;
> Or if it had been there, Your Eyes alone
> Have Pow'r to chase all Poyson, but their own.[7]   (ll. 80-89; IV, 1465K)

[7] Parallel lines in Dryden's translation of the *Pollio* are:

Unlabour'd Harvest shall the Fields adorn.

(l. 33; II, 888K)

No Plow shall hurt the Glebe, no Pruning-hook the Vine.

(l. 50; II, 888K)

The Serpents Brood shall die; the sacred ground
Shall Weeds and pois'nous Plants refuse to bear.

(ll. 28-29; II, 888K)

Tradition saw in the *Pollio* a mystical occurrence of Christian prophecy
in a Classical context, and Dryden's poem takes complete advantage of
this parallelism of Christian and Classical predication, fortifying the suggestion with a clear biblical signature (*Your second Coming*) in the opening line. Speaking with the tongues of Classical tradition and Christian
revelation, of Virgil and the prophets, Dryden's poem says anew what has
been said before. There is no competition or discord, only concentration
upon the one statement, coincidence of images in one predication. The
ordering of experience is a recurrent poetic problem, and the major cycles
of experience are always like and unlike the cycles that have preceded.
The second voyage repeats the first and each in turn repeats the great
voyages of experience and prophecy that poetry has recorded and imagined. Language and imagery, Dryden shows us, can be used to uphold and
preserve the continuity of experience. This is the way to be greatly
original, not original narrowly in terms of self, but largely original,
making the sources of poetry flow in the present. The present subject of
poetry is the old subject:

From the same Point of Heav'n their Course advance,
And move in Measures of their former Dance.

Poetic ordering of experience as conceived in this poem is congruent with
universal order. The Duchess figures in the order and movement of the
heavens, the macrocosm in which she is like the sun. She figures also as
microcosm, the faultless frame of the four governed elements, and the
cycle from disorder to restoration which has been run in social terms, in
terms of Ireland and of mankind, can be run in individual terms, in
terms of sickness and the restoration to health. The imagery of this
process, however, makes us look from end to end of the order, from
macrocosm to microcosm, while we examine disease in the individual.
First there are the macrocosmic images:

Rest here a while, Your Lustre to restore,
That they may see You as You shone before:
For yet, th'Eclipse not wholly past, You wade
Thro' some Remains, and Dimness of a Shade.   (ll. 103-06; IV, 1466K)

Then there is the disease imaged in the microcosm:

> Now past the Danger, let the Learn'd begin
> Th'Enquiry, where Disease could enter in;
> How those malignant Atoms forc'd their Way,
> What in the faultless Frame they found to make their Prey?
> Where ev'ry Element was weigh'd so well,
> That Heav'n alone, who mix'd the Mass, could tell
> Which of the Four Ingredients could rebel;
> And where, imprison'd in so sweet a Cage,
> A Soul might well be pleas'd to pass an Age.   (ll. 111-19; IV, 1466K)

The poem not only makes us see the problem of order at a number of different levels by a series of concentric movements, circling the universe of divine creation, but also enacts for us the parallel problems of poetic order. This double process is continuous through the whole poem and sharply present in this passage where overt consideration of the problems of creativity, the elements and the faultless frame, merges the activities of God and the poet. One poetic voice after another speaks in the couplet that images God-perfected creation of man:

> And where, imprison'd in so sweet a Cage,
> A Soul might well be pleas'd to pass an Age.

The poets, too, have labored to perfect their sweet cage.

The conclusion of Dryden's poem praises the restoration of all order in the restored health of the Duchess; by this act, Heaven renews the life and ordered movement of all conditions of men, including the condition of poet:

> Bless'd be the Pow'r which has at once restor'd
> The Hopes of lost Succession to Your Lord,
> Joy to the first, and last of each Degree,
> Vertue to Courts, and what I long'd to see,
> To You the Graces, and the Muse to me.   (ll. 146-50; IV, 1467K)

The completion of the cycle of the poem returns to the beginning and renews the initial expression of the poem's central symbol as seen by Chaucer, Virgil, and Homer. From *The Knight's Tale* comes the imagery of red and white, Mars and Venus, ordered in Theseus' banner as here in the warlike Duke of Ormond and his fair consort, together, and individually in the symbolic Duchess:

> O Daughter of the Rose, whose Cheeks unite
> The diff'ring Titles of the Red and White.   (ll. 151-52; IV, 1467K)

The Duchess renews virtues of Homer's Penelope:

> All is Your Lord's alone; ev'n absent, He
> Employs the Care of Chast *Penelope*.   (ll. 157-58; IV, 1467K)

And of Virgil's Dido:

> For him Your curious Needle paints the Flow'rs:
> Such Works of Old Imperial Dames were taught;
> Such for *Ascanius*, fair *Elisa* wrought.   (ll. 160-62; IV, 1467K)

The major predications in the imagery of the poem return in this passage with marvelously concentrated force and expression; the Duchess is, first and last, the sun and the stars in their courses. The lights of day and night are smoothly evoked from Chaucer's imagery and presented in a couplet that suggests the cycle of a day:

> Who Heav'ns alternate Beauty well display,
> The Blush of Morning, and the Milky Way.   (ll. 153-54; IV, 1467K)

A blend of Milton and Metaphysical boldness resumes the biblical imagery that has gone into the creation of the symbol:

> Whose Face is Paradise, but fenc'd from Sin:
> For God in either Eye has plac'd a Cherubin.   (ll. 155-56; IV, 1467K)

With the summation of these cycles of imagery reminiscent of all the ways in which the poem has presented the cycles of experience and suggesting the perfection of the completed circle, a point of rest, the poem faces the future and suggests the renewal of the past as the new generation moves on the metaled ways of past and future:

> All other Parts of Pious Duty done,
> You owe Your *Ormond* nothing but a Son:
> To fill in future Times his Father's Place,
> And wear the Garter of his Mother's Race.   (ll. 165-68; IV, 1467K)

The *pietàs* which recognizes obligations to past and future and manages to resolve and harmonize these duties in the present is a Classical ideal; it provides the method of Dryden's imagery. This ideal governs Dryden's practice as a poet, and this poem is a signature of that ideal, one of its triumphs.

Canons Ashby

by David Wright

County of squares and spires, in the middle of England,
   Where with companions I was used to rove,
Country containing the cedar of John Dryden,
   Cedar, in whose shadow of thunder and love
I saw those Caroline lawns, and musical
I heard, inaudible, those waters fall, fall

Triumphs and miseries, last poet of a golden
   Order, and under whose laurel I desire
To plant a leaf of bay, and by whose building
   To tune irregular strings, his stronger lyre
Plunging, a swan to alight, upon a clear
Music of language I delight to hear.

Not a hundred yards from where my substance wastes
   Nightly in London, John Dryden died on tick.
The air clouded, and in his garden gusts
   Shook the cedar tree; as I watched its branches flick
In a windy prolegomenon to autumn
While a sky marshalled engines to a storm,

I no longer heard those falling waters fall,
   Silence like Iris descended from a cloud,
And lawns grew dark, as that once musical
   Shadow of a cedar faded in the loud
Shades of thunder-cumuli on the grass,
Till we left the garden empty as it was.

"Canons Ashby." From *Moral Stories* (London: Derek Verschoyle, Ltd., 1954) by David Wright. Reprinted by permission of the author, Andre Deutsch, Ltd., and A. D. Peters.

Chronology of Important Dates

1631	John Dryden born at Aldwinckle, Northamptonshire, August 9.
1649	While a student at Westminster School, London, publishes an elegy "Upon the Death of Lord Hastings."
1654	Cambridge, Trinity College, B.A. degree. Death of Dryden's father.
1658	The elegy "Heroic Stanzas" on the death of Cromwell.
1660-1662	Early poems to the King, Sir Robert Howard, Clarendon, and Charleton. Election to the Royal Society.
1663	Dryden's first play, a comedy *The Wild Gallant.* December 1, he marries Lady Elizabeth Howard, sister of Sir Robert Howard.
1666	Dryden publishes the chronicle poem *Annus Mirabilis,* and is dropped from the Royal Society for not paying his dues.
1667	Continues success in the theater and is able to lend Charles II £500.
1668	Publishes *An Essay of Dramatic Poesy,* becomes Poet Laureate, renews loan to Charles II.
1670	Dryden becomes Historiographer Royal, with yearly pension of £200.
1671-1672	Appearance of Buckingham's *Rehearsal,* a satire on heroic plays, especially Dryden's *Conquest of Granada.* Dryden as Poet Laureate is lampooned in the character "Mr. Bayes."
1673-1674	Prologues and Epilogues to the University of Oxford. *The State of Innocence,* an opera on the theme of *Paradise Lost.* Dryden's loan to Charles II repaid with interest.
1677	*All for Love.* Dryden's pension increased to £300, but only half paid over the next seven years.
1679	Dryden is suspected of writing Mulgrave's *An Essay on Satire* which attacks Rochester and two royal mistresses. He is beaten by thugs in Rose Alley, Covent Garden.
1680	*The Spanish Fryar,* a tragicomedy. "Preface" to *Ovid's Epistles* by several hands: the volume also contains Dryden's first verse translation.
1681	*Absalom and Achitophel.*
1682	*The Medall,* attacking Shaftesbury. *Religio Laici.*
1684	*Miscellany Poems* published, containing satires, translations, and the elegy "To the Memory of Mr. Oldham."
1685	Death of Charles II. Publication of *Sylvae, or the Second Part of Poetical Miscellanies. To the Memory of Anne Killigrew.* Dryden becomes a Roman Catholic.
687	*The Hind and the Panther,* "A Song for St. Cecilia's Day."

1688   James II dethroned, succeeded by William III. Dryden dismissed as Poet Laureate and Historiographer Royal.

1692   *Satires of Juvenal and Persius.*

1693   Dryden writes his last play, *Love Triumphant,* and publishes *Examen Poeticum: Being the Third Part of Miscellany Poems.*

1697   Translation of *The Works of Virgil,* "Alexander's Feast."

1700   Publication of the *Fables* with a famous "Preface," and containing poems, with translations from Chaucer, Boccaccio, and Ovid. Death of Dryden, May 1.

Notes on the Editor and Authors

BERNARD N. SCHILLING, the editor, teaches in the English and Comparative Literature Departments of the University of Rochester. He has written on various aspects of the teaching profession, Voltaire's reception in England, and the major Victorians, as well as on Dryden.

T. S. ELIOT, poet and playwright, is respected among scholars as much for his many critical essays on poets and dramatists of the seventeenth century as for his considerable creative writing. His achievement is revealed in the volume in this series edited by Hugh Kenner.

LOUIS I. BREDVOLD has now retired after teaching in the University of Michigan. His writings include many standard articles on Dryden in addition to the volume represented here.

JAMES M. OSBORN is Research Associate in the Yale University Library. He has recently published a modern spelling edition of Thomas Whythorne's *Autobiography*.

REUBEN A. BROWER is Professor of English and Master of Adams House at Harvard University. Among his earlier works is *The Fields of Light* (1951).

EDWIN MORGAN is a Lecturer in English at the Glasgow University.

EARL WASSERMAN teaches at Johns Hopkins University. His list of publications includes *Elizabethan Poetry in the Eighteenth Century* (1947) and *Epistle to Bathurst: A Critical Reading* (1960).

R. J. KAUFMANN teaches English and Comparative Literature courses at the University of Rochester. His work on English Drama includes *Richard Brome: Caroline Playwright* (1961) and the editing of *Elizabethan Drama: Modern Essays in Criticism* (1961).

MOODY E. PRIOR, long a teacher of English at Northwestern University, is now also Dean of the Graduate School at Northwestern. His latest book is *Science and the Humanities*.

EARL MINER teaches at the University of California at Los Angeles and is one of the editors of the definitive "California" Edition of Dryden's works.

EDWARD N. HOOKER, before his death in 1956, taught at the University of California at Los Angeles. In addition to founding the "California" Edition of Dryden's works, he has edited *The Critical Works of John Dennis* (1939-43).

E. M. W. TILLYARD was Master of Jesus College, Cambridge, England, before his recent death. Among his many books, two of which are interesting to students of the seventeenth century, are *The Elizabethan World Picture* (1943) and *The Miltonic Setting* (1938).

JOHN HOLLANDER teaches at Yale University. His poetry has appeared in *Poetry*, the *New Yorker*, and *The New Republic*, and his latest work is *Movie-going and Other Poems* (1962).

ARTHUR W. HOFFMAN began teaching at Yale and is now Professor of English at Syracuse University. He has written on Chaucer as well as on Dryden.

DAVID WRIGHT is a South African poet now living in London. In addition to the book represented by "Canons Ashby," Wright's poems have appeared regularly in *Poetry*.

Selected Bibliography

Since the renewal of interest in Dryden after 1920-21, a great deal of work has been done on various aspects of the poet's life and achievement. Samuel H. Monk has compiled a bibliography entitled *John Dryden: A List of Critical Studies—1895 to 1948* (1950) and has given a star to every item of special value. But if we omit the work of writers already represented in our selection, we shall find little to recommend of general critical and interpretive interest. Eliot himself contributed *John Dryden: The Poet, the Dramatist, the Critic* (1932) and Mr. Bonamy Dobrée has written with pleasant enthusiasm of Dryden in *A Variety of Ways* (1932). Mr. Leavis' essay on *Antony and Cleopatra* and *All for Love* may be recommended (*Scrutiny* V [1936], 158-69). Mr. Ian Jack's *Augustan Satire* (1952) contains readable chapters on *Mac Flecknoe* and *Absalom and Achitophel*.

When completed, the great "California" Edition of *The Works of John Dryden*, now under the general editorship of H. T. Swedenberg, Jr., will be indispensable. So far two volumes have appeared with excellent notes and commentary. Until this edition is completed, the Oxford Edition of *The Poems of John Dryden*, in four volumes, by James Kinsley (1958) offers a highly readable text. *The Life of John Dryden* by Charles E. Ward (1961) has become the standard biography, but the reader may still consult Dr. Samuel Johnson with profit on Dryden in his *Lives of the Poets*. Material used in the editor's introduction to this volume is more fully treated in his *Dryden and the Conservative Myth* (1961).

The general introduction to the second edition of *Poetical Works of John Dryden* (1950) by George R. Noyes is well balanced and sound, offering a great deal of information on all aspects of Dryden's career. *The Best of Dryden* (1933), edited by Louis I. Bredvold, and *Selected Works of John Dryden*, edited by William Frost in the Rinehart paperback series (1953), are to be recommended for judicious selection and valuable commentary.